MznLnx

Missing Links Exam Preps

Exam Prep for

Essentials of Geology

Chernicoff & Fox, 3rd Edition

The MznLnx Exam Prep is your link from the texbook and lecture to your exams.
The MznLnx Exam Preps are unauthorized and comprehensive reviews of your textbooks.

All material provided by MznLnx and Rico Publications (c) 2010
Textbook publishers and textbook authors do not particpate in or contribute to these reviews.

MznLnx

Rico
Publications

Exam Prep for Essentials of Geology
3rd Edition
Chernicoff & Fox

Publisher: Raymond Houge
Assistant Editor: Michael Rouger
Text and Cover Designer: Lisa Buckner
Marketing Manager: Sara Swagger
Project Manager, Editorial Production: Jerry Emerson
Art Director: Vernon Lowerui

Product Manager: Dave Mason
Editorial Assitant: Rachel Guzmanji
Pedagogy: Debra Long
Cover Image: Jim Reed/Getty Images
Text and Cover Printer: City Printing, Inc.
Compositor: Media Mix, Inc.

(c) 2010 Rico Publications

ALL RIGHTS RESERVED. No part of this work covered by the copyright may be reproduced or used in any form or by an means--graphic, electronic, or mechanical, including photocopying, recording, taping, Web distribution, information storage, and retrieval systems, or in any other manner--without the written permission of the publisher.

For more information about our products, contact us at:

Dave.Mason@RicoPublications.com

For permission to use material from this text or

product, submit a request online to:

Dave.Mason@RicoPublications.com

Printed in the United States
ISBN:

Contents

CHAPTER 1
A First Look at Planet Earth — 1

CHAPTER 2
Minerals — 10

CHAPTER 3
Igneous Processes and Igneous Rocks — 16

CHAPTER 4
Volcanoes and Volcanism — 25

CHAPTER 5
Weathering - The Breakdown of Rocks — 34

CHAPTER 6
Sedimentatio and Sedimentary Rocks — 42

CHAPTER 7
Metamorphism and Metamorphic Rocks — 51

CHAPTER 8
Telling Time Geologically — 57

CHAPTER 9
Folds, Faults, and Mountains — 65

CHAPTER 10
Earthquakes and the Earth's Interior — 72

CHAPTER 11
Plate Tectonics: Creating Oceans and Continents — 79

CHAPTER 12
Mass Movement — 88

CHAPTER 13
Streams and Floods — 93

CHAPTER 14
Groundwater, Caves, and Karst — 98

CHAPTER 15
Glaciers and Ice Ages — 104

CHAPTER 16
Deserts and Wind Action — 115

CHAPTER 17
Shores and Coastal Processes — 120

CHAPTER 18
Human Use of the Earth's Resources — 125

CHAPTER 19
A Brief History of Earth and Its Life Forms — 131

ANSWER KEY — 143

TO THE STUDENT

COMPREHENSIVE

The *MznLnx* Exam Prep series is designed to help you pass your exams. Editors at MznLnx review your textbooks and then prepare these practice exams to help you master the textbook material. Unlike study guides, workbooks, and practice tests provided by the texbook publisher and textbook authors, *MznLnx* gives you **all** of the material in each chapter in exam form, not just samples, so you can be sure to nail your exam.

MECHANICAL

The MznLnx Exam Prep series creates exams that will help you learn the subject matter as well as test you on your understanding. Each question is designed to help you master the concept. Just working through the exams, you gain an understanding of the subject--its a simple mechanical process that produces success.

INTEGRATED STUDY GUIDE AND REVIEW

MznLnx is not just a set of exams designed to test you, its also a comprehensive review of the subject content. Each exam question is also a review of the concept, making sure that you will get the answer correct without having to go to other sources of material. You learn as you go! Its the easiest way to pass an exam.

HUMOR

Studying can be tedious and dry. MznLnx's instructional design includes moderate humor within the exam questions on occassion, to break the tedium and revitalize the brain

Chapter 1. A First Look at Planet Earth

1. _____ is water located beneath the ground surface in soil pore spaces and in the fractures of lithologic formations. A unit of rock or an unconsolidated deposit is called an aquifer when it can yield a usable quantity of water. The depth at which soil pore spaces or fractures and voids in rock become completely saturated with water is called the water table.
    a. 1509 Istanbul earthquake
    b. 1700 Cascadia earthquake
    c. Groundwater
    d. Depression focused recharge

2. _____ are the largest glaciers, enormous masses of ice that are not visibly affected by the landscape and that cover the entire surface beneath them, except possibly on the margins where they are thinnest. Antarctica and Greenland are the only places where continental _____ currently exist. These regions contain vast quantities of fresh water.
    a. AL 333
    b. AL 129-1
    c. AASHTO Soil Classification System
    d. Ice sheets

3. The _____ is a long, fringing ice shelf in the northwest part of the Weddell Sea, extending along the east coast of Antarctic Peninsula from Cape Longing to the area just southward of Hearst Island.

   In finer detail, the _____ is a series of three shelves that occupy (or occupied) distinct embayments along the coast.

    a. 1703 Genroku earthquake
    b. 1700 Cascadia earthquake
    c. 1509 Istanbul earthquake
    d. Larsen Ice Shelf

4. A _____ is a large, slow-moving mass of ice, formed from compacted layers of snow, that slowly deforms and flows in response to gravity and high pressure.

   _____ ice is the largest reservoir of fresh water on Earth, and second only to oceans as the largest reservoir of total water.

    a. Glacier
    b. Geologic temperature record
    c. Keeling Curve
    d. Little Ice Age

5. _____ is a landscape shaped by the dissolution of a layer or layers of soluble bedrock, usually carbonate rock such as limestone or dolomite.

   Due to subterranean drainage, there may be very limited surface water, even to the absence of all rivers and lakes. Many karst regions display distinctive surface features, with sinkholes or dolines being the most common.

    a. Amblypoda
    b. Ambulocetus
    c. Andrija Mohorovičić
    d. Karst topography

6. The general term '_____' or, more precisely, 'glacial age' denotes a geological period of long-term reduction in the temperature of the Earth's surface and atmosphere, resulting in an expansion of continental ice sheets, polar ice sheets and alpine glaciers. Within a long-term _____, individual pulses of extra cold climate are termed 'glaciations'. Glaciologically, _____ implies the presence of extensive ice sheets in the northern and southern hemispheres; by this definition we are still in an _____
    a. AL 333
    b. AASHTO Soil Classification System
    c. Ice age
    d. AL 129-1

Chapter 1. A First Look at Planet Earth

7. The _____ is a a term for a geologic period 65 million to 1.8 million years ago. The _____ covered the time span between the superseded Secondary period and an out-of-date definition of the Quaternary period. The period began with the demise of the non-avian dinosaurs in the Cretaceous-_____ extinction event, at start of the Cenozoic era, spanning to beginning of the most recent Ice Age, at the end of the Pliocene epoch.
   a. Rockall
   b. Suspended load
   c. Historical geology
   d. Tertiary

8. _____ is the idea that Earth has been affected in the past by sudden, short-lived, violent events, possibly worldwide in scope.

The dominant paradigm of modern geology, in contrast, is uniformitarianism (also sometimes described as gradualism), in which slow incremental changes, such as erosion, create the Earth's appearance. This view holds that the present is the key to the past, and that all things continue as they were from the beginning of the world.

   a. 1509 Istanbul earthquake
   b. 1703 Genroku earthquake
   c. 1700 Cascadia earthquake
   d. Catastrophism

9. _____ is the principle that the same scientific laws and processes are constant throughout space and time. It applies specifically to sciences that require a long timescale such as geology, astronomy, and paleontology. It was first defined by Charles Lyell (1797 - 1875), who incorporated James Hutton's gradualism into the idea of _____.
   a. AASHTO Soil Classification System
   b. Uniformitarianism
   c. AL 333
   d. AL 129-1

10. An _____ is the result of a sudden release of energy in the Earth's crust that creates seismic waves. They are recorded with a seismometer or the related and mostly obsolete Richter magnitude, with a magnitude 3 or lower _____ being mostly imperceptible and magnitude 7 causing serious damage over large areas.
    a. AASHTO Soil Classification System
    b. Earthquake
    c. AL 333
    d. AL 129-1

11. The _____ is a cosmological model of the initial conditions and subsequent development of the universe. It is supported by the most comprehensive and accurate explanations from current scientific evidence and observation. As used by cosmologists, the term _____ generally refers to the idea that the universe has expanded from a primordial hot and dense initial condition at some finite time in the past, and continues to expand to this day.
    a. 1700 Cascadia earthquake
    b. 1703 Genroku earthquake
    c. 1509 Istanbul earthquake
    d. Big Bang

12. _____, is the process of coastal sediments returning to the visible portion of a beach or foreshore following a submersion event. A sustainable beach or foreshore often goes through a cycle of submersion during rough weather then _____ during calmer periods. If a coastline is not in a healthy sustainable condition, then erosion can be more serious and _____ does not fully restore the original volume of the visible beach or foreshore leading to permanent beach or foreshore loss.
    a. AL 333
    b. AL 129-1
    c. Accretion
    d. AASHTO Soil Classification System

13.

Chapter 1. A First Look at Planet Earth 3

A widely accepted theory of planet formation, the so-called _____ hypothesis of Viktor Safronov, states that planets form out of dust grains that collide and stick to form larger and larger bodies. When the bodies reach sizes of approximately one kilometer, then they can attract each other directly through their mutual gravity, aiding further growth into moon-sized protoplanets enormously.

   a. 1509 Istanbul earthquake
   b. 1703 Genroku earthquake
   c. 1700 Cascadia earthquake
   d. Planetesimal

14. Two important classifications of weathering processes exist -- physical and _____. Mechanical or physical weathering involves the breakdown of rocks and soils through direct contact with atmospheric conditions, such as heat, water, ice and pressure. The second classification, _____, involves the direct effect of atmospheric chemicals or biologically produced chemicals (also known as biological weathering) in the breakdown of rocks, soils and minerals.
   a. 1700 Cascadia earthquake
   b. 1509 Istanbul earthquake
   c. 1703 Genroku earthquake
   d. Chemical weathering

15. _____ describes the large scale motions of Earth's lithosphere. The theory encompasses the older concepts of continental drift, developed during the first decades of the 20th century by Alfred Wegener, and seafloor spreading, understood during the 1960s.

The outermost part of the Earth's interior is made up of two layers: the lithosphere and the asthenosphere.

   a. Copperbelt Province
   b. Plate tectonics
   c. Thrust fault
   d. Subduction

16. _____ is the decomposition of Earth rocks, soils and their minerals through direct contact with the planet's atmosphere. _____ occurs in situ, or 'with no movement', and thus should not be confused with erosion, which involves the movement of rocks and minerals by agents such as water, ice, wind and gravity.

Two important classifications of _____ processes exist -- physical and chemical _____.

   a. 1700 Cascadia earthquake
   b. 1703 Genroku earthquake
   c. 1509 Istanbul earthquake
   d. Weathering

17. The _____ is the mechanically weak ductily-deforming region of the upper mantle of the Earth. It lies below the lithosphere, at depths between 100 and 200 km (~ 62 and 124 miles) below the surface, but perhaps extending as deep as 400 km (~ 249 miles.)

The _____ is a portion of the upper mantle just below the lithosphere that is involved in plate movements and isostatic adjustments. In spite of its heat, pressures keep it plastic, and it has a relatively low density. Seismic waves pass relatively slowly through the _____, compared to the overlying lithospheric mantle, thus it has been called the low-velocity zone. This was the observation that originally alerted seismologists to its presence and gave some information about its physical properties, as the speed of seismic waves decreases with decreasing rigidity.

a. AASHTO Soil Classification System
c. AL 129-1
b. AL 333
d. Asthenosphere

18. The _____ is a chronologic schema (or idealized model) relating stratigraphy to time that is used by geologists, paleontologists and other earth scientists to describe the timing and relationships between events that have occurred during the history of the Earth. The table of geologic time spans presented here agrees with the dates and nomenclature proposed by the International Commission on Stratigraphy, and uses the standard color codes of the United States Geological Survey.

Evidence from radiometric dating indicates that the Earth is about 4.570 billion years old.

a. Geologic time scale
c. 1703 Genroku earthquake
b. 1700 Cascadia earthquake
d. 1509 Istanbul earthquake

19. The _____ is the rigid outermost shell of a rocky planet.

In the Earth, the _____ includes the crust and the uppermost mantle, which constitute the hard and rigid outer layer of the planet. The _____ is underlain by the asthenosphere, the weaker, hotter, and deeper part of the upper mantle.

a. Continental crust
c. Continental drift
b. Thrust fault
d. Lithosphere

20. The _____, is a geologic eon before the Proterozoic and Paleoproterozoic, before 2.5 Ga (billion years ago, or 2,500 Ma.) Instead of being based on stratigraphy, this date is defined chronometrically. The lower boundary (starting point) has not been officially recognized by the International Commission on Stratigraphy, but it is usually set to 3.8 Ga, at the end of the Hadean eon.

a. AL 333
c. AASHTO Soil Classification System
b. Archean
d. AL 129-1

21. _____ are the preserved remains or traces of animals, plants, and other organisms from the remote past. The totality of _____, both discovered and undiscovered, and their placement in fossiliferous rock formations and sedimentary layers (strata) is known as the fossil record. The study of _____ across geological time, how they were formed, and the evolutionary relationships between taxa (phylogeny) are some of the most important functions of the science of paleontology.

a. Fossils
c. 1703 Genroku earthquake
b. 1700 Cascadia earthquake
d. 1509 Istanbul earthquake

22. _____ is one of the three main rock types (the others being sedimentary and metamorphic rock.) _____ is formed by magma (molten rock) being cooled and becoming solid . They may form with or without crystallization, either below the surface as intrusive (plutonic) rocks or on the surface as extrusive (volcanic) rocks. They make up approximately 95% of the upper part of the Earth's crust, but their great abundance is hidden on the Earth's surface by a relatively thin but widespread layer of sedimentary and metamorphic rocks.

a. AL 129-1
c. AL 333
b. AASHTO Soil Classification System
d. Igneous rock

Chapter 1. A First Look at Planet Earth

23. _____ is the result of the transformation of an existing rock type, the protolith, in a process called metamorphism, which means 'change in form'. The protolith is subjected to heat and pressure (temperatures greater than 150 to 200 >°C and pressures of 1500 bars) causing profound physical and/or chemical change. The protolith may be sedimentary rock, igneous rock or another older _____.

   a. Petrology
   b. Pluton
   c. Metamorphic rock
   d. Large igneous provinces

24. _____ is the process of determining a specific date for an archaeological or palaeontological site or artifact. Some archaeologists prefer the terms chronometric or calendar dating, as use of the word 'absolute' implies a certainty and precision that is rarely possible in archaeology. _____ is usually based on the physical or chemical properties of the materials of artifacts, buildings, or other items that have been modified by humans.

   a. AASHTO Soil Classification System
   b. Erathem
   c. Uranium-lead dating
   d. Absolute dating

25. Before the advent of absolute dating in the 20th century, archaeologists and geologists were largely limited to the use of the _____ techniques. It estimates the order of prehistoric and geological events determined by using basic stratigraphic rules, and by observing where fossil organisms lay in the geological record, often in horizontal, stratified bands of rocks present throughout the world.

Though _____ can determine the sequential order in which a series of events occurred, not when they occur, it is in no way inferior to radiometric dating; in fact, _____ by biostratigraphy is the preferred method in paleontology, and is in some respects more accurate (Stanley, 167-9.)

   a. Milankovitch Theory
   b. Stage
   c. Relative dating
   d. Global Boundary Stratotype Section and Point

26. The _____ is a fundamental concept in geology that describes the dynamic transitions through geologic time among the three main rock types: sedimentary, metamorphic, and igneous. Each type of rock is altered or destroyed when it is forced out of its equilibrium conditions. An igneous rock such as basalt may break down and dissolve when exposed to the atmosphere, or melt as it is subducted under a continent.

   a. Migmatite
   b. Rock cycle
   c. Tephra
   d. Serpentinite

27. _____ is any particulate matter that can be transported by fluid flow, and which eventually is deposited.

They are most often transported by water (fluvial processes) transported by wind (aeolian processes) and glaciers. Beach sands and river channel deposits are examples of fluvial transport and deposition, though _____ also often settles out of slow-moving or standing water in lakes and oceans.

   a. Brickearth
   b. Bovey Beds
   c. Sediment
   d. Dry quicksand

28. _____ is one of the three main rock types (the others being igneous and metamorphic rock.) _____ is formed by deposition and consolidation of mineral and organic material and from precipitation of minerals from solution. The processes that form _____ occur at the surface of the Earth and within bodies of water.

a. Felsic
b. Sedimentary rock
c. Rock cycle
d. Serpentinite

29. The _____ is a tectonic plate covering most of North America, Greenland and part of Siberia. It extends eastward to the Mid-Atlantic Ridge and westward to the Chersky Range in eastern Siberia. The plate includes both continental and oceanic crust. The interior of the main continental landmass includes an extensive granitic core called a craton. Along most of the edges of this craton are fragments of crustal material called terranes, accreted to the craton by tectonic actions over the long span of geologic time. It is believed that much of North America west of the Rockies is composed of such terranes.

a. North Bismarck Plate
b. Gorda Plate
c. North American plate
d. Conway Reef Plate

30. The _____ is the earliest of three geologic eras of the Phanerozoic eon. The _____ spanned from roughly 542 to 251 million years ago (ICS, 2004), and is subdivided into six geologic periods; from oldest to youngest they are: the Cambrian, Ordovician, Silurian, Devonian, Carboniferous, and Permian.

The _____ covers the time from the first appearance of abundant, soft-shelled fossils to the time when the continents were beginning to be dominated by large, relatively sophisticated reptiles and modern plants. The lower (oldest) boundary was classically set at the first appearance of creatures known as trilobites and archeocyathids.

a. 1700 Cascadia earthquake
b. 1509 Istanbul earthquake
c. 1703 Genroku earthquake
d. Paleozoic

31. The lithosphere is broken up into what are called _____. In the case of Earth, there are eight major and many minor plates The lithospheric plates ride on the asthenosphere. These plates move in relation to one another at one of three types of plate boundaries: convergent, or collisional boundaries; divergent boundaries, also called spreading centers; and transform boundaries.

a. Lithosphere
b. Juan de Fuca Ridge
c. Tectonic plates
d. Thrust fault

32. The _____ is a tectonic plate which includes most of the continent of Eurasia (a landmass consisting of the traditional continents of Europe and Asia), with the notable exceptions of the Indian subcontinent, the Arabian subcontinent, and the area east of the Chersky Range in East Siberia. It also includes oceanic crust extending westward to the Mid-Atlantic Ridge and northward to the Gakkel Ridge.

The easterly side is a boundary with the North American Plate to the north and a boundary with the Philippine Mobile Belt and the Philippine Sea Plate to the south, and possibly with the Okhotsk Plate and the Amurian Plate.

a. Arabian Plate
b. Intermontane Plate
c. Eurasian plate
d. Antarctic Plate

33. In plate tectonics, a _____ is a linear feature that exists between two tectonic plates that are moving away from each other. These areas can form in the middle of continents but eventually form ocean basins. Divergent boundaries within continents initially produce rifts which produce rift valleys. Therefore, most active divergent plate boundaries are between oceanic plates and are often called mid-oceanic ridges. Divergent boundaries also form Volcanic Islands which occur when the plates move apart to produce gaps which molten lava rises to fill. Thus creating a shield volcano which would eventually build up to become a volcanic island.
   a. Divergent boundary
   b. 1509 Istanbul earthquake
   c. 1703 Genroku earthquake
   d. 1700 Cascadia earthquake

34. The _____ is a name given in the late 19th century by British explorer John Walter Gregory to the continuous geographic trough, approximately 6,000 kilometres (3,700 mi) in length, that runs from northern Syria in Southwest Asia to central Mozambique in East Africa. The name continues in some usages, although it is today considered geologically imprecise as it includes what are today regarded as separate, since 1869 due to the Suez Canal Company project, although related rift and fault systems. Today, the term is most often used to refer to the valley of the East African Rift, the divergent plate boundary which extends from the Afar Triple Junction southward across eastern Africa, and is in the process of splitting the African Plate into two new separate plates.
   a. 1700 Cascadia earthquake
   b. 1703 Genroku earthquake
   c. 1509 Istanbul earthquake
   d. Great Rift Valley

35. _____ is molten rock that is found beneath the surface of the Earth, and may also exist on other terrestrial planets. Besides molten rock, _____ may also contain suspended crystals and gas bubbles. _____ often collects in a _____ chamber inside a volcano. _____ is capable of intrusion into adjacent rocks, extrusion onto the surface as lava, and explosive ejection as tephra to form pyroclastic rock.
   a. Metamorphic zone
   b. Large igneous provinces
   c. Metamorphic rock
   d. Magma

36. A _____ is an underwater mountain range, typically having a valley known as a rift running along its spine, formed by plate tectonics. This type of oceanic ridge is characteristic of what is known as an oceanic spreading center, which is responsible for seafloor spreading. The uplifted sea floor results from convection currents which rise in the mantle as magma at a linear weakness in the oceanic crust, and emerge as lava, creating new crust upon cooling.
   a. Downcutting
   b. Wave pounding
   c. Spheroidal weathering
   d. Mid-ocean ridge

37. In geology, a _____ is a place where the Earth's crust and lithosphere are being pulled apart and is an example of extensional tectonics.

Typical _____ features are a central linear downdropped fault segment, called a graben, with parallel normal faulting and _____-flank uplifts on either side forming a _____ valley, where the _____ remains above sea level. The axis of the _____ area commonly contains volcanic rocks and active volcanism is a part of many, but not all active _____ systems.

   a. 1700 Cascadia earthquake
   b. 1703 Genroku earthquake
   c. 1509 Istanbul earthquake
   d. Rift

38. _____ occurs at mid-ocean ridges, where new oceanic crust is formed through volcanic activity and then gradually moves away from the ridge. _____ helps explain continental drift in the theory of plate tectonics.

Earlier theories (e.g., by Alfred Wegener) of continental drift were that continents 'plowed' through the sea. The idea that the seafloor itself moves (and carries the continents with it) as it expands from a central axis was proposed by Harry Hess from Princeton University in the 1960s. The theory is well-accepted now, and the phenomenon is known to be caused by convection currents in the plastic, very weak upper mantle, or asthenosphere.

- a. 1700 Cascadia earthquake
- b. 1703 Genroku earthquake
- c. 1509 Istanbul earthquake
- d. Seafloor spreading

39. The _____ is an oceanic tectonic plate beneath the Pacific Ocean.

To the north the easterly side is a divergent boundary with the Explorer Plate, the Juan de Fuca Plate and the Gorda Plate forming respectively the Explorer Ridge, the Juan de Fuca Ridge and the Gorda Ridge. In the middle the easterly side is a transform boundary with the North American Plate along the San Andreas Fault and a boundary with the Cocos Plate.

- a. Bird's Head Plate
- b. Niuafo'ou Plate
- c. New Hebrides Plate
- d. Pacific plate

40. The _____ is a tectonic plate which includes the continent of Africa, as well as oceanic crust which lies between the continent and various surrounding ocean ridges.

The westerly side is a divergent boundary with the North American Plate to the north and the South American Plate to the south forming the central and southern part of the Mid-Atlantic Ridge. The _____ is bounded on the northeast by the Arabian Plate, the southeast by the Indo-Australian Plate, the north by the Eurasian Plate and the Anatolian Plate, and on the south by the Antarctic Plate.

- a. Arabian Plate
- b. African plate
- c. Eurasian Plate
- d. Easter Plate

41. A _____ is a phenomenon of fluid dynamics that occurs in situations where there are temperature differences within a body of liquid or gas.

Fluids are materials that exhibit the property of flow. Both gases and liquids have fluid properties, and in sufficient quantity, even particulate solids such as salt, grain, and gravel show some fluid properties. When a volume of fluid is heated, it expands and becomes less dense and thus more buoyant than the surrounding fluid. The colder, denser fluid settles underneath the warmer, less dense fluid and forces it to rise. Such movement is called convection, and the moving body of liquid is referred to as a _____.

- a. Convection cell
- b. 1700 Cascadia earthquake
- c. 1703 Genroku earthquake
- d. 1509 Istanbul earthquake

Chapter 1. A First Look at Planet Earth

42. In plate tectonics, a _____ is an actively deforming region where two tectonic plates or fragments of lithosphere move toward one another and collide. As a result of pressure and friction and plate material melting in the mantle, earthquakes and volcanoes are common near convergent boundaries.
    a. Convergent boundary
    b. Plate tectonics
    c. Mirovia
    d. Thrust fault

43. The _____ is a tectonic plate that was originally a part of the ancient continent of Gondwanaland from which it split off, eventually becoming a major plate. About 50 to 55 million years ago, it fused with the adjacent Australian Plate. It is today part of the major Indo-Australian Plate, and includes the subcontinent of India and a portion of the basin under the Indian Ocean.
    a. AL 129-1
    b. AL 333
    c. AASHTO Soil Classification System
    d. Indian plate

44. A _____ is a mountain rising from the ocean seafloor that does not reach to the water's surface (sea level), and thus is not an island. These are typically formed from extinct volcanoes, that rise abruptly and are usually found rising from a seafloor of 1,000-4,000 meters depth. They are defined by oceanographers as independent features that rise to at least 1,000 meters above the seafloor.
    a. 1700 Cascadia earthquake
    b. 1509 Istanbul earthquake
    c. 1703 Genroku earthquake
    d. Seamount

45. In geology, _____ is the process that takes place at convergent boundaries by which one tectonic plate moves under another tectonic plate, sinking into the Earth's mantle, as the plates converge. A _____ zone is an area on Earth where two tectonic plates move towards one another and _____ occurs. Rates of _____ are typically measured in centimeters per year, with the average rate of convergence being approximately 2 to 8 centimeters per year (about the rate a fingernail grows.)
    a. Plate tectonics
    b. Subduction
    c. Continental crust
    d. Mirovia

46. A _____ or transform boundary is a fault which runs along the boundary of a tectonic plate. The relative motion of such plates is horizontal in either sinistral or dextral direction. Typically, some vertical motion may also exist, but the principal vectors in a _____ are oriented horizontally.
    a. 1509 Istanbul earthquake
    b. 1703 Genroku earthquake
    c. Transform fault
    d. 1700 Cascadia earthquake

47. A _____ is an opening in a planet's surface or crust, which allows hot, molten rock, ash, and gases to escape from below the surface. Volcanic activity involving the extrusion of rock tends to form mountains or features like mountains over a period of time.
    a. 1703 Genroku earthquake
    b. Volcano
    c. 1509 Istanbul earthquake
    d. 1700 Cascadia earthquake

Chapter 2. Minerals

1. _____ is a silvery white and ductile member of the boron group of chemical elements. It has the symbol Al; its atomic number is 13. It is not soluble in water under normal circumstances. _____ is the most abundant metal in the Earth's crust, and the third most abundant element therein, after oxygen and silicon. It makes up about 8% by weight of the Earth'e;s solid surface.
    a. AL 129-1
    b. AASHTO Soil Classification System
    c. AL 333
    d. Aluminum

2. _____ is the most important aluminium ore. It consists largely of the minerals gibbsite $Al(OH)_3$, boehmite >γ-AlO(OH), and diaspore >α-AlO(OH), together with the iron oxides goethite and hematite, the clay mineral kaolinite and small amounts of anatase TiO_2. It was named after the village Les Baux in southern France, where it was first discovered in 1821 by the geologist Pierre Berthier.
    a. 1703 Genroku earthquake
    b. Bauxite
    c. 1509 Istanbul earthquake
    d. 1700 Cascadia earthquake

3. _____ is a carbonate mineral and the most stable polymorph of calcium carbonate ($CaCO_3$.) The other polymorphs are the minerals aragonite and vaterite. Aragonite will change to _____ at 470>°C, and vaterite is even less stable.

_____ is a common constituent of sedimentary rocks, limestone in particular, much of which is formed from the shells of dead marine organisms. Approximately 10% of sedimentary rock is limestone.

    a. Calcite
    b. 1509 Istanbul earthquake
    c. 1703 Genroku earthquake
    d. 1700 Cascadia earthquake

4. _____ is the chemical element with the symbol Ca and atomic number 20. It has an atomic mass of 40.078 amu. _____ is a soft grey alkaline earth metal, and is the fifth most abundant element by mass in the Earth's crust.
    a. 1703 Genroku earthquake
    b. 1700 Cascadia earthquake
    c. 1509 Istanbul earthquake
    d. Calcium

5. _____ is a clay mineral with the chemical composition $Al_2Si_2O_5(OH)_4$. It is a layered silicate mineral, with one tetrahedral sheet linked through oxygen atoms to one octahedral sheet of alumina octahedra. Rocks that are rich in _____ are known as china clay or kaolin. _____ clay occurs in abundance in soils that have formed from the chemical weathering of rocks in hot, moist climates - for example in tropical rainforest areas
    a. 1700 Cascadia earthquake
    b. Kaolinite
    c. 1509 Istanbul earthquake
    d. 1703 Genroku earthquake

6. _____ is the second most abundant mineral in the Earth's continental crust . It is made up of a framework of silicon-oxygen tetrahedra SiO_4, with each silicon shared between two oxygens to give the overall formula SiO_2. _____ has a hardness of 7 on the Mohs scale and a density of 2.65 g/cmÂ³.
    a. 1703 Genroku earthquake
    b. 1700 Cascadia earthquake
    c. 1509 Istanbul earthquake
    d. Quartz

7. The _____, is a geologic eon before the Proterozoic and Paleoproterozoic, before 2.5 Ga (billion years ago, or 2,500 Ma.) Instead of being based on stratigraphy, this date is defined chronometrically. The lower boundary (starting point) has not been officially recognized by the International Commission on Stratigraphy, but it is usually set to 3.8 Ga, at the end of the Hadean eon.

Chapter 2. Minerals

a. AL 333
b. AL 129-1
c. AASHTO Soil Classification System
d. Archean

8. The unified _____, is a unit of mass used to express atomic and molecular masses. It is the approximate mass of a hydrogen atom, a proton, or a neutron.

The precise definition is that it is one twelfth of the mass of an isolated atom of carbon-12 ($>^{12}C$) at rest and in its ground state.

a. AL 333
b. AASHTO Soil Classification System
c. AL 129-1
d. Atomic mass unit

9. A _____ is a free neutron that is Boltzmann distributed with kT = 0.024 eV (4.0×10^{-21} J) at room temperature. This gives characteristic (not average, or median) speed of 2.2 km/s. The name 'thermal' comes from their energy being that of the room temperature gas or material they are permeating.
a. 1700 Cascadia earthquake
b. Thermal neutron
c. 1703 Genroku earthquake
d. 1509 Istanbul earthquake

10. A _____ is an atom with an unstable nucleus, which is a nucleus characterized by excess energy which is available to be imparted either to a newly-created radiation particle within the nucleus, or else to an atomic electron . The _____, in this process, undergoes radioactive decay, and emits a gamma ray(s) and/or subatomic particles. These particles constitute ionizing radiation.
a. 1509 Istanbul earthquake
b. 1703 Genroku earthquake
c. Radionuclide
d. 1700 Cascadia earthquake

11. _____ is the electromagnetic interaction between delocalized electrons, called conduction electrons, and the metallic nuclei within metals. Understood as the sharing of 'free' electrons among a lattice of positively-charged ions (cations), _____ is sometimes compared with that of molten salts; however, this simplistic view holds true for very few metals. In a more quantum-mechanical view, the conduction electrons divide their density equally over all atoms that function as neutral (non-charged) entities.
a. 1700 Cascadia earthquake
b. 1509 Istanbul earthquake
c. 1703 Genroku earthquake
d. Metallic bonding

12. _____ is water located beneath the ground surface in soil pore spaces and in the fractures of lithologic formations. A unit of rock or an unconsolidated deposit is called an aquifer when it can yield a usable quantity of water. The depth at which soil pore spaces or fractures and voids in rock become completely saturated with water is called the water table.
a. Depression focused recharge
b. 1700 Cascadia earthquake
c. 1509 Istanbul earthquake
d. Groundwater

13. Alpine glaciers form high on the mountain slopes and are niche, slope or cirque glaciers. As a mountain glacier increases in size it can begin to flow down valley, and are referred to as _____.
a. 1700 Cascadia earthquake
b. Valley glaciers
c. 1509 Istanbul earthquake
d. 1703 Genroku earthquake

14. A _____ is a large, slow-moving mass of ice, formed from compacted layers of snow, that slowly deforms and flows in response to gravity and high pressure.

_____ ice is the largest reservoir of fresh water on Earth, and second only to oceans as the largest reservoir of total water.

a. Keeling Curve
b. Little Ice Age
c. Geologic temperature record
d. Glacier

15. In mineralogy and crystallography, a _____ is a unique arrangement of atoms in a crystal. A _____ is composed of a motif, a set of atoms arranged in a particular way, and a lattice. Motifs are located upon the points of a lattice, which is an array of points repeating periodically in three dimensions.
a. 1700 Cascadia earthquake
b. Crystal structure
c. 1703 Genroku earthquake
d. 1509 Istanbul earthquake

16. A _____ is a mineral-like substance that does not demonstrate crystallinity. Mineraloids possess chemical compositions that vary beyond the generally accepted ranges for specific minerals. For example, obsidian is an amorphous glass and not a crystal.
a. 1700 Cascadia earthquake
b. Mineraloid
c. 1703 Genroku earthquake
d. 1509 Istanbul earthquake

17. _____ is a naturally occurring glass formed as an extrusive igneous rock. It is produced when felsic lava extruded from a volcano cools without crystal growth. _____ is commonly found within the margins of rhyolitic lava flows known as _____ flows, where the chemical composition (high silica content) induces a high viscosity and polymerization degree of the lava.
a. AASHTO Soil Classification System
b. AL 129-1
c. AL 333
d. Obsidian

18. The mineral _____ is a magnesium iron silicate with the formula $(Mg,Fe)_2SiO_4$. It is one of the most common minerals on Earth, and has also been identified in meteorites and on the Moon, Mars, and comet Wild 2.

The ratio of magnesium and iron varies between the two endmembers of the solid solution series: forsterite (Mg-endmember) and fayalite (Fe-endmember.)

a. Olivine
b. AASHTO Soil Classification System
c. AL 333
d. AL 129-1

19. The _____ of a mineral is the color of the powder produced when it is dragged across an unweathered surface. Unlike the apparent color of a mineral, which for most minerals can vary considerably, the trail of finely ground powder generally has a more consistent characteristic color, and is thus an important diagnostic tool in mineral identification. If no _____ seems to be made, the mineral's _____ is said to be white or colorless.
a. Streak
b. 1703 Genroku earthquake
c. 1509 Istanbul earthquake
d. 1700 Cascadia earthquake

20. _____ is a naturally occurring granular material composed of finely divided rock and mineral particles.

Chapter 2. Minerals

As the term is used by geologists, _____ particles range in diameter from 0.0625 (or >$^1\!/_{16}$ mm, or 62.5 micrometers) to 2 millimeters. An individual particle in this range size is termed a _____ grain.

a. 1509 Istanbul earthquake
b. 1700 Cascadia earthquake
c. Sand
d. 1703 Genroku earthquake

21. _____, in structural geology and related disciplines, describes the tendency of a rock to break along preferred planes of weakness.

Rocks deformed under very low to low metamorphic grade often develop planes along which the rock can easily be split. Slates are an example of a rock with a penetrative _____ caused partly by the realignment of phyllosilicate minerals with increasing flattening strain.

a. 1703 Genroku earthquake
b. 1509 Istanbul earthquake
c. 1700 Cascadia earthquake
d. Cleavage

22. In chemistry, a _____ is a salt or ester of carbonic acid.

To test for the presence of the _____ anion in a salt, the addition of dilute mineral acid (e.g. hydrochloric acid) will yield carbon dioxide gas.

_____-containing salts are industrially and mineralogically ubiquitous.

a. Carbonate
b. 1509 Istanbul earthquake
c. 1703 Genroku earthquake
d. 1700 Cascadia earthquake

23. The _____ characterizes the scratch resistance of various minerals through the ability of a harder material to scratch a softer material. It was created in 1812 by the German mineralogist Friedrich Mohs and is one of several definitions of hardness in materials science. The method, however, is of great antiquity, having first been mentioned by Theophrastus in his treatise On Stones in ca 300 BC, followed by Pliny the Elder in his Naturalis Historia circa A.D.

a. 1703 Genroku earthquake
b. Mohs scale of mineral hardness
c. 1509 Istanbul earthquake
d. 1700 Cascadia earthquake

24. _____ is defined as the ratio of the density of a given solid or liquid substance to the density of water at a specific temperature and pressure, typically at 4 >°C (39 >°F) and 1 atm (760.00 mmHg) , making it a dimensionless quantity Substances with a _____ greater than one are denser than water, and so (ignoring surface tension effects) will sink in it, and those with a _____ of less than one are less dense than water, and so will float in it. _____ is a special case of, or in some usages synonymous with, relative density, with the latter term often preferred in modern scientific writing.

a. 1700 Cascadia earthquake
b. 1509 Istanbul earthquake
c. 1703 Genroku earthquake
d. Specific gravity

Chapter 2. Minerals

25. A _____ is a compound containing an anion in which one or more central silicon atoms are surrounded by electronegative ligands. This definition is broad enough to include species such as hexafluorosilicate ('fluorosilicate'), $[SiF_6]^{2-}$, but the _____ species that are encountered most often consist of silicon with oxygen as the ligand. _____ anions, with a negative net electrical charge, must have that charge balanced by other cations to make an electrically neutral compound.
   a. 1509 Istanbul earthquake
   b. 1703 Genroku earthquake
   c. 1700 Cascadia earthquake
   d. Silicate

26. _____ defines an important group of generally dark-colored rock-forming inosilicate minerals, composed of double chain SiO_4 tetrahedra, linked at the vertices and generally containing ions of iron and/or magnesium in their structures. They crystallize into two crystal systems, monoclinic and orthorhombic. In chemical composition and general characteristics they are similar to the pyroxenes. They are minerals of either igneous or metamorphic origin; in the former case occurring as constituents (hornblende) of igneous rocks, such as granite, diorite, andesite and others. Those of metamorphic origin include examples such as those developed in limestones by contact metamorphism (tremolite) and those formed by the alteration of other ferromagnesian minerals (hornblende).
   a. Amphibole
   b. AL 129-1
   c. AASHTO Soil Classification System
   d. AL 333

27. The _____ are a group of important rock-forming silicate minerals found in many igneous and metamorphic rocks. They share a common structure consisting of single chains of silica tetrahedra and they crystallize in the monoclinic and orthorhombic systems. _____ have the general formula $XY(Si,Al)_2O_6$ (where X represents calcium, sodium, iron^{+2} and magnesium and more rarely zinc, manganese and lithium and Y represents ions of smaller size, such as chromium, aluminium, iron^{+3}, magnesium, manganese, scandium, titanium, vanadium and even iron^{+2}).
   a. 1700 Cascadia earthquake
   b. 1509 Istanbul earthquake
   c. 1703 Genroku earthquake
   d. Pyroxenes

28. _____ is a common phyllosilicate mineral within the mica group, with the approximate chemical formula $K(Mg, Fe)_3AlSi_3O_{10}(F, OH)_2$. More generally, it refers to the dark mica series, primarily a solid-solution series between the iron-endmember annite, and the magnesium-endmember phlogopite; more aluminous endmembers include siderophyllite.
   a. 1700 Cascadia earthquake
   b. Biotite
   c. 1509 Istanbul earthquake
   d. 1703 Genroku earthquake

29. _____ are a group of rock-forming tectosilicate minerals which make up as much as 60% of the Earth's crust.

_____ crystallize from magma in both intrusive and extrusive igneous rocks, as veins, and are also present in many types of metamorphic rock. Rock formed entirely of plagioclase feldspar is known as anorthosite.

   a. 1703 Genroku earthquake
   b. 1509 Istanbul earthquake
   c. 1700 Cascadia earthquake
   d. Feldspars

30. _____ is the name of a sedimentary carbonate rock and a mineral, both composed of calcium magnesium carbonate $CaMg_2$ found in crystals.

_____ rock (also dolostone) is composed predominantly of the mineral _____. Limestone that is partially replaced by _____ is referred to as dolomitic limestone, or in old U.S. geologic literature as magnesian limestone.

Chapter 2. Minerals

a. Jasperoid
b. Dolomite
c. Sandstone
d. Metasediment

31. _____, copper(I) sulfide (Cu_2S), is an important copper ore mineral. It is opaque, being colored dark-gray to black with a metallic luster. It has a hardness of 2½ - 3. It is a sulfide with an orthorhombic crystal system.

_____ is sometimes found as a primary vein mineral in hydrothermal veins. However, most _____ occurs in the supergene enriched environment below the oxidation zone of copper deposits as a result of the leaching of copper from the oxidized minerals.

a. 1700 Cascadia earthquake
b. 1509 Istanbul earthquake
c. 1703 Genroku earthquake
d. Chalcocite

32. _____ is a crystalline form of aluminium oxide (>α-Al_2O_3) and is one of the rock-forming minerals. It is naturally clear, but can have different colors when impurities are present. Transparent specimens are used as gems, called ruby if red, while all other colors are called sapphire.

a. 1700 Cascadia earthquake
b. 1509 Istanbul earthquake
c. Corundum
d. 1703 Genroku earthquake

33. A _____ or gem is a piece of attractive mineral, which -- when cut and polished -- is used to make jewelry or other adornments. However certain rocks, and organic materials are not minerals, but are still used for jewelry, and are therefore often considered to be gemstones as well. Most gemstones are hard, but some soft minerals are used in jewelry because of their lustre or other physical properties that have aesthetic value.

a. 1700 Cascadia earthquake
b. 1703 Genroku earthquake
c. Gemstone
d. 1509 Istanbul earthquake

34. _____ is a type of potassic volcanic rock best known for sometimes containing diamonds. It is named after the town of Kimberley in South Africa, where the discovery of an 83.5 carats (16.7 g) diamond in 1871 spawned a diamond rush, eventually creating the Big Hole.

_____ occurs in the Earth's crust in vertical structures known as _____ pipes.

a. 1509 Istanbul earthquake
b. 1703 Genroku earthquake
c. Kimberlite
d. 1700 Cascadia earthquake

Chapter 3. Igneous Processes and Igneous Rocks

1. _____ is an absorbent aluminium phyllosilicate, generally impure clay consisting mostly of montmorillonite. There are a few types of bentonites and their names depend on the dominant elements, such as K, Na, Ca, and Al. As noted in several places in the geologic literature, there are some nomenclatorial problems with the classification of _____ clays.
   a. 1509 Istanbul earthquake
   b. 1700 Cascadia earthquake
   c. Bentonite
   d. 1703 Genroku earthquake

2. _____ is a naturally occurring material composed primarily of fine-grained minerals, which show plasticity through a variable range of water content, and which can be hardened when dried and/or fired. _____ deposits are mostly composed of _____ minerals (phyllosilicate minerals), minerals which impart plasticity and harden when fired and/or dried, and variable amounts of water trapped in the mineral structure by polar attraction. Organic materials which do not impart plasticity may also be a part of _____ deposits.
   a. 1509 Istanbul earthquake
   b. 1700 Cascadia earthquake
   c. 1703 Genroku earthquake
   d. Clay

3. _____ are hydrous aluminium phyllosilicates, sometimes with variable amounts of iron, magnesium, alkali metals, alkaline earths and other cations. Clays have structures similar to the micas and therefore form flat hexagonal sheets. _____ are common weathering products (including weathering of feldspar) and low temperature hydrothermal alteration products.
   a. 1703 Genroku earthquake
   b. 1700 Cascadia earthquake
   c. Clay minerals
   d. 1509 Istanbul earthquake

4. _____ is one of the three main rock types (the others being sedimentary and metamorphic rock.) _____ is formed by magma (molten rock) being cooled and becoming solid . They may form with or without crystallization, either below the surface as intrusive (plutonic) rocks or on the surface as extrusive (volcanic) rocks. They make up approximately 95% of the upper part of the Earth's crust, but their great abundance is hidden on the Earth's surface by a relatively thin but widespread layer of sedimentary and metamorphic rocks.
   a. Igneous rock
   b. AL 333
   c. AASHTO Soil Classification System
   d. AL 129-1

5. _____ is molten rock expelled by a volcano during eruption. When first expelled from a volcanic vent, it is a liquid at temperatures from 700 >°C to 1,200 >°C (1,300 >°F to 2,200 >°F.) Although _____ is quite viscous, with about 100,000 times the viscosity of water, it can flow great distances before cooling and solidifying, because of both its thixotropic and shear thinning properties.
   a. Pyroclastic flow
   b. Pumice
   c. Lava
   d. Cinder

6. _____ is molten rock that is found beneath the surface of the Earth, and may also exist on other terrestrial planets. Besides molten rock, _____ may also contain suspended crystals and gas bubbles. _____ often collects in a _____ chamber inside a volcano. _____ is capable of intrusion into adjacent rocks, extrusion onto the surface as lava, and explosive ejection as tephra to form pyroclastic rock.
   a. Metamorphic zone
   b. Metamorphic rock
   c. Large igneous provinces
   d. Magma

7. _____ is a term usually used to refer to igneous rock grain size. It means that the size of matrix grains in the rock are large enough to be distinguished with the unaided eye as opposed to aphanitic This texture forms by slow cooling of magma deep underground in the plutonic environment.

Chapter 3. Igneous Processes and Igneous Rocks

a. 1509 Istanbul earthquake
c. 1703 Genroku earthquake
b. Phaneritic
d. 1700 Cascadia earthquake

8. _____ is a name given to certain typically dark-coloured igneous rocks which are so fine-grained that their component mineral crystals are not detected by the unaided eye. This texture results from rapid cooling in volcanic or hypabyssal environments.

They are commonly porphyritic, having large crystals embedded in the fine groundmass or matrix.

a. AL 333
c. AL 129-1
b. AASHTO Soil Classification System
d. Aphanite

9. The _____, is a geologic eon before the Proterozoic and Paleoproterozoic, before 2.5 Ga (billion years ago, or 2,500 Ma.) Instead of being based on stratigraphy, this date is defined chronometrically. The lower boundary (starting point) has not been officially recognized by the International Commission on Stratigraphy, but it is usually set to 3.8 Ga, at the end of the Hadean eon.

a. Archean
c. AL 333
b. AASHTO Soil Classification System
d. AL 129-1

10. _____ is a common extrusive volcanic rock. It is usually grey to black and fine-grained due to rapid cooling of lava at the surface of a planet. It may be porphyritic containing larger crystals in a fine matrix, or vesicular, or frothy scoria.

a. 1703 Genroku earthquake
c. 1509 Istanbul earthquake
b. 1700 Cascadia earthquake
d. Basalt

11. In geology, an _____ is a body of igneous rock that has crystallized from molten magma below the surface of the Earth. Bodies of magma that solidify underground before they reach the surface of the earth are called plutons the Roman god of the underworld. Correspondingly, rocks of this kind are also referred to as igneous plutonic rocks or igneous intrusive rocks.

a. AL 333
c. AASHTO Soil Classification System
b. AL 129-1
d. Intrusion

12. _____ is a very coarse-grained igneous rock that has a grain size of 20 mm or more; such rocks are referred to as pegmatitic.

Most _____ is composed of quartz, feldspar and mica; in essence a 'granite'. Rarer 'intermediate' and 'mafic' _____ containing amphibole, Ca-plagioclase feldspar, pyroxene and other minerals are known, found in recrystallised zones and apophyses associated with large layered intrusions.

a. 1703 Genroku earthquake
c. Pegmatite
b. 1700 Cascadia earthquake
d. 1509 Istanbul earthquake

13. A _____ is a large emplacement of igneous intrusive rock that forms from cooled magma deep in the Earth's crust. they are almost always made mostly of felsic or intermediate rock-types, such as granite, quartz monzonite, or diorite

Although they may appear uniform, batholiths are in fact structures with complex histories and compositions.

a. Scoria
b. Charnockite
c. Flood basalt
d. Batholith

14. _____ is an igneous rock of volcanic origin. They are usually fine-grained or aphanitic to glassy in texture. They often contain clasts of other rocks and phenocrysts.

a. Tephra
b. Felsic
c. Volcanic rock
d. Metamorphic zone

15. _____ is a term used in geology to refer to silicate minerals, magma, and rocks which are enriched in the lighter elements such as silicon, oxygen, aluminium, sodium, and potassium. _____ minerals are usually light in color and have specific gravities less than 3. Common _____ minerals include quartz, muscovite, orthoclase, and the sodium-rich plagioclase feldspars.

a. Felsic
b. Volcanic rock
c. Metamorphic rock
d. Pluton

16. _____ is an adjective describing a silicate mineral or rock that is rich in magnesium and iron; the term was derived by contracting 'magnesium' and 'ferric'. Most _____ minerals are dark in color and the specific gravity is greater than 3. Common rock-forming _____ minerals include olivine, pyroxene, amphibole, and biotite.

_____ lava, before cooling, has a low viscosity, in comparison to felsic lava, due to the lower silica content in _____ magma. Water and other volatiles can more easily and gradually escape from _____ lava, so eruptions of volcanoes made of _____ lavas are less explosively violent than felsic lava eruptions.

a. 1700 Cascadia earthquake
b. 1703 Genroku earthquake
c. 1509 Istanbul earthquake
d. Mafic

17. _____ is a naturally occurring glass formed as an extrusive igneous rock. It is produced when felsic lava extruded from a volcano cools without crystal growth. _____ is commonly found within the margins of rhyolitic lava flows known as _____ flows, where the chemical composition (high silica content) induces a high viscosity and polymerization degree of the lava.

a. AASHTO Soil Classification System
b. AL 129-1
c. AL 333
d. Obsidian

18. The mineral _____ is a magnesium iron silicate with the formula $(Mg,Fe)_2SiO_4$. It is one of the most common minerals on Earth, and has also been identified in meteorites and on the Moon, Mars, and comet Wild 2.

The ratio of magnesium and iron varies between the two endmembers of the solid solution series: forsterite (Mg-endmember) and fayalite (Fe-endmember.)

a. AASHTO Soil Classification System
b. AL 129-1
c. AL 333
d. Olivine

Chapter 3. Igneous Processes and Igneous Rocks

19. A _____ is a dense, coarse-grained igneous rock, consisting mostly of the minerals olivine and pyroxene. _____ is ultramafic, as the rock contains less than 45% silica. It is high in magnesium, reflecting the high proportions of magnesium-rich olivine, with appreciable iron.

_____ is the dominant rock of the upper part of the Earth's mantle. The compositions of _____ nodules found in certain basalts and diamond pipes (kimberlites) are of special interest, because they provide samples of the Earth's Mantle roots of continents brought up from depths from about 30 km or so to depths at least as great as about 200 km.

   a. 1703 Genroku earthquake
   b. 1509 Istanbul earthquake
   c. 1700 Cascadia earthquake
   d. Peridotite

20. _____ is a textural term for a volcanic rock that is a solidified frothy lava typically created when super-heated, highly pressurized rock is violently ejected from a volcano. It can be formed when lava and water are mixed. This unusual formation is due to the simultaneous actions of rapid cooling and rapid depressurization.
   a. Pumice
   b. Pyroclastic flow
   c. Volcanic ash
   d. Cinder

21. _____ refers to a large group of dark, coarse-grained, intrusive igneous rocks chemically equivalent to basalt. The rocks are plutonic, formed when molten magma is trapped beneath the Earth's surface and cools into a crystalline mass.

The vast majority of the Earth's surface is underlain by _____ within the oceanic crust, produced by basalt magmatism at mid-ocean ridges.

   a. 1700 Cascadia earthquake
   b. 1703 Genroku earthquake
   c. 1509 Istanbul earthquake
   d. Gabbro

22. _____ is an igneous, volcanic rock, of intermediate composition, with aphanitic to porphyritic texture. The mineral assemblage is typically dominated by plagioclase plus pyroxene and/or hornblende. Magnetite, zircon, apatite, ilmenite, biotite, and garnet are common accessory minerals.
   a. AASHTO Soil Classification System
   b. Andesite
   c. AL 333
   d. AL 129-1

23. _____ is a process of melting that takes place in the Earth's mantle. The melting temperatures are unlikely high enough to melt the entire source rock, and only portions of or some of the minerals they contain melt.
   a. Raton hotspot
   b. Submarine eruption
   c. Volcanic blocks
   d. Partial melting

24. _____ is an igneous, volcanic (extrusive) rock, of felsic (silicon-rich) composition. It may have any texture from aphanitic to porphyritic. The mineral assemblage is usually quartz, alkali feldspar and plagioclase. Biotite and hornblende are common accessory minerals.

_____ can be considered as the extrusive equivalent to the plutonic granite rock, and consequently, outcroppings of it often bear a resemblance to granite. Due to their high content of silica and low iron and magnesium contents, _____ melts are highly polymerized and form highly viscous lavas.

a. Rhyolite
b. 1703 Genroku earthquake
c. 1700 Cascadia earthquake
d. 1509 Istanbul earthquake

25. _____ is the (natural or artificial) process of formation of solid crystals precipitating from a solution, melt or more rarely deposited directly from a gas. _____ is also a chemical solid-liquid separation technique, in which mass transfer of a solute from the liquid solution to a pure solid crystalline phase occurs.

The _____ process consists of two major events, nucleation and crystal growth.

a. 1700 Cascadia earthquake
b. 1703 Genroku earthquake
c. 1509 Istanbul earthquake
d. Crystallization

26. In geology, _____ refers to heat sources within the planet. _____ is technically an adjective (e.g., _____ energy) but in U.S. English the word has attained frequent use as a noun.

The planet's internal heat was originally generated during its accretion, due to gravitational binding energy, and since then additional heat has continued to be generated by decay heat from the radioactive decay of elements.

a. Combe
b. Geothermal
c. Diamond Head
d. Compaction

27. The _____ is the rate of increase in temperature per unit depth in the Earth. It varies with location and is typically measured by determining the bottom open-hole temperature after borehole drilling. To achieve accuracy the drilling fluid needs time to reach the ambient temperature.

a. Geothermal heat pump
b. Hot Dry Rock Geothermal Energy
c. Geothermal power
d. Geothermal gradient

28. _____ is water located beneath the ground surface in soil pore spaces and in the fractures of lithologic formations. A unit of rock or an unconsolidated deposit is called an aquifer when it can yield a usable quantity of water. The depth at which soil pore spaces or fractures and voids in rock become completely saturated with water is called the water table.

a. 1509 Istanbul earthquake
b. Groundwater
c. Depression focused recharge
d. 1700 Cascadia earthquake

29. _____ is a silvery white and ductile member of the boron group of chemical elements. It has the symbol Al; its atomic number is 13. It is not soluble in water under normal circumstances. _____ is the most abundant metal in the Earth's crust, and the third most abundant element therein, after oxygen and silicon. It makes up about 8% by weight of the Earth'e;s solid surface.

a. AASHTO Soil Classification System
b. AL 333
c. Aluminum
d. AL 129-1

30. _____ are a group of rock-forming tectosilicate minerals which make up as much as 60% of the Earth's crust.

_____ crystallize from magma in both intrusive and extrusive igneous rocks, as veins, and are also present in many types of metamorphic rock. Rock formed entirely of plagioclase feldspar is known as anorthosite.

Chapter 3. Igneous Processes and Igneous Rocks

a. 1703 Genroku earthquake
c. 1509 Istanbul earthquake
b. Feldspars
d. 1700 Cascadia earthquake

31. _____ is a naturally occurring granular material composed of finely divided rock and mineral particles.

As the term is used by geologists, _____ particles range in diameter from 0.0625 (or $>^1\!\!/_{16}$ mm, or 62.5 micrometers) to 2 millimeters. An individual particle in this range size is termed a _____ grain.

a. 1700 Cascadia earthquake
c. Sand
b. 1703 Genroku earthquake
d. 1509 Istanbul earthquake

32. The chemical compound silicon dioxide, also known as _____ , is an oxide of silicon with a chemical formula of SiO_2 and has been known for its hardness since antiquity. _____ is most commonly found in nature as sand or quartz, as well as in the cell walls of diatoms. It is a principal component of most types of glass and substances such as concrete.

a. Silica
c. 1700 Cascadia earthquake
b. 1703 Genroku earthquake
d. 1509 Istanbul earthquake

33. A _____ is a type of intrusion in which a more mobile and ductily-deformable material is forced into brittle overlying rocks. Depending on the tectonic environment, they can range from idealized mushroom-shaped Rayleigh-Taylor instability-type structures in regions with low tectonic stress such as in the Gulf of Mexico to narrow dike (geology) dikes of material that move along tectonically-induced fractures in surrounding rock. The term was introduced by the Romanian geologist Ludovic Mrazek, who was the first to understand the principle of salt intrusion and plasticity.

a. Skarn
c. Diapir
b. Slyne-Erris Trough
d. Rockall Basin

34. A _____ is a mountain rising from the ocean seafloor that does not reach to the water's surface (sea level), and thus is not an island. These are typically formed from extinct volcanoes, that rise abruptly and are usually found rising from a seafloor of 1,000-4,000 meters depth. They are defined by oceanographers as independent features that rise to at least 1,000 meters above the seafloor.

a. 1509 Istanbul earthquake
c. 1700 Cascadia earthquake
b. 1703 Genroku earthquake
d. Seamount

35. A _____ is a rock fragment which becomes enveloped in a larger rock during the latter's development and hardening. In geology, the term _____ is almost exclusively used to describe inclusions in igneous rock during magma emplacement and eruption. Xenoliths may be engulfed along the margins of a magma chamber, torn loose from the walls of an erupting lava conduit or explosive diatreme or picked up along the base of a flowing lava on Earth's surface.

a. 1700 Cascadia earthquake
c. 1703 Genroku earthquake
b. Xenolith
d. 1509 Istanbul earthquake

36. _____ is a geological term meaning the rock native to an area. It is similar and in many cases interchangeable with the terms basement and wall rocks.

The term is used to denote the usual strata of a region in relation to the rock which is being discussed or observed.

Chapter 3. Igneous Processes and Igneous Rocks

a. 1703 Genroku earthquake
b. 1509 Istanbul earthquake
c. Country rock
d. 1700 Cascadia earthquake

37. A _____ or dyke in geology is a type of sheet intrusion referring to any geologic body that cuts discordantly across

- planar wall rock structures, such as bedding or foliation
- massive rock formations, like igneous/magmatic intrusions and salt diapirs.

They can therefore be either intrusive or sedimentary in origin.

An intrusive _____ is an igneous body with a very high aspect ratio, which means that its thickness is usually much smaller than the other two dimensions. Thickness can vary from sub-centimeter scale to many meters and the lateral dimensions can extend over many kilometers. A _____ is an intrusion into an opening cross-cutting fissure, shouldering aside other pre-existing layers or bodies of rock; this implies that a _____ is always younger than the rocks that contain it.

a. Fossil beach
b. Duricrust
c. Mineral hydration
d. Dike

38. A _____ in geology is an intrusive igneous rock body that crystallized from a magma slowly cooling below the surface of the Earth. Plutons include batholiths, dikes, sills, laccoliths, lopoliths, and other igneous bodies. In practice, '_____' usually refers to a distinctive mass of igneous rock, typically kilometers in dimension, without a tabular shape like those of dikes and sills.

a. Pluton
b. Magma
c. Sedimentary rock
d. Petrology

39. A _____ is a volcanic landform created when magma hardens within a vent on an active volcano. When forming, a _____ can cause an extreme build-up of pressure if volatile-charged magma is trapped beneath it, and this can sometimes lead to an explosive eruption. If a plug is preserved, erosion may remove the surrounding rock while the erosion-resistant plug remains, producing a distinctive landform.

a. 1509 Istanbul earthquake
b. 1700 Cascadia earthquake
c. 1703 Genroku earthquake
d. Volcanic plug

40. A _____ is an igneous intrusion (or concordant pluton) that has been injected between two layers of sedimentary rock. The pressure of the magma is high enough that the overlying strata are forced upward, giving the _____ a dome or mushroom-like form with a generally planar base.

They tend to form at relatively shallow depths and are typically formed by relatively viscous magmas, such as those that crystallize to diorite, granodiorite, and granite. Cooling underground takes place slowly, giving time for larger crystals to form in the cooling magma. The surface rock above the _____ often erodes away completely, leaving the core mound of igneous rock.

a. 1700 Cascadia earthquake
b. 1509 Istanbul earthquake
c. 1703 Genroku earthquake
d. Laccolith

41. A _____ is a large igneous intrusion which is lenticular in shape with a depressed central region. They are generally concordant with the intruded strata with dike or funnel-shaped feeder bodies below the body. The term was first defined and used by Frank Fitch Grout during the early 1900s in describing the Duluth gabbro complex in northern Minnesota and adjacent Ontario.
    a. Lopolith
    b. 1700 Cascadia earthquake
    c. 1703 Genroku earthquake
    d. 1509 Istanbul earthquake

42. _____, (Navajo: >Ts>é Bit'a'>í, 'rock with wings' or 'winged rock') is a rock formation rising nearly 1,800 feet (550 m) above the high-desert plain on the Navajo Nation and in San Juan County, New Mexico.

_____ is composed of fractured volcanic breccia and black dikes of igneous rock called 'minette'. It is the erosional remnant of the throat of a volcano, and the volcanic breccia formed in a diatreme. The exposed rock probably was originally formed 2,500-3000 feet (750-1,000 meters) below the earth's surface, but it was exposed after millions of years of erosion. Wall-like sheets of minette, known as dikes, radiate away from the central formation. Radiometric age determinations of the minette establish that these volcanic rocks solidified about 27 million years ago.

    a. 1509 Istanbul earthquake
    b. Shiprock
    c. 1700 Cascadia earthquake
    d. 1703 Genroku earthquake

43. _____ describes the large scale motions of Earth's lithosphere. The theory encompasses the older concepts of continental drift, developed during the first decades of the 20th century by Alfred Wegener, and seafloor spreading, understood during the 1960s.

The outermost part of the Earth's interior is made up of two layers: the lithosphere and the asthenosphere.

    a. Thrust fault
    b. Subduction
    c. Plate tectonics
    d. Copperbelt Province

44. The _____ is the most significant regional geologic distinction in the Pacific Ocean basin. It separates the mafic basaltic volcanic rocks of the Central Pacific Basin from the partially submerged continental areas of more felsic andesitic volcanic rock on its margins. The _____ parallels the subduction zones and deep oceanic trenches around the Pacific basin.
    a. Andesite line
    b. AASHTO Soil Classification System
    c. AL 333
    d. AL 129-1

45. A _____ is an underwater mountain range, typically having a valley known as a rift running along its spine, formed by plate tectonics. This type of oceanic ridge is characteristic of what is known as an oceanic spreading center, which is responsible for seafloor spreading. The uplifted sea floor results from convection currents which rise in the mantle as magma at a linear weakness in the oceanic crust, and emerge as lava, creating new crust upon cooling.
    a. Wave pounding
    b. Mid-ocean ridge
    c. Downcutting
    d. Spheroidal weathering

46. _____ is a phaneritic, intrusive igneous rock characterized by a predominance of plagioclase feldspar, and a minimal mafic component (0-10%.) Pyroxene, ilmenite, magnetite, and olivine are the mafic minerals most commonly present.

_____ on Earth can be divided into two types: Proterozoic _____ and Archean _____.

   a. AL 129-1
   c. AL 333
   b. AASHTO Soil Classification System
   d. Anorthosite

47. In geology, _____ is the process that takes place at convergent boundaries by which one tectonic plate moves under another tectonic plate, sinking into the Earth's mantle, as the plates converge. A _____ zone is an area on Earth where two tectonic plates move towards one another and _____ occurs. Rates of _____ are typically measured in centimeters per year, with the average rate of convergence being approximately 2 to 8 centimeters per year (about the rate a fingernail grows.)
   a. Continental crust
   c. Plate tectonics
   b. Subduction
   d. Mirovia

Chapter 4. Volcanoes and Volcanism

1. A _____ is an opening in a planet's surface or crust, which allows hot, molten rock, ash, and gases to escape from below the surface. Volcanic activity involving the extrusion of rock tends to form mountains or features like mountains over a period of time.
   a. 1703 Genroku earthquake
   b. Volcano
   c. 1509 Istanbul earthquake
   d. 1700 Cascadia earthquake

2. A _____ is a mountain rising from the ocean seafloor that does not reach to the water's surface (sea level), and thus is not an island. These are typically formed from extinct volcanoes, that rise abruptly and are usually found rising from a seafloor of 1,000-4,000 meters depth. They are defined by oceanographers as independent features that rise to at least 1,000 meters above the seafloor.
   a. 1703 Genroku earthquake
   b. 1700 Cascadia earthquake
   c. 1509 Istanbul earthquake
   d. Seamount

3. A _____ is a fissure in a planet's surface from which geothermally heated water issues. they are commonly found near volcanically active places, areas where tectonic plates are moving apart, ocean basins, and hotspots.

   They are locally very common because the earth is both geologically active and has large amounts of water on its surface and within its crust. Common land types include hot springs, fumaroles and geysers. The most famous _____ system on land is probably within Yellowstone National Park in the United States.

   a. 1703 Genroku earthquake
   b. 1509 Istanbul earthquake
   c. 1700 Cascadia earthquake
   d. Hydrothermal vent

4. _____ are the preserved remains or traces of animals, plants, and other organisms from the remote past. The totality of _____, both discovered and undiscovered, and their placement in fossiliferous rock formations and sedimentary layers (strata) is known as the fossil record. The study of _____ across geological time, how they were formed, and the evolutionary relationships between taxa (phylogeny) are some of the most important functions of the science of paleontology.
   a. 1700 Cascadia earthquake
   b. Fossils
   c. 1509 Istanbul earthquake
   d. 1703 Genroku earthquake

5. _____ is a term used in geology to refer to silicate minerals, magma, and rocks which are enriched in the lighter elements such as silicon, oxygen, aluminium, sodium, and potassium. _____ minerals are usually light in color and have specific gravities less than 3. Common _____ minerals include quartz, muscovite, orthoclase, and the sodium-rich plagioclase feldspars.
   a. Volcanic rock
   b. Metamorphic rock
   c. Pluton
   d. Felsic

6. _____ is an adjective describing a silicate mineral or rock that is rich in magnesium and iron; the term was derived by contracting 'magnesium' and 'ferric'. Most _____ minerals are dark in color and the specific gravity is greater than 3. Common rock-forming _____ minerals include olivine, pyroxene, amphibole, and biotite.

   _____ lava, before cooling, has a low viscosity, in comparison to felsic lava, due to the lower silica content in _____ magma. Water and other volatiles can more easily and gradually escape from _____ lava, so eruptions of volcanoes made of _____ lavas are less explosively violent than felsic lava eruptions.

a. 1700 Cascadia earthquake
b. 1703 Genroku earthquake
c. 1509 Istanbul earthquake
d. Mafic

7. _____ is molten rock that is found beneath the surface of the Earth, and may also exist on other terrestrial planets. Besides molten rock, _____ may also contain suspended crystals and gas bubbles. _____ often collects in a _____ chamber inside a volcano. _____ is capable of intrusion into adjacent rocks, extrusion onto the surface as lava, and explosive ejection as tephra to form pyroclastic rock.
   a. Metamorphic zone
   b. Metamorphic rock
   c. Large igneous provinces
   d. Magma

8. _____ is a measure of the resistance of a fluid which is being deformed by either shear stress or extensional stress. In everyday terms (and for fluids only), _____ is 'thickness'. Thus, water is 'thin', having a lower _____, while honey is 'thick' having a higher _____.
   a. 1700 Cascadia earthquake
   b. 1703 Genroku earthquake
   c. 1509 Istanbul earthquake
   d. Viscosity

9. _____ is an igneous, volcanic rock, of intermediate composition, with aphanitic to porphyritic texture. The mineral assemblage is typically dominated by plagioclase plus pyroxene and/or hornblende. Magnetite, zircon, apatite, ilmenite, biotite, and garnet are common accessory minerals.
   a. AASHTO Soil Classification System
   b. AL 333
   c. AL 129-1
   d. Andesite

10. _____ is a common extrusive volcanic rock. It is usually grey to black and fine-grained due to rapid cooling of lava at the surface of a planet. It may be porphyritic containing larger crystals in a fine matrix, or vesicular, or frothy scoria.
    a. 1700 Cascadia earthquake
    b. 1509 Istanbul earthquake
    c. 1703 Genroku earthquake
    d. Basalt

11. _____ is molten rock expelled by a volcano during eruption. When first expelled from a volcanic vent, it is a liquid at temperatures from 700 >°C to 1,200 >°C (1,300 >°F to 2,200 >°F.) Although _____ is quite viscous, with about 100,000 times the viscosity of water, it can flow great distances before cooling and solidifying, because of both its thixotropic and shear thinning properties.
    a. Pumice
    b. Cinder
    c. Pyroclastic flow
    d. Lava

12. _____ is basaltic lava that has a smooth, billowy, undulating, or ropy surface. These surface features are due to the movement of very fluid lava under a congealing surface crust.
    a. 1700 Cascadia earthquake
    b. Pahoehoe lava
    c. 1509 Istanbul earthquake
    d. 1703 Genroku earthquake

13. _____ are natural conduits through which lava travels beneath the surface of a lava flow, expelled by a volcano during an eruption. They can be actively draining lava from a source, or can be extinct, meaning the lava flow has ceased and the rock has cooled and left a long, cave-like channel.

_____ are formed when an active low-viscosity lava flow develops a continuous and hard crust,which thickens and forms a roof above the still-flowing lava stream.

Chapter 4. Volcanoes and Volcanism

a. 1700 Cascadia earthquake
c. 1509 Istanbul earthquake
b. Lava tubes
d. 1703 Genroku earthquake

14. _____ are pillow-shaped structures sometimes seen in lavas and are attributed to the congealment of lava under water, or subaqeous extrusion. A pillow structure in certain extrusive igneous rock is characterized by discontinuous pillow-shaped masses, commonly up to 1 metre in diameter. _____ commonly occur at Constructive plate boundaries, forming part of a mid-ocean ridge.
   a. Medical geology
   c. Paralithic
   b. Pillow lava
   d. Geological survey

15. _____ is an igneous, volcanic (extrusive) rock, of felsic (silicon-rich) composition. It may have any texture from aphanitic to porphyritic. The mineral assemblage is usually quartz, alkali feldspar and plagioclase. Biotite and hornblende are common accessory minerals.

_____ can be considered as the extrusive equivalent to the plutonic granite rock, and consequently, outcroppings of it often bear a resemblance to granite. Due to their high content of silica and low iron and magnesium contents, _____ melts are highly polymerized and form highly viscous lavas.

   a. 1700 Cascadia earthquake
   c. Rhyolite
   b. 1703 Genroku earthquake
   d. 1509 Istanbul earthquake

16. _____ is a textural term for macrovesicular volcanic rock. It is commonly, but not exclusively, basaltic or andesitic in composition. _____ is light as a result of numerous macroscopic ellipsoidal vesicles, but most _____ has a specific gravity greater than 1, and sinks in water.
   a. Coldwell Complex
   c. Great Dyke
   b. Charnockite
   d. Scoria

17. _____ is a volcanic rock texture characterised by, or containing many vesicles. The texture is often found in extrusive aphanitic igneous rock. The vesicles are small cavities formed by the expansion of bubbles of gas or steam during the solidification of the rock.
   a. 1700 Cascadia earthquake
   c. 1703 Genroku earthquake
   b. 1509 Istanbul earthquake
   d. Vesicular texture

18. _____ consists of small tephra, which are bits of pulverized rock and glass created by volcanic eruptions, less than 2 millimetres (0.079 in) in diameter. There are three mechanisms of _____ formation: gas release under decompression causing magmatic eruptions; thermal contraction from chilling on contact with water causing phreatomagmatic eruptions and ejection of entrained particles during steam eruptions causing phreatic eruptions. The violent nature of volcanic eruptions involving steam results in the magma and solid rock surrounding the vent being torn into particles of clay to sand size.
   a. Pit crater
   c. Supervolcano
   b. Cinder
   d. Volcanic ash

19. A _____ is a pyroclastic material. They are extrusive igneous rocks, and are similar to pumice, which has so many cavities and is such low-density that it can float on water.

Chapter 4. Volcanoes and Volcanism

a. Cinder
b. Supervolcano
c. Lava
d. Pit crater

20. _____ is a size classification term for tephra, which is material that falls out of the air during a volcanic eruption. They are in some senses similar to ooids or pisoids in calcareous sediments.

By definition _____ range in size from 2 mm to 64 mm in diameter. A pyroclastic particle greater than 64 mm in diameter is correctly known as a volcanic bomb when molten, or a volcanic block when solid.

a. 1703 Genroku earthquake
b. 1509 Istanbul earthquake
c. 1700 Cascadia earthquake
d. Lapilli

21. A _____ is a common and devastating result of some explosive volcanic eruptions. The flows are fast-moving currents of hot gas and rock (collectively known as tephra), which travel away from the volcano at speeds generally as great as 700 km/hr (450 mi/h.) The gas can reach temperatures of about 1,000 >°C (1,830 >°F). The flows normally hug the ground and travel downhill, or spread laterally under gravity. Their speed depends upon the density of the current, the volcanic output rate, and the gradient of the slope.

a. Pit crater
b. Cinder
c. Supervolcano
d. Pyroclastic flow

22. _____ are clastic rocks composed solely or primarily of volcanic materials. Where the volcanic material has been transported and reworked through mechanical action, such as by wind or water, these rocks are termed volcaniclastic. Commonly associated with explosive volcanic activity - such as Plinian or krakatoan eruption styles, or phreatomagmatic eruptions - pyroclastic deposits are commonly formed from airborne ash, lapilli and bombs or blocks ejected from the volcano itself, mixed in with shattered country rock.

a. Great Dyke
b. Charnockite
c. Coldwell Complex
d. Pyroclastic rocks

23. _____ is air-fall material produced by a volcanic eruption regardless of composition or fragment size. _____ is typically rhyolitic in composition, as most explosive volcanoes are the product of the more viscous felsic or high silica magmas.

Volcanologists also refer to airborne fragments as pyroclasts.

a. Volcanic rock
b. Sedimentary rock
c. Metamorphic rock
d. Tephra

24. _____ are fragments of rock which measure more than 64mm in size and are erupted in a solid condition.

_____ are formed from material from previous eruptions or from country rock and are therefore mostly accessory or accidental in origin. Blocks also occur due to the impact and breakage of volcanic bombs (a bomb is a block with streamlined appearance, often expelled in a molten state).

a. Submarine eruption
b. Raton hotspot
c. Volcanic blocks
d. Partial melting

Chapter 4. Volcanoes and Volcanism

25. A _____ is a mass of molten rock (tephra) larger than 65 mm (2.5 inches) in diameter, formed when a volcano ejects viscous fragments of lava during an eruption. They cool into solid fragments before they reach the ground. Lava bombs can be thrown many kilometres from an erupting vent, and often acquire aerodynamic shapes during their flight.
   a. Volcanic bomb
   b. 1509 Istanbul earthquake
   c. 1703 Genroku earthquake
   d. 1700 Cascadia earthquake

26. A _____ is a cauldron-like volcanic feature usually formed by the collapse of land following a volcanic eruption such as the one at Yellowstone National Park. They are sometimes confused with volcanic craters.
   a. 1700 Cascadia earthquake
   b. 1509 Istanbul earthquake
   c. Caldera
   d. 1703 Genroku earthquake

27. A _____ is a type of mudflow or landslide composed of pyroclastic material and water that flows down from a volcano, typically along a river valley. The term '_____' originated in the Javanese language of Indonesia. They can be best described as volcanic mudflows. They may not necessarily be caused by volcanic activity, but at the very least do originate from some type of volcanism.
   a. Lahar
   b. 1703 Genroku earthquake
   c. 1509 Istanbul earthquake
   d. 1700 Cascadia earthquake

28. A _____ or mudslide is the most rapid (up to 80 km/h, or 50 mph) and fluid type of downhill mass wasting. It is a rapid movement of a large mass of mud formed from loose earth and water. Similar terms are mudslide (not very liquid), mud stream, debris flow (e.g. in high mountains), jökulhlaup, and lahar
   a. 1703 Genroku earthquake
   b. 1509 Istanbul earthquake
   c. 1700 Cascadia earthquake
   d. Mudflow

29. _____ are among the simplest volcano formations in the world. They are built by ejecta from a volcanic vent, piling up around the vent in the shape of a cone with a central crater. _____ are of different types, depending upon the nature and size of the fragments ejected during the eruption.
   a. Ambulocetus
   b. Amblypoda
   c. Andrija Mohorovičić
   d. Volcanic cones

30. _____ is a pyroclastic rock, of any origin, that was sufficiently hot at the time of deposition to weld together. Strictly speaking, if the rock contains scattered pea-sized fragments or fiamme in it, it is called a welded lapilli-tuff. They (and welded lapilli-tuffs) can be of fallout origin, or deposited from pyroclastic density currents, as in the case of ignimbrites.
   a. Welded tuff
   b. 1509 Istanbul earthquake
   c. 1703 Genroku earthquake
   d. 1700 Cascadia earthquake

31. _____ is a type of rock consisting of consolidated volcanic ash ejected from vents during a volcanic eruption. _____ is sometimes called tufa, particularly when used as construction material, although tufa also refers to a quite different rock.

The products of a volcanic eruption are volcanic gases, lava, steam, and tephra. Magma is blown apart when it interacts violently with volcanic gases and steam. Solid material produced and thrown into the air by such volcanic eruptions is called tephra, regardless of composition or fragment size. If the resulting pieces of ejecta are small enough, the material is called volcanic ash, defined as such particles less than 2 mm in diameter, sand-sized or smaller.

Chapter 4. Volcanoes and Volcanism

a. Tuff
c. 1509 Istanbul earthquake
b. 1703 Genroku earthquake
d. 1700 Cascadia earthquake

32. A _____ is a type of volcanic eruption where lava flows from the vent in a relative gentle, low level eruption, so called because it is characteristic of Hawaiian volcanoes. Typically they are effusive eruptions, with basaltic magmas of low viscosity, low content of gases, and high temperature at the vent. Very little amount of volcanic ash is produced.

a. 1509 Istanbul earthquake
c. 1703 Genroku earthquake
b. 1700 Cascadia earthquake
d. Hawaiian eruption

33. A _____ is generally a large area of exposed Precambrian crystalline igneous and high-grade metamorphic rocks that form tectonically stable areas. In all cases, the age of these rocks is greater than 570 million years and sometimes dates back 2 to 3.5 billion years. They have been little affected by tectonic events following the end of the Precambrian Era, and are relatively flat regions where mountain building, faulting, and other tectonic processes are greatly diminished compared with the activity that occurs at the margins of the shields and the boundaries between tectonic plates.

a. Shield
c. 1700 Cascadia earthquake
b. 1703 Genroku earthquake
d. 1509 Istanbul earthquake

34. A _____ is a large volcano with shallow-sloping sides.

They are formed by lava flows of low viscosity - lava that flows easily. Consequently, a volcanic mountain having a broad profile is built up over time by flow after flow of relatively fluid basaltic lava issuing from vents or fissures on the surface of the volcano

a. 1703 Genroku earthquake
c. 1700 Cascadia earthquake
b. Shield volcano
d. 1509 Istanbul earthquake

35. The _____ is a geologic and geographic region that lies across parts of the U.S. states of Washington, Oregon, and Idaho. It is a wide flood basalt plateau between the Cascade and Rocky Mountains, cut through by the Columbia River.

During late Miocene and early Pliocene times, one of the largest flood basalts ever to appear on the earth's surface engulfed about 63,000 square miles (160,000 km^2) of the Pacific Northwest, forming a large igneous province. Over a period of perhaps 10 to 15 million years lava flow after lava flow poured out, eventually accumulating to a thickness of more than 6,000 feet . As the molten rock came to the surface, the earth's crust gradually sank into the space left by the rising lava. The subsidence of the crust produced a large, slightly depressed lava plain now known as the Columbia Basin or Plateau.

a. 1509 Istanbul earthquake
c. Columbia River plateau
b. 1700 Cascadia earthquake
d. 1703 Genroku earthquake

36. A _____ or trap basalt is the result of a giant volcanic eruption or series of eruptions that coats large stretches of land or the ocean floor with basalt lava. Flood basalts have occurred on continental scales (large igneous provinces) in prehistory, creating great plateaus and mountain ranges. Flood basalts have erupted at random intervals throughout geological history and are clear evidence that the Earth undergoes periods of enhanced activity rather than being in a uniform steady state.

Chapter 4. Volcanoes and Volcanism

a. Coldwell Complex
b. Pyroclastic rocks
c. Scoria
d. Flood basalt

37. A volcanic plateau is a plateau produced by volcanic activity. There are two main types: _____ and pyroclastic plateaus.

_____ are formed by highly fluid (runny) basaltic lava during numerous successive eruptions through numerous vents without violent explosions (quiet eruptions). These eruptions are quiet because of low viscosity of mafic lava, so that it is very fluid and contains small amount of trapped gases. The resulting sheet lava flows may be extruded from linear fissures or rifts or gigantic volcanic eruptions through multiple vents characteristic of the prehistoric era which produced giant flood basalts.

a. 1509 Istanbul earthquake
b. 1700 Cascadia earthquake
c. 1703 Genroku earthquake
d. Lava plateaus

38. _____ is the largest volcano on earth in terms of area covered and one of five volcanoes that form the Island of Hawaii in the U.S. state of Hawai>Ê»i in the Pacific Ocean. It is an active shield volcano, with a volume estimated at approximately 18,000 cubic miles (75,000 kmÂ³), although its peak is about 120 feet (37 m) lower than that of its neighbor, Mauna Kea. The Hawaiian name '_____' means 'Long Mountain'.

a. 1703 Genroku earthquake
b. Mauna Loa
c. 1509 Istanbul earthquake
d. 1700 Cascadia earthquake

39. A _____ is a type of volcanic eruption where lava erupts under an ocean. Most of the Earth's volcanic eruptions are of this type, but few have been documented because of the difficulty in monitoring them. They usually occur at mid-oceanic ridges.

a. Raton hotspot
b. Volcanic blocks
c. Partial melting
d. Submarine eruption

40. _____ is a caldera lake located in the U.S. state of Oregon. It is the main feature of _____ National Park and famous for its deep blue color and water clarity. The lake partly fills a nearly 1,958 foot (597 m) deep caldera that was formed around 7,700 (>± 150) BC by the collapse of the volcano Mount Mazama.

a. Crater Lake
b. 1703 Genroku earthquake
c. 1700 Cascadia earthquake
d. 1509 Istanbul earthquake

41. A _____ or scoria cone is a steep conical hill of volcanic fragments that accumulate around and downwind from a volcanic vent. The rock fragments, often called cinders or scoria, are glassy and contain numerous gas bubbles 'frozen' into place as magma exploded into the air and then cooled quickly. Cinder cones range in size from tens to hundreds of meters tall.

a. Cinder cone
b. 1703 Genroku earthquake
c. 1700 Cascadia earthquake
d. 1509 Istanbul earthquake

42. In geology, a _____ is a location on the Earth's surface that has experienced active volcanism for a long period of time.

J. Tuzo Wilson came up with the idea in 1963 that volcanic chains like the Hawaiian Islands result from the slow movement of a tectonic plate across a 'fixed' _____ deep beneath the surface of the planet.

a. 1703 Genroku earthquake
b. 1700 Cascadia earthquake
c. Hotspot
d. 1509 Istanbul earthquake

43. The _____ is the earliest of three geologic eras of the Phanerozoic eon. The _____ spanned from roughly 542 to 251 million years ago (ICS, 2004), and is subdivided into six geologic periods; from oldest to youngest they are: the Cambrian, Ordovician, Silurian, Devonian, Carboniferous, and Permian.

The _____ covers the time from the first appearance of abundant, soft-shelled fossils to the time when the continents were beginning to be dominated by large, relatively sophisticated reptiles and modern plants. The lower (oldest) boundary was classically set at the first appearance of creatures known as trilobites and archeocyathids.

a. 1509 Istanbul earthquake
b. 1703 Genroku earthquake
c. Paleozoic
d. 1700 Cascadia earthquake

44. In geology, a _____ is a place where the Earth's crust and lithosphere are being pulled apart and is an example of extensional tectonics.

Typical _____ features are a central linear downdropped fault segment, called a graben, with parallel normal faulting and _____-flank uplifts on either side forming a _____ valley, where the _____ remains above sea level. The axis of the _____ area commonly contains volcanic rocks and active volcanism is a part of many, but not all active _____ systems.

a. 1703 Genroku earthquake
b. 1700 Cascadia earthquake
c. 1509 Istanbul earthquake
d. Rift

45. In geology, _____ is the process that takes place at convergent boundaries by which one tectonic plate moves under another tectonic plate, sinking into the Earth's mantle, as the plates converge. A _____ zone is an area on Earth where two tectonic plates move towards one another and _____ occurs. Rates of _____ are typically measured in centimeters per year, with the average rate of convergence being approximately 2 to 8 centimeters per year (about the rate a fingernail grows.)

a. Mirovia
b. Continental crust
c. Plate tectonics
d. Subduction

46. A _____, sometimes called a composite volcano, is a tall, conical volcano with many layers (strata) of hardened lava, tephra, and volcanic ash. They are characterized by a steep profile and periodic, explosive eruptions. The lava that flows from a _____ tends to be viscous; it cools and hardens before spreading far.

a. 1700 Cascadia earthquake
b. 1509 Istanbul earthquake
c. 1703 Genroku earthquake
d. Stratovolcano

47. _____ is a geologic term for a type of topography characterized by a series of separate and parallel mountain ranges with broad valleys interposed, extending over a more or less wide area. It is typified by the topography found in the Great Basin in the western United States, which is part of a larger regional topography known as the _____ Province. _____ topography results from crustal extension.

Chapter 4. Volcanoes and Volcanism

a. Cap carbonates
c. Cross-cutting relationships
b. Bediasite
d. Basin and Range

48. The _____ is a large geologic province which includes parts of the southwestern United States and northwestern Mexico, typified by basin and range topography.

The topography of the _____ is a result of crustal extension within this part of the North American Plate. The cause of this extension is as yet not fully understood, although several hypotheses have been offered. The crust here has been stretched up to 100% of its original width. In fact, the crust underneath the _____, especially under the Great Basin, is some of the thinnest in the world.

a. Canadian Shield
c. Musgrave Block
b. Basin and Range province
d. Yilgarn Craton

49. The _____ is a tectonic plate covering most of North America, Greenland and part of Siberia. It extends eastward to the Mid-Atlantic Ridge and westward to the Chersky Range in eastern Siberia. The plate includes both continental and oceanic crust. The interior of the main continental landmass includes an extensive granitic core called a craton. Along most of the edges of this craton are fragments of crustal material called terranes, accreted to the craton by tectonic actions over the long span of geologic time. It is believed that much of North America west of the Rockies is composed of such terranes.
a. North Bismarck Plate
c. Conway Reef Plate
b. North American plate
d. Gorda Plate

50. A _____ is an instrument designed to measure very small changes from the horizontal level, either on the ground or in structures. A similar term, in less common usage, is the inclinometer. They are used extensively for monitoring volcanos, the response of dams to filling, the small movements of potential landslides, the orientation and volume of hydraulic fractures, and the response of structures to various influences such as loading and foundation settlement.
a. 1703 Genroku earthquake
c. 1700 Cascadia earthquake
b. 1509 Istanbul earthquake
d. Tiltmeter

51. An _____ is the result of a sudden release of energy in the Earth's crust that creates seismic waves. They are recorded with a seismometer or the related and mostly obsolete Richter magnitude, with a magnitude 3 or lower _____ being mostly imperceptible and magnitude 7 causing serious damage over large areas.
a. Earthquake
c. AL 333
b. AASHTO Soil Classification System
d. AL 129-1

52. _____ describes a long-duration release of seismic energy with distinct spectral (harmonic) lines that and often precedes or accompanies volcanic eruptions. More generally, volcanic tremor, is a sustained signal that may or may not possess these harmonic spectral features.

_____ is a sustained release of seismic and/or infrasonic energy typically associated with the underground movement or venting of magma and/or volcanic gases.

a. Fault friction
c. Strong ground motion
b. Harmonic tremor
d. Shadow zone

Chapter 5. Weathering - The Breakdown of Rocks

1. _____ is the removal of solids (sediment, soil, rock and other particles) in the natural environment. It usually occurs due to transport by wind, water, or ice; by down-slope creep of soil and other material under the force of gravity; or by living organisms, such as burrowing animals, in the case of bioerosion.

   _____ is distinguished from weathering, which is the process of chemical or physical breakdown of the minerals in the rocks, although the two processes may occur concurrently.

   a. AL 333
   b. AASHTO Soil Classification System
   c. AL 129-1
   d. Erosion

2. _____ is the decomposition of Earth rocks, soils and their minerals through direct contact with the planet's atmosphere. _____ occurs in situ, or 'with no movement', and thus should not be confused with erosion, which involves the movement of rocks and minerals by agents such as water, ice, wind and gravity.

   Two important classifications of _____ processes exist -- physical and chemical _____.

   a. 1703 Genroku earthquake
   b. Weathering
   c. 1509 Istanbul earthquake
   d. 1700 Cascadia earthquake

3. Two important classifications of weathering processes exist -- _____ and chemical weathering. Mechanical or _____ involves the breakdown of rocks and soils through direct contact with atmospheric conditions, such as heat, water, ice and pressure. The second classification, chemical weathering, involves the direct effect of atmospheric chemicals or biologically produced chemicals (also known as biological weathering) in the breakdown of rocks, soils and minerals.
   a. 1703 Genroku earthquake
   b. 1700 Cascadia earthquake
   c. 1509 Istanbul earthquake
   d. Physical weathering

4. _____ is any particulate matter that can be transported by fluid flow, and which eventually is deposited.

   They are most often transported by water (fluvial processes) transported by wind (aeolian processes) and glaciers. Beach sands and river channel deposits are examples of fluvial transport and deposition, though _____ also often settles out of slow-moving or standing water in lakes and oceans.

   a. Dry quicksand
   b. Brickearth
   c. Bovey Beds
   d. Sediment

5. Two important classifications of weathering processes exist -- physical and _____. Mechanical or physical weathering involves the breakdown of rocks and soils through direct contact with atmospheric conditions, such as heat, water, ice and pressure. The second classification, _____, involves the direct effect of atmospheric chemicals or biologically produced chemicals (also known as biological weathering) in the breakdown of rocks, soils and minerals.
   a. 1509 Istanbul earthquake
   b. 1700 Cascadia earthquake
   c. Chemical Weathering
   d. 1703 Genroku earthquake

6. _____ can also be called frost shattering or frost-wedging. This type of weathering is common in mountain areas where the temperature is around freezing point. Frost induced weathering, although often attributed to the expansion of freezing water captured in cracks, is generally independent of the water-to-ice expansion. It has long been known that moist soils expand or frost heave upon freezing as a result of water migrating along from unfrozen areas via thin films to collect at growing ice lenses. This same phenomena occurs within pore spaces of rocks.

Chapter 5. Weathering - The Breakdown of Rocks

   a. 1703 Genroku earthquake
   b. 1509 Istanbul earthquake
   c. 1700 Cascadia earthquake
   d. Frost disintegration

7. A _____ column (or _____) is a column of rising air in the lower altitudes of the Earth's atmosphere. They are created by the uneven heating of the Earth's surface from solar radiation, and an example of convection. The Sun warms the ground, which in turn warms the air directly above it.
   a. 1700 Cascadia earthquake
   b. 1703 Genroku earthquake
   c. Thermal
   d. 1509 Istanbul earthquake

8. _____ is mechanical scraping of a rock surface by friction between rocks and moving particles during their transport in wind, glacier, waves, gravity or running water, after friction, the moving particles dislodge loose and weak debris from the side of the rock, these particles can be dissolved in the water source.

The intensity of _____ depends on the hardness, concentration, velocity and mass of moving particles.

A virtually smooth marine platform cut by the ocean waves at a coastline.

   a. AL 129-1
   b. AASHTO Soil Classification System
   c. AL 333
   d. Abrasion

9. _____ is water located beneath the ground surface in soil pore spaces and in the fractures of lithologic formations. A unit of rock or an unconsolidated deposit is called an aquifer when it can yield a usable quantity of water. The depth at which soil pore spaces or fractures and voids in rock become completely saturated with water is called the water table.
   a. Depression focused recharge
   b. 1700 Cascadia earthquake
   c. 1509 Istanbul earthquake
   d. Groundwater

10. _____ or tree-ring dating is the method of scientific dating based on the analysis of tree-ring growth patterns. This technique was developed during the first half of the 20th century originally by the astronomer A. E. Douglass, the founder of the Laboratory of Tree-Ring Research at the University of Arizona. Douglass sought to better understand cycles of sunspot activity and reasoned that changes in solar activity would affect climate patterns on earth which would subsequently be recorded by tree-ring growth patterns (i.e., sunspots >→ climate >→ tree rings.)
   a. 1509 Istanbul earthquake
   b. Dendrochronology
   c. 1700 Cascadia earthquake
   d. 1703 Genroku earthquake

11. _____ defines an important group of generally dark-colored rock-forming inosilicate minerals, composed of double chain SiO_4 tetrahedra, linked at the vertices and generally containing ions of iron and/or magnesium in their structures. They crystallize into two crystal systems, monoclinic and orthorhombic. In chemical composition and general characteristics they are similar to the pyroxenes. They are minerals of either igneous or metamorphic origin; in the former case occurring as constituents (hornblende) of igneous rocks, such as granite, diorite, andesite and others. Those of metamorphic origin include examples such as those developed in limestones by contact metamorphism (tremolite) and those formed by the alteration of other ferromagnesian minerals (hornblende).
   a. AL 333
   b. AASHTO Soil Classification System
   c. AL 129-1
   d. Amphibole

12. The _____, is a geologic eon before the Proterozoic and Paleoproterozoic, before 2.5 Ga (billion years ago, or 2,500 Ma.) Instead of being based on stratigraphy, this date is defined chronometrically. The lower boundary (starting point) has not been officially recognized by the International Commission on Stratigraphy, but it is usually set to 3.8 Ga, at the end of the Hadean eon.

   a. AL 333
   b. AL 129-1
   c. AASHTO Soil Classification System
   d. Archean

13. _____ is a common extrusive volcanic rock. It is usually grey to black and fine-grained due to rapid cooling of lava at the surface of a planet. It may be porphyritic containing larger crystals in a fine matrix, or vesicular, or frothy scoria.

   a. 1700 Cascadia earthquake
   b. 1703 Genroku earthquake
   c. 1509 Istanbul earthquake
   d. Basalt

14. _____ is a naturally occurring material composed primarily of fine-grained minerals, which show plasticity through a variable range of water content, and which can be hardened when dried and/or fired. _____ deposits are mostly composed of _____ minerals (phyllosilicate minerals), minerals which impart plasticity and harden when fired and/or dried, and variable amounts of water trapped in the mineral structure by polar attraction. Organic materials which do not impart plasticity may also be a part of _____ deposits.

   a. 1700 Cascadia earthquake
   b. 1509 Istanbul earthquake
   c. Clay
   d. 1703 Genroku earthquake

15. _____ are hydrous aluminium phyllosilicates, sometimes with variable amounts of iron, magnesium, alkali metals, alkaline earths and other cations. Clays have structures similar to the micas and therefore form flat hexagonal sheets. _____ are common weathering products (including weathering of feldspar) and low temperature hydrothermal alteration products.

   a. Clay minerals
   b. 1700 Cascadia earthquake
   c. 1703 Genroku earthquake
   d. 1509 Istanbul earthquake

16. _____ are a group of rock-forming tectosilicate minerals which make up as much as 60% of the Earth's crust.

   _____ crystallize from magma in both intrusive and extrusive igneous rocks, as veins, and are also present in many types of metamorphic rock. Rock formed entirely of plagioclase feldspar is known as anorthosite.

   a. 1509 Istanbul earthquake
   b. 1700 Cascadia earthquake
   c. 1703 Genroku earthquake
   d. Feldspars

17. _____ refers to a large group of dark, coarse-grained, intrusive igneous rocks chemically equivalent to basalt. The rocks are plutonic, formed when molten magma is trapped beneath the Earth's surface and cools into a crystalline mass.

   The vast majority of the Earth's surface is underlain by _____ within the oceanic crust, produced by basalt magmatism at mid-ocean ridges.

   a. 1700 Cascadia earthquake
   b. 1703 Genroku earthquake
   c. 1509 Istanbul earthquake
   d. Gabbro

Chapter 5. Weathering - The Breakdown of Rocks

18. The _____ is a chronologic schema (or idealized model) relating stratigraphy to time that is used by geologists, paleontologists and other earth scientists to describe the timing and relationships between events that have occurred during the history of the Earth. The table of geologic time spans presented here agrees with the dates and nomenclature proposed by the International Commission on Stratigraphy, and uses the standard color codes of the United States Geological Survey.

Evidence from radiometric dating indicates that the Earth is about 4.570 billion years old.

   a. 1700 Cascadia earthquake   b. 1509 Istanbul earthquake
   c. Geologic time scale   d. 1703 Genroku earthquake

19. _____ is a clay mineral with the chemical composition $Al_2Si_2O_5(OH)_4$. It is a layered silicate mineral, with one tetrahedral sheet linked through oxygen atoms to one octahedral sheet of alumina octahedra. Rocks that are rich in _____ are known as china clay or kaolin. _____ clay occurs in abundance in soils that have formed from the chemical weathering of rocks in hot, moist climates - for example in tropical rainforest areas

   a. 1509 Istanbul earthquake   b. 1703 Genroku earthquake
   c. Kaolinite   d. 1700 Cascadia earthquake

20. The mineral _____ is a magnesium iron silicate with the formula $(Mg,Fe)_2SiO_4$. It is one of the most common minerals on Earth, and has also been identified in meteorites and on the Moon, Mars, and comet Wild 2.

The ratio of magnesium and iron varies between the two endmembers of the solid solution series: forsterite (Mg-endmember) and fayalite (Fe-endmember.)

   a. AL 129-1   b. AL 333
   c. AASHTO Soil Classification System   d. Olivine

21. A _____ is a dense, coarse-grained igneous rock, consisting mostly of the minerals olivine and pyroxene. _____ is ultramafic, as the rock contains less than 45% silica. It is high in magnesium, reflecting the high proportions of magnesium-rich olivine, with appreciable iron.

_____ is the dominant rock of the upper part of the Earth's mantle. The compositions of _____ nodules found in certain basalts and diamond pipes (kimberlites) are of special interest, because they provide samples of the Earth's Mantle roots of continents brought up from depths from about 30 km or so to depths at least as great as about 200 km.

   a. 1509 Istanbul earthquake   b. 1700 Cascadia earthquake
   c. 1703 Genroku earthquake   d. Peridotite

22. The _____ are a group of important rock-forming silicate minerals found in many igneous and metamorphic rocks. They share a common structure consisting of single chains of silica tetrahedra and they crystallize in the monoclinic and orthorhombic systems. _____ have the general formula $XY(Si,Al)_2O_6$ (where X represents calcium, sodium, iron^{+2} and magnesium and more rarely zinc, manganese and lithium and Y represents ions of smaller size, such as chromium, aluminium, iron^{+3}, magnesium, manganese, scandium, titanium, vanadium and even iron^{+2}).

   a. 1703 Genroku earthquake   b. 1509 Istanbul earthquake
   c. 1700 Cascadia earthquake   d. Pyroxenes

Chapter 5. Weathering - The Breakdown of Rocks

23. The _____ is a a term for a geologic period 65 million to 1.8 million years ago. The _____ covered the time span between the superseded Secondary period and an out-of-date definition of the Quaternary period. The period began with the demise of the non-avian dinosaurs in the Cretaceous-_____ extinction event, at start of the Cenozoic era, spanning to beginning of the most recent Ice Age, at the end of the Pliocene epoch.
    a. Suspended load
    b. Historical geology
    c. Rockall
    d. Tertiary

24. _____ is a sedimentary rock composed largely of the mineral calcite (calcium carbonate: $CaCO_3$.) The deposition of _____ strata is often a by-product and indicator of biological activity in the geologic record. Calcium (along with nitrogen, phosphorus, and potassium) is a key mineral to plant nutrition: soils overlying _____ bedrock tend to be pre-fertilized with calcium.
    a. 1509 Istanbul earthquake
    b. 1700 Cascadia earthquake
    c. 1703 Genroku earthquake
    d. Limestone

25. _____ is a silvery white and ductile member of the boron group of chemical elements. It has the symbol Al; its atomic number is 13. It is not soluble in water under normal circumstances. _____ is the most abundant metal in the Earth's crust, and the third most abundant element therein, after oxygen and silicon. It makes up about 8% by weight of the Earth'e;s solid surface.
    a. AL 333
    b. AL 129-1
    c. AASHTO Soil Classification System
    d. Aluminum

26. _____ is the most important aluminium ore. It consists largely of the minerals gibbsite $Al(OH)_3$, boehmite >γ-AlO(OH), and diaspore >α-AlO(OH), together with the iron oxides goethite and hematite, the clay mineral kaolinite and small amounts of anatase TiO_2. It was named after the village Les Baux in southern France, where it was first discovered in 1821 by the geologist Pierre Berthier.
    a. 1700 Cascadia earthquake
    b. 1703 Genroku earthquake
    c. Bauxite
    d. 1509 Istanbul earthquake

27. In stratigraphy, _____ is the native consolidated rock underlying the surface of a terrestrial planet, usually the Earth. Above the _____ is usually an area of broken and weathered unconsolidated rock in the basal subsoil. The top of the _____ is known as rockhead and identifying this, via excavations, drilling or geophysical methods, is an important task in most civil engineering projects.
    a. Biozones
    b. Cyclostratigraphy
    c. Principle of original horizontality
    d. Bedrock

28. _____ is a layer of loose, heterogeneous material covering solid rock. It includes dust, soil, broken rock, and other related materials and is present on Earth, the Moon, some asteroids, and other planets. The term was first defined by George P. Merrill in 1897 who stated, 'In places this covering is made up of material originating through rock-weathering or plant growth in situ. In other instances it is of fragmental and more or less decomposed matter drifted by wind, water or ice from other sources. This entire mantle of unconsolidated material, whatever its nature or origin, it is proposed to call the _____.'
    a. 1703 Genroku earthquake
    b. 1509 Istanbul earthquake
    c. 1700 Cascadia earthquake
    d. Regolith

29. _____ is the naturally occurring, unconsolidated or loose covering on the Earth's surface. _____ is composed of particles of broken rock that have been altered by chemical, biological and environmental processes including weathering and erosion. _____ is different from its parent rock(s) source(s), altered by interactions between the lithosphere, hydrosphere, atmosphere, and the biosphere.
  a. Topsoil
  b. 1509 Istanbul earthquake
  c. Soil
  d. 1700 Cascadia earthquake

30. _____ is a type of chemical weathering that creates rounded boulders and helps to create domed monoliths. This should not be confused with stream abrasion, a physical process which also creates rounded rocks on a much smaller scale. A good example of _____ can be found in the Alabama Hills area of eastern California.
  a. Hydrothermal circulation
  b. Spheroidal weathering
  c. Wave pounding
  d. Hydraulic action

31. The _____ is the earliest of three geologic eras of the Phanerozoic eon. The _____ spanned from roughly 542 to 251 million years ago (ICS, 2004), and is subdivided into six geologic periods; from oldest to youngest they are: the Cambrian, Ordovician, Silurian, Devonian, Carboniferous, and Permian.

The _____ covers the time from the first appearance of abundant, soft-shelled fossils to the time when the continents were beginning to be dominated by large, relatively sophisticated reptiles and modern plants. The lower (oldest) boundary was classically set at the first appearance of creatures known as trilobites and archeocyathids.

  a. Paleozoic
  b. 1700 Cascadia earthquake
  c. 1509 Istanbul earthquake
  d. 1703 Genroku earthquake

32. _____ is the process by which soil is created. It is the major topic of the science of pedology, whose other aspects include the soil morphology, classification (taxonomy) of soils, and their distribution in nature, present and past (soil geography and paleopedology).
  a. Soil structure
  b. Soil horizon
  c. 1509 Istanbul earthquake
  d. Pedogenesis

33. The _____ Era is one of three geologic eras of the Phanerozoic eon. The division of time into eras dates back to Giovanni Arduino, in the 18th century, although his original name for the era now called the '_____' was 'Secondary' (making the modern era the 'Tertiary'.)

The _____ was a time of tectonic, climatic and evolutionary activity. The continents gradually shifted from a state of connectedness into their present configuration; the drifting provided for speciation and other important evolutionary developments.

  a. Mesozoic
  b. 1703 Genroku earthquake
  c. 1700 Cascadia earthquake
  d. 1509 Istanbul earthquake

34. _____ is the upper, outermost layer of soil, usually the top 2 inches (5.1 cm) to 8 inches (20 cm.) It has the highest concentration of organic matter and microorganisms and is where most of the Earth's biological soil activity occurs. Plants generally concentrate their roots in and obtain most of their nutrients from this layer.

Chapter 5. Weathering - The Breakdown of Rocks

a. 1509 Istanbul earthquake
b. 1700 Cascadia earthquake
c. Soil
d. Topsoil

35. A _____ is a specific layer in the soil which measures parallel to the soil surface and possesses physical characteristics which differ from the layers above and beneath. Horizon formation is a function of a range of geological, chemical, and biological processes and occurs over long time periods. Soils vary in the degree to which horizons are expressed.
   a. 1703 Genroku earthquake
   b. 1509 Istanbul earthquake
   c. 1700 Cascadia earthquake
   d. Soil horizon

36. _____ is determined by how individual soil granules clump or bind together and aggregate, and therefore, the arrangement of soil pores between them. _____ has a major influence on water and air movement, biological activity, root growth and seedling emergence.

_____ describes the arrangement of the solid parts of the soil and of the pore space located between them (Marshall ' Holmes, 1979).

   a. Pedogenesis
   b. 1509 Istanbul earthquake
   c. Soil horizon
   d. Soil structure

37. _____ is a sedimentary rock, a hardened deposit of calcium carbonate. This calcium carbonate cements together other materials, including gravel, sand, clay, and silt. It is found in aridisol and mollisol soil orders.
   a. Caliche
   b. 1509 Istanbul earthquake
   c. 1703 Genroku earthquake
   d. 1700 Cascadia earthquake

38. '_____' is degraded organic material in soil, which causes some soil layers to be dark brown or black.

In soil science, _____ refers to any organic matter that has reached a point of stability, where it will break down no further and might, if conditions do not change, remain essentially as it is for centuries, if not millennia.

   a. Humus
   b. 1509 Istanbul earthquake
   c. 1703 Genroku earthquake
   d. 1700 Cascadia earthquake

39. _____ is material displaced across a soil profile, from one layer to another one, by the action of rainwater. The removal of material from a soil layer is called eluviation. The transport of the material may be either mechanical or chemical.
   a. AL 333
   b. AL 129-1
   c. AASHTO Soil Classification System
   d. Illuvium

40. An _____ is the result of a sudden release of energy in the Earth's crust that creates seismic waves. They are recorded with a seismometer or the related and mostly obsolete Richter magnitude, with a magnitude 3 or lower _____ being mostly imperceptible and magnitude 7 causing serious damage over large areas.
   a. AASHTO Soil Classification System
   b. AL 333
   c. AL 129-1
   d. Earthquake

41. In geology, a _____ or _____ line is a planar fracture in rock in which the rock on one side of the fracture has moved with respect to the rock on the other side. Large faults within the Earth's crust are the result of differential or shear motion and active _____ zones are the causal locations of most earthquakes. Earthquakes are caused by energy release during rapid slippage along a _____.
   a. 1700 Cascadia earthquake
   b. 1509 Istanbul earthquake
   c. 1703 Genroku earthquake
   d. Fault

42. The _____ is a major seismic zone in the Southern and Midwestern United States stretching to the southwest from New Madrid, Missouri.

The New Madrid fault system was responsible for the 1812 New Madrid Earthquake and has the potential to produce damaging earthquakes on an average of every 300 to 500 years. Since 1812 frequent smaller intraplate earthquakes were recorded for the area.

The _____ is made up of reactivated faults that formed when North America began to split or rift apart during the breakup of the supercontinent Rodinia in the Neoproterozoic Era (about 750 million years ago). The resulting rift system failed but remained as an aulacogen (a scar or zone of weakness).

   a. 1700 Cascadia earthquake
   b. 1509 Istanbul earthquake
   c. 1703 Genroku earthquake
   d. New Madrid Seismic Zone

43. The _____ is a continental transform fault that runs a length of roughly 800 miles (1,300 km) through California in the United States. The fault's motion is right-lateral strike-slip (horizontal motion.) It forms the tectonic boundary between the Pacific Plate and the North American Plate.
   a. 1509 Istanbul earthquake
   b. San Andreas fault
   c. 1703 Genroku earthquake
   d. 1700 Cascadia earthquake

Chapter 6. Sedimentatio and Sedimentary Rocks

1. _____ is one of the three main rock types (the others being igneous and metamorphic rock.) _____ is formed by deposition and consolidation of mineral and organic material and from precipitation of minerals from solution. The processes that form _____ occur at the surface of the Earth and within bodies of water.
   a. Felsic
   b. Rock cycle
   c. Serpentinite
   d. Sedimentary rock

2. _____ is any particulate matter that can be transported by fluid flow, and which eventually is deposited.

They are most often transported by water (fluvial processes) transported by wind (aeolian processes) and glaciers. Beach sands and river channel deposits are examples of fluvial transport and deposition, though _____ also often settles out of slow-moving or standing water in lakes and oceans.

   a. Brickearth
   b. Sediment
   c. Dry quicksand
   d. Bovey Beds

3. _____ is the geological process by which material is added to a landform or land mass. Fluids such as wind and water, as well as sediment gravity flows, transport previously eroded sediment, which, at the loss of enough kinetic energy in the fluid, is deposited, building up layers of sediment.

_____ occurs when the forces responsible for sediment transportation are no longer sufficient to overcome the forces of particle weight and friction, which resist motion.

   a. Headward erosion
   b. Seafloor spreading
   c. Deposition
   d. Permineralization

4. _____ is a geological term used to describe particles of rock derived from pre-existing rock through processes of weathering and erosion. Thesel particles can consist of lithic fragments (particles of recognisable rock), or of monomineralic fragments (mineral grains.) These particles are often transported through sedimentary processes into depositional systems such as riverbeds, lakes or the ocean forming sedimentary successions.
   a. Geodiversity
   b. Gibraltar Arc
   c. Riegel
   d. Detritus

5. In geology a _____ is the smallest division of a geologic formation or stratigraphic rock series marked by well-defined divisional planes (bedding planes) separating it from layers above and below. A _____ is the smallest lithostratigraphic unit, usually ranging in thickness from a centimeter to several meters and distinguishable from beds above and below it. Beds can be differentiated in various ways, including rock or mineral type and particle size.
   a. 1700 Cascadia earthquake
   b. 1703 Genroku earthquake
   c. 1509 Istanbul earthquake
   d. Bed

6. _____ are those structures formed during sediment deposition.

_____ such as cross bedding, graded bedding and ripple marks are utilized in stratigraphic studies to indicate original position of strata in geologically complex terranes.

There are two kinds of flow regimes, which at varying speeds and velocities produce different structures.

a. 1703 Genroku earthquake
c. 1509 Istanbul earthquake
b. Sedimentary structures
d. 1700 Cascadia earthquake

7. _____ is a paramount and base concept in archaeology, especially in the course of excavation. It is largely based on the Law of Superposition. When archaeological finds are below the surface of the ground (as is most commonly the case), the identification of the context of each find is vital in enabling the archaeologist to draw conclusions about the site and about the nature and date of its occupation.
   a. 1509 Istanbul earthquake
   c. Stratification
   b. 1700 Cascadia earthquake
   d. 1703 Genroku earthquake

8. In geology, _____ are sedimentary structures that indicate agitation by water (current or waves) or wind. _____ formed by water consist of two basic types:

   1. Current _____ are asymmetrical in profile, with a gentle up-current slope and a steeper down-current slope. The down-current slope depends on the shape of the sediment, with 33>° being typical.
   2. Wave-formed _____ have a symmetrical, almost sinusoidal profile; they indicate an environment with weak currents where water motion is dominated by wave oscillations.

Ripples will not form in sediment larger than course sand.

   a. 1700 Cascadia earthquake
   c. 1509 Istanbul earthquake
   b. Ripple marks
   d. 1703 Genroku earthquake

9. _____ refers to the process by which a sediment progressively loses its porosity due to the effects of loading. This forms part of the process of lithification. When a layer of sediment is originally deposited, it contains an open framework of particles with the pore space being usually filled with water.
   a. Combe
   c. Compaction
   b. Submersion
   d. Fault

10. _____ is the process in which sediments compact under pressure, expel connate fluids, and gradually become solid rock. Essentially, _____ is a process of porosity destruction through compaction and cementation. _____ includes all the processes which convert unconsolidated sediments into sedimentary rocks.
    a. 1703 Genroku earthquake
    c. 1700 Cascadia earthquake
    b. Lithification
    d. 1509 Istanbul earthquake

11. In geology, _____ are a body of rock with specified characteristics. Ideally, a _____ is a distinctive rock unit that forms under certain conditions of sedimentation, reflecting a particular process or environment.

The term _____ was introduced by the Swiss geologist Amanz Gressly in 1838 and was part of his significant contribution to the foundations of modern stratigraphy, [Cross and Homewood (1997)] which replaced the earlier notions of Neptunism.

   a. Mylonite
   c. Granulites
   b. Foliation
   d. Facies

Chapter 6. Sedimentatio and Sedimentary Rocks

12. _____ rocks are composed of fragments of pre-existing rock. The term is most commonly, but not uniquely, applied to sedimentary rocks.

_____ metamorphic rocks include breccias formed in faults, as well as some protomylonite and pseudotachylite.

a. 1703 Genroku earthquake
b. 1700 Cascadia earthquake
c. Clastic
d. 1509 Istanbul earthquake

13. _____ is a fine grained sedimentary rock whose original constituents were clays or muds. Grain size is up to 0.0625 mm with individual grains too small to be distinguished without a microscope. With increased pressure over time the platey clay minerals may become aligned, with the appearance of fissility or parallel layering.

a. Metasediment
b. Concretion
c. Superficial deposits
d. Mudstone

14. _____ is the second most abundant mineral in the Earth's continental crust. It is made up of a framework of silicon-oxygen tetrahedra SiO_4, with each silicon shared between two oxygens to give the overall formula SiO_2. _____ has a hardness of 7 on the Mohs scale and a density of 2.65 g/cm³.

a. Quartz
b. 1509 Istanbul earthquake
c. 1703 Genroku earthquake
d. 1700 Cascadia earthquake

15. In geology, solid-state _____ is a metamorphic process that occurs under situations of intense temperature and pressure where grains, atoms or molecules of a rock or mineral are packed closer together, creating a new crystal structure. The basic composition remains the same. This process can be illustrated by observing how snow recrystallizes to ice without melting.

a. 1700 Cascadia earthquake
b. 1703 Genroku earthquake
c. 1509 Istanbul earthquake
d. Recrystallization

16. _____ is a sedimentary rock composed mainly of sand-size mineral or rock grains. Most _____ is composed of quartz and/or feldspar because these are the most common minerals in the Earth's crust. Like sand, _____ may be any color, but the most common colors are tan, brown, yellow, red, gray and white.

a. Dolomite
b. Sandstone
c. Mudstone
d. Jasperoid

17. _____ is a fine-grained sedimentary rock whose original constituents were clay minerals or muds. It is characterized by thin laminae breaking with an irregular curving fracture, often splintery and usually parallel to the often-indistinguishable bedding plane. This property is called fissility.

a. Sandstone
b. Dolomite
c. Dolostone
d. Shale

18. _____ is a rock composed of angular fragments of minerals or rocks in a matrix (cementing material), that may be similar or different in composition to the fragments. A _____ may have a variety of different origins, as indicated by the named types including sedimentary _____, tectonic _____, igneous _____, impact _____ and hydrothermal _____.

Chapter 6. Sedimentatio and Sedimentary Rocks

Sedimentary breccias are a type of clastic sedimentary rock which are composed of angular to subangular, randomly oriented clasts of other sedimentary rocks.

a. Ventifacts
b. 1509 Istanbul earthquake
c. Coprolite
d. Breccia

19. A _____ is a rock consisting of individual stones that have become cemented together. They are sedimentary rocks consisting of rounded fragments and are thus differentiated from breccias, which consist of angular clasts. Both conglomerates and breccias are characterized by clasts larger than sand (>2 mm).
    a. Jasperoid
    b. Shale
    c. Dolostone
    d. Conglomerate

20. The _____, is a geologic eon before the Proterozoic and Paleoproterozoic, before 2.5 Ga (billion years ago, or 2,500 Ma.) Instead of being based on stratigraphy, this date is defined chronometrically. The lower boundary (starting point) has not been officially recognized by the International Commission on Stratigraphy, but it is usually set to 3.8 Ga, at the end of the Hadean eon.
    a. Archean
    b. AL 129-1
    c. AASHTO Soil Classification System
    d. AL 333

21. A _____ is a substance produced by life processes. It may be either constituents, or secretions, of plants or animals.

Examples

- Coal and oil are possible examples of constituents which may have undergone changes over geologic time periods.
- Chalk and limestone are examples of secretions (marine animal shells) which are of geologic age.
- Cotton and wood are biogenic constituents of contemporary origin.
- Pearls, silk and ambergris are examples of secretions of contemporary origin.

a. Deposition
b. Transgression
c. Biogenic substance
d. Wave pounding

22. _____ or dolomite rock is a sedimentary carbonate rock that contains a high percentage of the mineral dolomite. In old U.S.G.S. publications it was referred to as magnesian limestone. Most _____ formed as a magnesium replacement of limestone or lime mud prior to lithification.
    a. Shale
    b. Dolomite
    c. Concretion
    d. Dolostone

23. _____ are water-soluble mineral sediments that result from the evaporation of bodies of surficial water. _____ are considered sedimentary rocks.

Although all water bodies on the surface and in aquifers contain dissolved salts, the water must evaporate into the atmosphere for the minerals to precipitate.

a. AL 129-1
b. AL 333
c. Evaporites
d. AASHTO Soil Classification System

24. Traditionally, _____ compounds are considered to be of a mineral, not biological, origin. Complementarily, most organic compounds are traditionally viewed as being of biological origin. Over the past century, the precise classification of _____ vs organic compounds has become less important to scientists, primarily because the majority of known compounds are synthetic and not of natural origin.

Minerals are mainly oxides and sulfides, which are strictly _____. In fact, most of the earth and the universe is _____. Although the components of the Earth's crust are well elucidated, the processes of mineralization and the composition of the deep mantle remain active areas of investigation, which are mainly covered in geology-oriented venues.

a. AASHTO Soil Classification System
b. Inorganic
c. AL 333
d. AL 129-1

25. _____ is a sedimentary rock composed largely of the mineral calcite (calcium carbonate: $CaCO_3$.) The deposition of _____ strata is often a by-product and indicator of biological activity in the geologic record. Calcium (along with nitrogen, phosphorus, and potassium) is a key mineral to plant nutrition: soils overlying _____ bedrock tend to be pre-fertilized with calcium.

a. 1703 Genroku earthquake
b. Limestone
c. 1509 Istanbul earthquake
d. 1700 Cascadia earthquake

26. _____ is a sedimentary rock. It is a natural chemical precipitate of carbonate minerals; typically aragonite, but often recrystallized to, or primarily, calcite.

_____ forms as calcium carbonate is deposited from the water of mineral springs or rivulets that are saturated with dissolved calcium bicarbonate. The spring water from which the calcium carbonate precipitates can be hot, warm or cold. The rate of deposition increases with the temperature of the water, or alternatively, when biotic material accelerates the process of precipitation.

a. 1509 Istanbul earthquake
b. 1700 Cascadia earthquake
c. 1703 Genroku earthquake
d. Travertine

27. The _____ are a 159 square mile (412 km^2) salt flat in northwestern Utah. The depth of the salt has been recorded at 6 feet (1.8 m) in many areas. A remnant of the ancient Lake Bonneville of glacial times, the salt flats are now public land managed by the Bureau of Land Management.

a. 1509 Istanbul earthquake
b. 1703 Genroku earthquake
c. Bonneville Salt Flats
d. 1700 Cascadia earthquake

28. _____ is a carbonate mineral and the most stable polymorph of calcium carbonate ($CaCO_3$.) The other polymorphs are the minerals aragonite and vaterite. Aragonite will change to _____ at 470>°C, and vaterite is even less stable.

_____ is a common constituent of sedimentary rocks, limestone in particular, much of which is formed from the shells of dead marine organisms. Approximately 10% of sedimentary rock is limestone.

Chapter 6. Sedimentatio and Sedimentary Rocks

a. 1703 Genroku earthquake
c. Calcite

b. 1700 Cascadia earthquake
d. 1509 Istanbul earthquake

29. _____ is a fine-grained silica-rich microcrystalline, cryptocrystalline or microfibrous sedimentary rock that may contain small fossils. It varies greatly in color (from white to black), but most often manifests as gray, brown, grayish brown and light green to rusty red; its color is an expression of trace elements present in the rock, and both red and green are most often related to traces of iron (in its oxidized and reduced forms respectively.)

_____ occurs as oval to irregular nodules in greensand, limestone, chalk, and dolostone formations as a replacement mineral, where it is formed as a result of some type of diagenesis.

a. 1703 Genroku earthquake
c. 1509 Istanbul earthquake

b. Chert
d. 1700 Cascadia earthquake

30. A _____ in petrology or mineralogy is a secondary structure, generally spherical or irregularly rounded in shape. They are typically solid replacement bodies of chert or iron oxides formed during diagenesis of a sedimentary rock. They may be hollow as geodes or vugs or filled with crystals and intricate geometric shrinkage patterns as in septarian nodules.

a. 1703 Genroku earthquake
c. 1509 Istanbul earthquake

b. Nodule
d. 1700 Cascadia earthquake

31. _____ is a hard, compact variety of mineral coal that has a high lustre. It has the highest carbon count and contains the fewest impurities of all coals, despite its lower calorific content.

_____ is the highest of the metamorphic rank, in which the carbon content is between 92% and 98%.

a. AL 333
c. AASHTO Soil Classification System

b. AL 129-1
d. Anthracite

32. _____ is a relatively soft coal containing a tarlike substance called bitumen. It is of higher quality than lignite coal but of poorer quality than anthracite coal.

_____ is a sedimorphic rock formed by diagenetic and submetamorphic compression of peat bog material.

a. 1703 Genroku earthquake
c. 1509 Istanbul earthquake

b. 1700 Cascadia earthquake
d. Bituminous coal

33. _____ are the preserved remains or traces of animals, plants, and other organisms from the remote past. The totality of _____, both discovered and undiscovered, and their placement in fossiliferous rock formations and sedimentary layers (strata) is known as the fossil record. The study of _____ across geological time, how they were formed, and the evolutionary relationships between taxa (phylogeny) are some of the most important functions of the science of paleontology.

a. 1703 Genroku earthquake
c. 1509 Istanbul earthquake

b. 1700 Cascadia earthquake
d. Fossils

Chapter 6. Sedimentatio and Sedimentary Rocks

34. _____ is an accumulation of partially decayed vegetation matter. _____ forms in wetlands or peatlands, variously called bogs, moors, muskegs, pocosins, mires, and _____ swamp forests. By volume there are about 4 trillion mÂÂ³ of _____ in the world covering a total of around 2% of global land mass (about 3 million km^2), containing about 8 billion terajoules of energy.
  a. 1700 Cascadia earthquake
  b. 1509 Istanbul earthquake
  c. Peat
  d. 1703 Genroku earthquake

35. The phrase _____ is used to describe the movement of solid particles (sediment) and the processes that govern their motion. _____ is typically due to a combination of the force of gravity acting on the sediment, and/or the movement of the fluid in which the sediment is entrained. This is typically studied in natural systems, where the particles are clastic rocks (sand, gravel, boulders, etc.), mud, or clay; the fluid is air, water, or ice; and the force of gravity is due to the sloping surface on which the particles are resting.
  a. 1703 Genroku earthquake
  b. 1509 Istanbul earthquake
  c. 1700 Cascadia earthquake
  d. Sediment transport

36. _____ are those that accumulate in the abyssal plain of the deep ocean, far away from terrestrial sources that provide terrigenous sediments; the latter are primarily limited to the continental shelf, and deposited by rivers. _____ that are mixed with terrigenous sediments are known as hemipelagic.

There are three main types of _____:

    1.) Siliceous oozes
    2.) Calcareous oozes
    3.) Red clays

  a. Conglomerate
  b. Sandstone
  c. Metasediment
  d. Pelagic sediments

37. An _____ is a fan-shaped deposit formed where a fast flowing stream flattens, slows, and spreads typically at the exit of a canyon onto a flatter plain. A convergence of neighboring fans into a single apron of deposits against a slope is called a bajada, or compound _____.
  a. AL 129-1
  b. Alluvial fan
  c. AASHTO Soil Classification System
  d. AL 333

38. The _____ Period is the last geological period of the Neoproterozoic Era and of the Proterozoic Eon, immediately preceding the Cambrian Period, the first period of the Paleozoic Era and of the Phanerozoic Eon. Its status as an official geological period was ratified in 2004 by the International Union of Geological Sciences (IUGS), making it the first new geological period declared in 120 years. The type section is in the Flinders Ranges in South Australia.
  a. AL 129-1
  b. Ediacaran
  c. AASHTO Soil Classification System
  d. AL 333

39. _____ describes the large scale motions of Earth's lithosphere. The theory encompasses the older concepts of continental drift, developed during the first decades of the 20th century by Alfred Wegener, and seafloor spreading, understood during the 1960s.

The outermost part of the Earth's interior is made up of two layers: the lithosphere and the asthenosphere.

Chapter 6. Sedimentatio and Sedimentary Rocks 49

a. Subduction
b. Plate tectonics
c. Thrust fault
d. Copperbelt Province

40. The _____ is a name given in the late 19th century by British explorer John Walter Gregory to the continuous geographic trough, approximately 6,000 kilometres (3,700 mi) in length, that runs from northern Syria in Southwest Asia to central Mozambique in East Africa. The name continues in some usages, although it is today considered geologically imprecise as it includes what are today regarded as separate, since 1869 due to the Suez Canal Company project, although related rift and fault systems. Today, the term is most often used to refer to the valley of the East African Rift, the divergent plate boundary which extends from the Afar Triple Junction southward across eastern Africa, and is in the process of splitting the African Plate into two new separate plates.

a. 1700 Cascadia earthquake
b. 1509 Istanbul earthquake
c. Great Rift Valley
d. 1703 Genroku earthquake

41. In geology, a _____ or _____ line is a planar fracture in rock in which the rock on one side of the fracture has moved with respect to the rock on the other side. Large faults within the Earth's crust are the result of differential or shear motion and active _____ zones are the causal locations of most earthquakes. Earthquakes are caused by energy release during rapid slippage along a _____.

a. 1509 Istanbul earthquake
b. 1700 Cascadia earthquake
c. 1703 Genroku earthquake
d. Fault

42. The _____ is the earliest of three geologic eras of the Phanerozoic eon. The _____ spanned from roughly 542 to 251 million years ago (ICS, 2004), and is subdivided into six geologic periods; from oldest to youngest they are: the Cambrian, Ordovician, Silurian, Devonian, Carboniferous, and Permian.

The _____ covers the time from the first appearance of abundant, soft-shelled fossils to the time when the continents were beginning to be dominated by large, relatively sophisticated reptiles and modern plants. The lower (oldest) boundary was classically set at the first appearance of creatures known as trilobites and archeocyathids.

a. 1703 Genroku earthquake
b. Paleozoic
c. 1509 Istanbul earthquake
d. 1700 Cascadia earthquake

43. The _____ is a continental transform fault that runs a length of roughly 800 miles (1,300 km) through California in the United States. The fault's motion is right-lateral strike-slip (horizontal motion.) It forms the tectonic boundary between the Pacific Plate and the North American Plate.

a. 1700 Cascadia earthquake
b. 1703 Genroku earthquake
c. 1509 Istanbul earthquake
d. San Andreas fault

44. In geology, a _____ is a place where the Earth's crust and lithosphere are being pulled apart and is an example of extensional tectonics.

Typical _____ features are a central linear downdropped fault segment, called a graben, with parallel normal faulting and _____-flank uplifts on either side forming a _____ valley, where the _____ remains above sea level. The axis of the _____ area commonly contains volcanic rocks and active volcanism is a part of many, but not all active _____ systems.

a. 1700 Cascadia earthquake
b. 1509 Istanbul earthquake
c. 1703 Genroku earthquake
d. Rift

45. The _____ a natural area in New York State northwest of New York City and southwest of Albany, are a mature dissected plateau, an uplifted region that was subsequently eroded into sharp relief. They are an eastward continuation, and the highest representation, of the Allegheny Plateau.

The history of the _____ is a geologic story come full circle, from erosion, deposition and uplift back to erosion. The _____ are more of a dissected plateau than a series of mountain ranges. The sediments that make up the rocks in the Catskills were deposited when the ancient Acadian Mountains in the east were rising and subsequently eroding. The sediments traveled westward and formed a great delta into the sea that was in the area at that time.

a. Catskill Mountains
b. 1703 Genroku earthquake
c. 1509 Istanbul earthquake
d. 1700 Cascadia earthquake

46. _____ is the decomposition of Earth rocks, soils and their minerals through direct contact with the planet's atmosphere. _____ occurs in situ, or 'with no movement', and thus should not be confused with erosion, which involves the movement of rocks and minerals by agents such as water, ice, wind and gravity.

Two important classifications of _____ processes exist -- physical and chemical _____.

a. 1509 Istanbul earthquake
b. 1700 Cascadia earthquake
c. Weathering
d. 1703 Genroku earthquake

47. A _____ is a large, slow-moving mass of ice, formed from compacted layers of snow, that slowly deforms and flows in response to gravity and high pressure.

_____ ice is the largest reservoir of fresh water on Earth, and second only to oceans as the largest reservoir of total water.

a. Little Ice Age
b. Geologic temperature record
c. Keeling Curve
d. Glacier

Chapter 7. Metamorphism and Metamorphic Rocks

1. A _____ is a mountain rising from the ocean seafloor that does not reach to the water's surface (sea level), and thus is not an island. These are typically formed from extinct volcanoes, that rise abruptly and are usually found rising from a seafloor of 1,000-4,000 meters depth. They are defined by oceanographers as independent features that rise to at least 1,000 meters above the seafloor.

   a. 1703 Genroku earthquake   b. 1700 Cascadia earthquake
   c. 1509 Istanbul earthquake   d. Seamount

2. _____ is the result of the transformation of an existing rock type, the protolith, in a process called metamorphism, which means 'change in form'. The protolith is subjected to heat and pressure (temperatures greater than 150 to 200 >°C and pressures of 1500 bars) causing profound physical and/or chemical change. The protolith may be sedimentary rock, igneous rock or another older _____.

   a. Large igneous provinces   b. Metamorphic rock
   c. Petrology   d. Pluton

3. _____ is the solid-state recrystallization of pre-existing rocks due to changes in physical and chemical conditions, primarily heat, pressure, and the introduction of chemically active fluids. Both mineralogical, chemical and crystallographic changes can occur during this process.

Three types of _____ exist: dynamic, contact and regional.

   a. Geomicrobiology   b. Geotechnics
   c. Slope Mass Rating   d. Metamorphism

4. _____ is a rock that forms by the metamorphism of basalt and rocks with similar composition at high pressures and low temperatures, approximately corresponding to a depth of 15 to 30 kilometers and 200 to ~500 degrees Celsius. The blue color of the rock comes from the presence of the mineral glaucophane.

They are typically found within orogenic belts as terranes of lithology in faulted contact with greenschist or rarely eclogite facies rocks.

   a. Jadeitite   b. Granoblastic
   c. Prehnite-pumpellyite facies   d. Blueschist

5. _____ is a naturally occurring material composed primarily of fine-grained minerals, which show plasticity through a variable range of water content, and which can be hardened when dried and/or fired. _____ deposits are mostly composed of _____ minerals (phyllosilicate minerals), minerals which impart plasticity and harden when fired and/or dried, and variable amounts of water trapped in the mineral structure by polar attraction. Organic materials which do not impart plasticity may also be a part of _____ deposits.

   a. 1703 Genroku earthquake   b. 1700 Cascadia earthquake
   c. 1509 Istanbul earthquake   d. Clay

6. _____ are hydrous aluminium phyllosilicates, sometimes with variable amounts of iron, magnesium, alkali metals, alkaline earths and other cations. Clays have structures similar to the micas and therefore form flat hexagonal sheets. _____ are common weathering products (including weathering of feldspar) and low temperature hydrothermal alteration products.

Chapter 7. Metamorphism and Metamorphic Rocks

a. 1703 Genroku earthquake
b. 1509 Istanbul earthquake
c. 1700 Cascadia earthquake
d. Clay minerals

7. _____ are a group of rock-forming tectosilicate minerals which make up as much as 60% of the Earth's crust.

_____ crystallize from magma in both intrusive and extrusive igneous rocks, as veins, and are also present in many types of metamorphic rock. Rock formed entirely of plagioclase feldspar is known as anorthosite.

a. 1700 Cascadia earthquake
b. 1509 Istanbul earthquake
c. 1703 Genroku earthquake
d. Feldspars

8. Overburden pressure, _____, and vertical stress are terms that denote the pressure or stress imposed on a layer of soil or rock by the weight of overlying material.

The overburden pressure at a depth z is given by

where $>\rho(z)$ is the density of the overlying rock at depth z and g is the acceleration due to gravity. p_0 is the datum pressure, like the pressure at the surface.

a. 1703 Genroku earthquake
b. Lithostatic pressure
c. 1509 Istanbul earthquake
d. 1700 Cascadia earthquake

9. _____ is molten rock that is found beneath the surface of the Earth, and may also exist on other terrestrial planets. Besides molten rock, _____ may also contain suspended crystals and gas bubbles. _____ often collects in a _____ chamber inside a volcano. _____ is capable of intrusion into adjacent rocks, extrusion onto the surface as lava, and explosive ejection as tephra to form pyroclastic rock.

a. Large igneous provinces
b. Metamorphic zone
c. Metamorphic rock
d. Magma

10. _____ is any penetrative planar fabric present in rocks. _____ is common to rocks affected by regional metamorphic compression typical of orogenic belts. Rocks exhibiting _____ include the typical metamorphic rock sequence of slate, phyllite, schist and gneiss.

a. Mylonite
b. Granulites
c. Cataclasite
d. Foliation

11. The _____, is a geologic eon before the Proterozoic and Paleoproterozoic, before 2.5 Ga (billion years ago, or 2,500 Ma.) Instead of being based on stratigraphy, this date is defined chronometrically. The lower boundary (starting point) has not been officially recognized by the International Commission on Stratigraphy, but it is usually set to 3.8 Ga, at the end of the Hadean eon.

a. AL 333
b. AL 129-1
c. Archean
d. AASHTO Soil Classification System

Chapter 7. Metamorphism and Metamorphic Rocks

12. _____ is the decomposition of Earth rocks, soils and their minerals through direct contact with the planet's atmosphere. _____ occurs in situ, or 'with no movement', and thus should not be confused with erosion, which involves the movement of rocks and minerals by agents such as water, ice, wind and gravity.

Two important classifications of _____ processes exist -- physical and chemical _____.

a. 1703 Genroku earthquake
b. 1509 Istanbul earthquake
c. 1700 Cascadia earthquake
d. Weathering

13. In geology, a _____ or _____ line is a planar fracture in rock in which the rock on one side of the fracture has moved with respect to the rock on the other side. Large faults within the Earth's crust are the result of differential or shear motion and active _____ zones are the causal locations of most earthquakes. Earthquakes are caused by energy release during rapid slippage along a _____.

a. Fault
b. 1703 Genroku earthquake
c. 1700 Cascadia earthquake
d. 1509 Istanbul earthquake

14. _____ is a common and widely distributed type of rock formed by high-grade regional metamorphic processes from pre-existing formations that were originally either igneous or sedimentary rocks. Gneissic rocks are usually medium to coarse foliated and largely recrystallized but do not carry large quantities of micas, chlorite or other platy minerals. Gneisses that are metamorphosed igneous rocks or their equivalent are termed granite gneisses, diorite gneisses, etc.

a. 1700 Cascadia earthquake
b. 1703 Genroku earthquake
c. 1509 Istanbul earthquake
d. Gneiss

15. _____ is the group designation for a series of contact metamorphic rocks that have been baked and indurated by the heat of intrusive igneous masses and have been rendered massive, hard, splintery, and in some cases exceedingly tough and durable. Most _____ are fine-grained, and while the original rocks may have been more or less fissile owing to the presence of bedding or cleavage planes, this structure is effaced or rendered inoperative in the _____. Though they may show banding, due to bedding, etc., they break across this as readily as along it; in fact, they tend to separate into cubical fragments rather than into thin plates.

a. Jadeitite
b. Dalradian
c. Prehnite-pumpellyite facies
d. Hornfels

16. _____ is a fine grained sedimentary rock whose original constituents were clays or muds. Grain size is up to 0.0625 mm with individual grains too small to be distinguished without a microscope. With increased pressure over time the platey clay minerals may become aligned, with the appearance of fissility or parallel layering.

a. Metasediment
b. Concretion
c. Mudstone
d. Superficial deposits

17. _____ is a type of foliated metamorphic rock primarily composed of quartz, sericite mica, and chlorite; the rock represents a gradation in the degree of metamorphism between slate and mica schist. Minute crystals of graphite, sericite, or chlorite impart a silky, sometimes golden sheen to the surfaces of cleavage (or schistosity.) _____ is formed from the continued metamorphism of slate.

a. 1700 Cascadia earthquake
b. 1509 Istanbul earthquake
c. 1703 Genroku earthquake
d. Phyllite

Chapter 7. Metamorphism and Metamorphic Rocks

18. _____ is a hard metamorphic rock which was originally sandstone. Sandstone is converted into _____ through heating and pressure usually related to tectonic compression within orogenic belts. Pure _____ is usually white to grey, though quartzites often occur in various shades of pink and red due to varying amounts of iron oxide .
   a. Mylonite
   b. Geothermobarometry
   c. Dalradian
   d. Quartzite

19. _____ forms a group of medium-grade metamorphic rocks, chiefly notable for the preponderance of lamellar minerals such as micas, chlorite, talc, hornblende, graphite, and others. Quartz often occurs in drawn-out grains to such an extent that a particular form called quartz _____ is produced. By definition, _____ contains more than 50% platy and elongated minerals, often finely interleaved with quartz and feldspar.
   a. Jadeitite
   b. Mylonite
   c. Porphyroclast
   d. Schist

20. _____ is a fine-grained sedimentary rock whose original constituents were clay minerals or muds. It is characterized by thin laminae breaking with an irregular curving fracture, often splintery and usually parallel to the often-indistinguishable bedding plane. This property is called fissility.
   a. Dolostone
   b. Dolomite
   c. Shale
   d. Sandstone

21. _____ or impact metamorphism describes the effects of shock-wave related deformation and heating during impact events. The formation of similar features during explosive volcanism is generally discounted due to the lack of metamorphic effects unequivocally associated with explosions and the difficulty in reaching sufficient pressures during such an event.

Planar fractures are parallel sets of multiple planar cracks or cleavages in quartz grains; they develop at the lowest pressures characteristic of shock waves (~5-8 GPa) and a common feature of quartz grains found associated with impact structures.

   a. Quartzite
   b. Porphyroblast
   c. Geothermobarometry
   d. Shock metamorphism

22. _____ is a fine-grained, foliated, homogeneous metamorphic rock derived from an original shale-type sedimentary rock composed of clay or volcanic ash through low grade regional metamorphism. The result is a foliated rock in which the foliation may not correspond to the original sedimentary layering. _____ is frequently grey in colour especially when seen en masse covering roofs.
   a. Shock metamorphism
   b. Slate
   c. Facies
   d. Geothermobarometry

23. _____ is a feature of rocks containing platy minerals. Platy minerals include clay minerals and micas, with a long thin shape. When these align, they form a series of planes along which the rock tends to split.
   a. 1509 Istanbul earthquake
   b. 1703 Genroku earthquake
   c. 1700 Cascadia earthquake
   d. Slaty cleavage

24. _____, in structural geology and related disciplines, describes the tendency of a rock to break along preferred planes of weakness.

Chapter 7. Metamorphism and Metamorphic Rocks

Rocks deformed under very low to low metamorphic grade often develop planes along which the rock can easily be split. Slates are an example of a rock with a penetrative _____ caused partly by the realignement of phyllosilicate minerals with increasing flattening strain.

a. 1700 Cascadia earthquake
b. Cleavage
c. 1703 Genroku earthquake
d. 1509 Istanbul earthquake

25. _____ - also known as greenstone - is a general field petrologic term applied to metamorphic and/or altered mafic volcanic rock. The green is due to abundant green chlorite, actinolite and epidote minerals that dominate the rock. However, basalts may remain quite black if primary pyroxene does not revert to chlorite or actinolite.

a. Quartzite
b. Greenschist
c. Cataclasite
d. Granulites

26. _____ is one of the three main rock types (the others being sedimentary and metamorphic rock.) _____ is formed by magma (molten rock) being cooled and becoming solid . They may form with or without crystallization, either below the surface as intrusive (plutonic) rocks or on the surface as extrusive (volcanic) rocks. They make up approximately 95% of the upper part of the Earth's crust, but their great abundance is hidden on the Earth's surface by a relatively thin but widespread layer of sedimentary and metamorphic rocks.

a. AASHTO Soil Classification System
b. AL 333
c. AL 129-1
d. Igneous rock

27. _____ is a rock at the frontier between igneous and metamorphic rocks. They can also be known as diatexite.

_____ forms under extreme temperature conditions during prograde metamorphism, where partial melting occurs in pre-existing rocks.

a. Pluton
b. Petrology
c. Migmatite
d. Serpentinite

28. The _____ is an Archean-age migmatitic gneiss found in soutwestern Minnesota. It has been dated to 3.6 billion years ago, making it one of the oldest rock units on the planet. It is believed to have original been a granite before it was metamorphosed.

a. Fort Union Formation
b. Teilzone
c. Bediasite
d. Morton Gneiss

29. An _____ is used in geology to determine the degree of metamorphism a rock has experienced. Depending on the original composition of and the pressure and temperature experienced by the protolith (parent rock), chemical reactions between minerals in the solid state produce new minerals. When an _____ is found in a metamorphosed rock, it indicates the minimum pressure and temperature the protolith must have achieved in order for that mineral to form.

a. AASHTO Soil Classification System
b. AL 333
c. AL 129-1
d. Index mineral

30. The _____ Era is one of three geologic eras of the Phanerozoic eon. The division of time into eras dates back to Giovanni Arduino, in the 18th century, although his original name for the era now called the '_____' was 'Secondary' (making the modern era the 'Tertiary'.)

The _____ was a time of tectonic, climatic and evolutionary activity. The continents gradually shifted from a state of connectedness into their present configuration; the drifting provided for speciation and other important evolutionary developments.

a. 1703 Genroku earthquake
b. Mesozoic
c. 1509 Istanbul earthquake
d. 1700 Cascadia earthquake

31. _____ describes the large scale motions of Earth's lithosphere. The theory encompasses the older concepts of continental drift, developed during the first decades of the 20th century by Alfred Wegener, and seafloor spreading, understood during the 1960s.

The outermost part of the Earth's interior is made up of two layers: the lithosphere and the asthenosphere.

a. Plate tectonics
b. Copperbelt Province
c. Thrust fault
d. Subduction

32. _____ is a rock composed of one or more serpentine minerals. Minerals in this group are formed by serpentinization, a hydration and metamorphic transformation of ultramafic rock from the Earth's mantle. The alteration is particularly important at the sea floor at tectonic plate boundaries.

a. Rock cycle
b. Metamorphic zone
c. Metamorphic rock
d. Serpentinite

33. _____ is a metamorphic rock, a talc-schist. It is largely composed of the mineral talc and is rich in magnesium. It is produced by dynamothermal metamorphism and metasomatism, which occurs at the areas where tectonic plates are subducted, changing rocks by heat and pressure, with influx of fluids, but without melting.

a. 1509 Istanbul earthquake
b. 1700 Cascadia earthquake
c. 1703 Genroku earthquake
d. Soapstone

34. An _____ is the result of a sudden release of energy in the Earth's crust that creates seismic waves. They are recorded with a seismometer or the related and mostly obsolete Richter magnitude, with a magnitude 3 or lower _____ being mostly imperceptible and magnitude 7 causing serious damage over large areas.

a. AASHTO Soil Classification System
b. AL 129-1
c. Earthquake
d. AL 333

Chapter 8. Telling Time Geologically

1. The _____ is a chronologic schema (or idealized model) relating stratigraphy to time that is used by geologists, paleontologists and other earth scientists to describe the timing and relationships between events that have occurred during the history of the Earth. The table of geologic time spans presented here agrees with the dates and nomenclature proposed by the International Commission on Stratigraphy, and uses the standard color codes of the United States Geological Survey.

Evidence from radiometric dating indicates that the Earth is about 4.570 billion years old.

    a. 1703 Genroku earthquake   b. 1509 Istanbul earthquake
    c. 1700 Cascadia earthquake   d. Geologic time scale

2. _____ is the decomposition of Earth rocks, soils and their minerals through direct contact with the planet's atmosphere. _____ occurs in situ, or 'with no movement', and thus should not be confused with erosion, which involves the movement of rocks and minerals by agents such as water, ice, wind and gravity.

Two important classifications of _____ processes exist -- physical and chemical _____.

    a. 1509 Istanbul earthquake   b. 1703 Genroku earthquake
    c. Weathering   d. 1700 Cascadia earthquake

3. The _____, is a geologic eon before the Proterozoic and Paleoproterozoic, before 2.5 Ga (billion years ago, or 2,500 Ma.) Instead of being based on stratigraphy, this date is defined chronometrically. The lower boundary (starting point) has not been officially recognized by the International Commission on Stratigraphy, but it is usually set to 3.8 Ga, at the end of the Hadean eon.

    a. AL 333   b. AL 129-1
    c. AASHTO Soil Classification System   d. Archean

4. _____, is a phylum of bacteria that obtain their energy through photosynthesis. The name '_____' comes from the color of the bacteria. They are a significant component of the marine nitrogen cycle and an important primary producer in many areas of the ocean, but are also found in habitats other than the marine environment; in particular _____ are known to occur in both freshwater, hypersaline inland lakes and in arid areas where they are a major component of biological soil crusts.

Stromatolites of fossilized oxygen-producing _____ have been found from 2.8 billion years ago. The ability of _____ to perform oxygenic photosynthesis is thought to have converted the early reducing atmosphere into an oxidizing one, which dramatically changed the composition of life forms on Earth by provoking an explosion of biodiversity and leading to the near-extinction of oxygen-intolerant organisms.

    a. 1509 Istanbul earthquake   b. 1700 Cascadia earthquake
    c. 1703 Genroku earthquake   d. Cyanobacteria

5. _____ is the use of the principles of geology to reconstruct and understand the history of the Earth. It focuses on geologic processes that change the Earth's surface and subsurface; and the use of stratigraphy, structural geology and paleontology to tell the sequence of these events. It also focuses on the evolution of plants and animals during different time periods in the geological timescale.

    a. Historical geology   b. Suspended load
    c. Logarithmic Spiral Beach   d. Tertiary

6. _____ is one of the three main rock types (the others being sedimentary and metamorphic rock.) _____ is formed by magma (molten rock) being cooled and becoming solid . They may form with or without crystallization, either below the surface as intrusive (plutonic) rocks or on the surface as extrusive (volcanic) rocks. They make up approximately 95% of the upper part of the Earth's crust, but their great abundance is hidden on the Earth's surface by a relatively thin but widespread layer of sedimentary and metamorphic rocks.
   a. AL 333
   b. AASHTO Soil Classification System
   c. AL 129-1
   d. Igneous rock

7. _____ is the result of the transformation of an existing rock type, the protolith, in a process called metamorphism, which means 'change in form'. The protolith is subjected to heat and pressure (temperatures greater than 150 to 200 >°C and pressures of 1500 bars) causing profound physical and/or chemical change. The protolith may be sedimentary rock, igneous rock or another older _____.
   a. Metamorphic rock
   b. Large igneous provinces
   c. Petrology
   d. Pluton

8. _____ is the process of determining a specific date for an archaeological or palaeontological site or artifact. Some archaeologists prefer the terms chronometric or calendar dating, as use of the word 'absolute' implies a certainty and precision that is rarely possible in archaeology. _____ is usually based on the physical or chemical properties of the materials of artifacts, buildings, or other items that have been modified by humans.
   a. Erathem
   b. AASHTO Soil Classification System
   c. Uranium-lead dating
   d. Absolute dating

9. Before the advent of absolute dating in the 20th century, archaeologists and geologists were largely limited to the use of the _____ techniques. It estimates the order of prehistoric and geological events determined by using basic stratigraphic rules, and by observing where fossil organisms lay in the geological record, often in horizontal, stratified bands of rocks present throughout the world.

Though _____ can determine the sequential order in which a series of events occurred, not when they occur, it is in no way inferior to radiometric dating; in fact, _____ by biostratigraphy is the preferred method in paleontology, and is in some respects more accurate (Stanley, 167-9.)

   a. Milankovitch Theory
   b. Stage
   c. Global Boundary Stratotype Section and Point
   d. Relative dating

10. Two important classifications of weathering processes exist -- physical and _____. Mechanical or physical weathering involves the breakdown of rocks and soils through direct contact with atmospheric conditions, such as heat, water, ice and pressure. The second classification, _____, involves the direct effect of atmospheric chemicals or biologically produced chemicals (also known as biological weathering) in the breakdown of rocks, soils and minerals.
   a. 1509 Istanbul earthquake
   b. 1703 Genroku earthquake
   c. 1700 Cascadia earthquake
   d. Chemical weathering

11. The _____ Period is the last geological period of the Neoproterozoic Era and of the Proterozoic Eon, immediately preceding the Cambrian Period, the first period of the Paleozoic Era and of the Phanerozoic Eon. Its status as an official geological period was ratified in 2004 by the International Union of Geological Sciences (IUGS), making it the first new geological period declared in 120 years. The type section is in the Flinders Ranges in South Australia.

Chapter 8. Telling Time Geologically

a. AL 129-1
b. AASHTO Soil Classification System
c. AL 333
d. Ediacaran

12. _____ is the principle that the same scientific laws and processes are constant throughout space and time. It applies specifically to sciences that require a long timescale such as geology, astronomy, and paleontology. It was first defined by Charles Lyell (1797 - 1875), who incorporated James Hutton's gradualism into the idea of _____.

a. AL 333
b. AASHTO Soil Classification System
c. AL 129-1
d. Uniformitarianism

13. _____ is the geological process by which material is added to a landform or land mass. Fluids such as wind and water, as well as sediment gravity flows, transport previously eroded sediment, which, at the loss of enough kinetic energy in the fluid, is deposited, building up layers of sediment.

_____ occurs when the forces responsible for sediment transportation are no longer sufficient to overcome the forces of particle weight and friction, which resist motion.

a. Headward erosion
b. Deposition
c. Seafloor spreading
d. Permineralization

14. _____ are the preserved remains or traces of animals, plants, and other organisms from the remote past. The totality of _____, both discovered and undiscovered, and their placement in fossiliferous rock formations and sedimentary layers (strata) is known as the fossil record. The study of _____ across geological time, how they were formed, and the evolutionary relationships between taxa (phylogeny) are some of the most important functions of the science of paleontology.

a. 1509 Istanbul earthquake
b. 1703 Genroku earthquake
c. 1700 Cascadia earthquake
d. Fossils

15. _____ are fossils used to define and identify geologic periods They work on the premise that, although different sediments may look different depending on the conditions under which they were laid down, they may include the remains of the same species of fossil. If the species concerned were short-lived, then it is certain that the sediments in question were deposited within that narrow time period.

a. Invertebrate paleontology
b. Allotrioceras
c. Indian bead
d. Index fossils

16. The principle of _____ states that a rock or fault is younger than any rock (or fault) through which it cuts. This principle was developed by James Hutton.

In a series of horizontal sedimentary beds, there is an igneous dyke which cuts vertically through them. The dyke is younger than the sediment beds though which it crosses, as the beds would have had to be around before the dyke could have intruded.

a. Zechstein
b. Marine clay
c. Bediasite
d. Cross-cutting relationships

17. The _____ is based on the observation that sedimentary rock strata contain fossilised flora and fauna, and that these fossils succeed each other vertically in a specific, reliable order that can be identified over wide horizontal distances. A fossilized Neanderthal bone will never be found in the same stratum as a fossilised Megalosaurus, for example, because the two species lived during different geological periods, separated by many millions of years. This allows for strata to be identified and dated by the fossils found within.

   a. Trackway

   b. Labyrinthodont

   c. Principle of faunal succession

   d. Palynofacies

18. The _____ states that, with sedimentary rocks, if inclusions (or clasts) are found in a formation, then the inclusions must be older than the formation that contains them. For example, in sedimentary rocks, it is common for gravel from an older formation to be ripped up and included in a newer layer. A similar situation with igneous rocks occurs when xenoliths are found. These foreign bodies are picked up as magma or lava flows, and are incorporated, later to cool in the matrix. As a result, xenoliths are older than the rock which contains them.

   a. 1703 Genroku earthquake

   b. 1509 Istanbul earthquake

   c. Principle of inclusions and components

   d. 1700 Cascadia earthquake

19. The _____ was proposed by the Danish geological pioneer Nicholas Steno (1638-1686.) This principle states that layers of sediment are originally deposited horizontally. The principle is important to the analysis of folded and tilted strata.

   a. Cyclostratigraphy

   b. Principle of original horizontality

   c. Sequence stratigraphy

   d. Bedrock

20. The _____ is a key axiom based on observations of natural history that is a foundational principle of sedimentary stratigraphy and so of other geology dependent natural sciences: 'Sedimentary layers are deposited in a time sequence, with the oldest on the bottom and the youngest on the top.'

The principle was first proposed in the 11th century by the Persian geologist, Avicenna , and the law was later formulated more clearly in the 17th century by the Danish scientist Nicolas Steno.

While discussing the origins of mountains in The Book of Healing in 1027, Avicenna first outlined the principle of the superposition of strata.

   a. Stage

   b. Chronozone

   c. Cenomanian

   d. Law of superposition

21. The lithosphere is broken up into what are called _____. In the case of Earth, there are eight major and many minor plates The lithospheric plates ride on the asthenosphere. These plates move in relation to one another at one of three types of plate boundaries: convergent, or collisional boundaries; divergent boundaries, also called spreading centers; and transform boundaries.

   a. Juan de Fuca Ridge

   b. Lithosphere

   c. Thrust fault

   d. Tectonic plates

22. _____ is a volcanic rock texture characterised by, or containing many vesicles. The texture is often found in extrusive aphanitic igneous rock. The vesicles are small cavities formed by the expansion of bubbles of gas or steam during the solidification of the rock.

Chapter 8. Telling Time Geologically

a. 1703 Genroku earthquake
c. 1509 Istanbul earthquake
b. 1700 Cascadia earthquake
d. Vesicular texture

23. _____ is an igneous rock of volcanic origin.

They are usually fine-grained or aphanitic to glassy in texture. They often contain clasts of other rocks and phenocrysts.

a. Tephra
c. Metamorphic zone
b. Felsic
d. Volcanic rock

24. A _____ is a rock fragment which becomes enveloped in a larger rock during the latter's development and hardening. In geology, the term _____ is almost exclusively used to describe inclusions in igneous rock during magma emplacement and eruption. Xenoliths may be engulfed along the margins of a magma chamber, torn loose from the walls of an erupting lava conduit or explosive diatreme or picked up along the base of a flowing lava on Earth's surface.

a. 1509 Istanbul earthquake
c. 1703 Genroku earthquake
b. Xenolith
d. 1700 Cascadia earthquake

25. _____ is fossil tree resin, which is appreciated for its color and beauty. Good quality _____ is used for the manufacture of ornamental objects and jewelry. Although not mineralized, it is often classified as a gemstone.

A common misconception is that _____ is made of tree sap; it is not. Sap is the fluid that circulates through a plant's vascular system, while resin is the semi-solid amorphous organic substance secreted in pockets and canals through epithelial cells of the plant.

a. AL 129-1
c. AL 333
b. AASHTO Soil Classification System
d. Amber

26. A _____ is fossilized animal dung. They are classified as trace fossils as opposed to body fossils, as they give evidence for the animal's behavior (in this case, diet) rather than morphology. They were first described by William Buckland in 1829.

a. Fault breccia
c. 1509 Istanbul earthquake
b. Coprolite
d. Ventifacts

27. In geology, _____ or _____ soil is soil at or below the freezing point of water (0 >°C or 32 >°F) for two or more years. Ice is not always present, as may be in the case of nonporous bedrock, but it frequently occurs and it may be in amounts exceeding the potential hydraulic saturation of the ground material. Most _____ is located in high latitudes (i.e. land in close proximity to the North and South poles), but alpine _____ may exist at high altitudes in much lower latitudes.

a. 1700 Cascadia earthquake
c. 1509 Istanbul earthquake
b. Permafrost
d. 1703 Genroku earthquake

28. _____ are geological records of biological activity. _____ may be impressions made on the substrate by an organism: for example, burrows, borings, footprints and feeding marks, and root cavities. The term in its broadest sense also includes the remains of other organic material produced by an organism - for example coprolites or chemical markers - or sedimentological structures produced by biological means - for example, stromatolites.

Chapter 8. Telling Time Geologically

a. 1700 Cascadia earthquake
b. 1509 Istanbul earthquake
c. 1703 Genroku earthquake
d. Trace fossils

29. In geology, a _____ is a widespread sedimentary layer that formed at a single time, such that it is useful for geologic correlations and dating over a large area. Examples of these are massive ashfalls, such as those produced by nearby normal volcanic eruptions, and far away in supervolcanic eruptions, as well as tills deposited by continental glaciers, and the global iridium layer deposited at the K-T boundary.
a. 1703 Genroku earthquake
b. 1509 Istanbul earthquake
c. Key bed
d. 1700 Cascadia earthquake

30. In geology a _____ is the smallest division of a geologic formation or stratigraphic rock series marked by well-defined divisional planes (bedding planes) separating it from layers above and below. A _____ is the smallest lithostratigraphic unit, usually ranging in thickness from a centimeter to several meters and distinguishable from beds above and below it. Beds can be differentiated in various ways, including rock or mineral type and particle size.
a. 1703 Genroku earthquake
b. 1509 Istanbul earthquake
c. 1700 Cascadia earthquake
d. Bed

31. _____ is a technique used to date materials, usually based on a comparison between the observed abundance of a naturally occurring radioactive isotope and its decay products, using known decay rates. It is the principal source of information about the absolute age of rocks and other geological features, including the age of the Earth itself, and can be used to date a wide range of natural and man-made materials. Together with stratigraphic principles, _____ methods are used in geochronology to establish the geological time scale.
a. 1703 Genroku earthquake
b. 1509 Istanbul earthquake
c. Radiometric dating
d. 1700 Cascadia earthquake

32. A _____ is an atom with an unstable nucleus, which is a nucleus characterized by excess energy which is available to be imparted either to a newly-created radiation particle within the nucleus, or else to an atomic electron . The _____, in this process, undergoes radioactive decay, and emits a gamma ray(s) and/or subatomic particles. These particles constitute ionizing radiation.
a. 1700 Cascadia earthquake
b. Radionuclide
c. 1703 Genroku earthquake
d. 1509 Istanbul earthquake

33. _____ is one of the three main rock types (the others being igneous and metamorphic rock.) _____ is formed by deposition and consolidation of mineral and organic material and from precipitation of minerals from solution. The processes that form _____ occur at the surface of the Earth and within bodies of water.
a. Serpentinite
b. Felsic
c. Rock cycle
d. Sedimentary rock

34. _____ is a radiometric dating method used in geochronology and archeology. It is based on measuring the products of the radioactive decay of potassium (K), which is a common element found in materials such as micas, clay minerals, tephra, and evaporites. In the samples of interest, the decay product ^{40}Ar is not trapped by the molten rock, but is trapped and accumulated in the solid. Time since recrystallization is calculated by measuring the ratio of ^{40}Ar accumulated to ^{40}K remaining. The long half-life of ^{40}K allows the method to be used to calculate the absolute age of samples older than a few thousand years.

Chapter 8. Telling Time Geologically

a. 1700 Cascadia earthquake
b. 1509 Istanbul earthquake
c. Rubidium-strontium dating
d. Potassium-argon dating

35. The _____ method is a radiometric dating technique that geologists use to determine the age of rocks.

Development of this process was aided by Fritz Strassmann, who later moved onto discovering nuclear fission with Otto Hahn and Lise Meitner.

The utility of the rubidium-strontium isotope system results from the fact that ^{87}Rb decays to ^{87}Sr.

a. Rubidium-strontium dating
b. Potassium-argon dating
c. 1700 Cascadia earthquake
d. 1509 Istanbul earthquake

36. _____ is usually performed on the mineral zircon ($ZrSiO_4$), though it can be used on other minerals such as monazite, titanite, and baddeleyite. Zircon incorporates uranium and thorium atoms into its crystalline structure, but strongly rejects lead. Therefore we can assume that the entire lead content of the zircon is radiogenic. Where this is not the case, a correction must be applied. _____ techniques have also been applied to other minerals such as calcite/aragonite and other carbonate minerals. These minerals often produce lower precision ages than igneous and metamorphic minerals traditionally used for age dating, but are more common in the geologic record.

a. Eonothem
b. AASHTO Soil Classification System
c. Erathem
d. Uranium-lead dating

37. _____ or tree-ring dating is the method of scientific dating based on the analysis of tree-ring growth patterns. This technique was developed during the first half of the 20th century originally by the astronomer A. E. Douglass, the founder of the Laboratory of Tree-Ring Research at the University of Arizona. Douglass sought to better understand cycles of sunspot activity and reasoned that changes in solar activity would affect climate patterns on earth which would subsequently be recorded by tree-ring growth patterns (i.e., sunspots >→ climate >→ tree rings.)

a. 1509 Istanbul earthquake
b. 1703 Genroku earthquake
c. 1700 Cascadia earthquake
d. Dendrochronology

38. A _____ is an annual layer of sediment or sedimentary rock. Initially, _____ was used to describe the separate components of annual layers in glacial lake sediments, but at the 1910 Geological Congress, the Swedish geologist Gerard De Geer (1858-1943) proposed a new formal definition where _____ described the whole of any annual sedimentary layer.

a. Varve
b. 1700 Cascadia earthquake
c. 1509 Istanbul earthquake
d. 1703 Genroku earthquake

39. In archeology, paleontology, and geomorphology, _____ is a geomorphic method of geochronologic aging that uses lichen growth to determine the age of exposed rock: lichens increase in size radially at a constant rate as they grow. Measuring the diameter of the largest lichen on a rock surface can therefore be used to determine the amount of time that the rock has been exposed. Lichen can be preserved on old rock faces for up to 10,000 years, providing the maximum age limit of the technique, though is most accurate (within 10% error) when applied to surfaces that have been exposed for less than 1000 years.

a. Geologic record
b. Lichenometry
c. Cenomanian
d. Relative dating

40. _____ are rare isotopes created when a high-energy cosmic ray interacts with the nucleus of an in situ atom. These isotopes are produced within earth materials such as rocks or soil, in Earth's atmosphere, and in extraterrestrial items such as meteorites. By measuring _____, scientists are able to gain insight into a range of geological and astronomical processes.
   a. Cosmogenic isotopes
   b. 1700 Cascadia earthquake
   c. Nanogeoscience
   d. 1509 Istanbul earthquake

Chapter 9. Folds, Faults, and Mountains

1. In geology the term _____ refers to the system of forces that tend to decrease the volume of or shorten rocks. Compressive strength refers to the maximum compressive stress that can be applied to a material before failure occurs. In tectonics, plates are always subjected to compressive stress.
   a. Geological survey
   b. Paralithic
   c. Slope Mass Rating
   d. Compression

2. _____ refers to natural mountain building, and may be studied as a tectonic structural event, (b) as a geographical event, and (c) a chronological event. Orogenic events (a) cause distinctive structural phenomena and related tectonic activity, (b) affect certain regions of rocks and crust, and (c) happen within a specific period of time.
   a. Antler orogeny
   b. Orogeny
   c. Orogenesis
   d. Alice Springs Orogeny

3. The _____, is a geologic eon before the Proterozoic and Paleoproterozoic, before 2.5 Ga (billion years ago, or 2,500 Ma.) Instead of being based on stratigraphy, this date is defined chronometrically. The lower boundary (starting point) has not been officially recognized by the International Commission on Stratigraphy, but it is usually set to 3.8 Ga, at the end of the Hadean eon.
   a. AL 129-1
   b. AASHTO Soil Classification System
   c. AL 333
   d. Archean

4. The term _____ is used in geology when one or a stack of originally flat and planar surfaces, such as sedimentary strata, are bent or curved as a result of plastic (i.e. permanent) deformation. Synsedimentary folds are those due to slumping of sedimentary material before it is lithified. Folds in rocks vary in size from microscopic crinkles to mountain-sized folds.
   a. 1703 Genroku earthquake
   b. 1700 Cascadia earthquake
   c. Fold
   d. 1509 Istanbul earthquake

5. A _____ is a special-purpose map made to show geological features.

The stratigraphic contour lines are drawn on the surface of a selected deep stratum, so that they can show the topographic trends of the strata under the ground. It is not always possible to properly show this when the strata are extremely fractured, mixed, in some discontinuities, or where they are otherwise disturbed.

   a. Geologic map
   b. 1509 Istanbul earthquake
   c. 1700 Cascadia earthquake
   d. 1703 Genroku earthquake

6. In structural geology, an _____ is a fold that is convex up and has its oldest beds at its core. The term is not to be confused with antiform, which is a purely descriptive term for any fold that is convex up. Therefore if age relationships (i.e. younging direction) between various strata are unknown, the term antiform must be used.
   a. AL 129-1
   b. AL 333
   c. AASHTO Soil Classification System
   d. Anticline

7. In structural geology, a _____ is a downward-curving fold, with layers that dip toward the center of the structure. A synclinorium is a large _____ with superimposed smaller folds.

On a geologic map, they are recognized by a sequence of rock layers that grow progressively younger, followed by the youngest layer at the fold's center or hinge, and by a reverse sequence of the same rock layers on the opposite side of the hinge.

Chapter 9. Folds, Faults, and Mountains

a. 1700 Cascadia earthquake
c. Syncline
b. 1703 Genroku earthquake
d. 1509 Istanbul earthquake

8. In geology, a _____ is a large sheetlike body of rock that has been moved more than 2 km (1.2 miles) from its original position. Nappes form during continental plate collisions, when folds are sheared so much that they fold back over on themselves and break apart. The resulting structure is a large-scale recumbent fold.
   a. 1509 Istanbul earthquake
   c. 1700 Cascadia earthquake
   b. 1703 Genroku earthquake
   d. Nappe

9. An _____ is the result of a sudden release of energy in the Earth's crust that creates seismic waves. They are recorded with a seismometer or the related and mostly obsolete Richter magnitude, with a magnitude 3 or lower _____ being mostly imperceptible and magnitude 7 causing serious damage over large areas.
   a. AL 129-1
   c. AASHTO Soil Classification System
   b. AL 333
   d. Earthquake

10. In geology, a _____ or _____ line is a planar fracture in rock in which the rock on one side of the fracture has moved with respect to the rock on the other side. Large faults within the Earth's crust are the result of differential or shear motion and active _____ zones are the causal locations of most earthquakes. Earthquakes are caused by energy release during rapid slippage along a _____.
    a. 1509 Istanbul earthquake
    c. 1700 Cascadia earthquake
    b. 1703 Genroku earthquake
    d. Fault

11. _____ landforms (mountains, hills, ridges, etc.) are created when large areas of bedrock are widely broken up by faults creating large vertical displacements of continental crust.

Vertical motion of the resulting blocks, sometimes accompanied by tilting, can then lead to high escarpments. These mountains are formed by the earth's crust being stretched and extended by tensional forces. Fault block mountains commonly accompany rifting, another indicator of tensional tectonic forces.

   a. 1703 Genroku earthquake
   c. Fault-block
   b. 1700 Cascadia earthquake
   d. 1509 Istanbul earthquake

12. The _____ is a continental transform fault that runs a length of roughly 800 miles (1,300 km) through California in the United States. The fault's motion is right-lateral strike-slip (horizontal motion.) It forms the tectonic boundary between the Pacific Plate and the North American Plate.
    a. 1700 Cascadia earthquake
    c. 1703 Genroku earthquake
    b. 1509 Istanbul earthquake
    d. San Andreas fault

13. The fault surface of _____ is usually near vertical and the footwall moves either left or right or laterally with very little vertical motion. _____ with left-lateral motion are also known as sinistral faults. Those with right-lateral motion are also known as dextral faults.
    a. 1509 Istanbul earthquake
    c. 1700 Cascadia earthquake
    b. 1703 Genroku earthquake
    d. Strike-slip faults

14. _____ can be again classified into the types 'reverse' and 'normal'. A normal fault occurs when the crust is extended. Alternatively such a fault can be called an extensional fault.

Chapter 9. Folds, Faults, and Mountains

a. 1509 Istanbul earthquake
c. Dip-slip faults
b. 1703 Genroku earthquake
d. 1700 Cascadia earthquake

15. A _____ is a depressed block of land bordered by parallel faults.

A _____ is the result of a block of land being downthrown producing a valley with a distinct scarp on each side.

_____ are produced from parallel normal faults, where the hanging wall is downthrown and the footwall is upthrown. The faults typically dip toward the center of the _____ from both sides.

a. Sag pond
c. Shear
b. Molasse basin
d. Graben

16. Since faults do not usually consist of a single, clean fracture, the term fault zone is used when referring to the zone of complex deformation that is associated with the fault plane. The two sides of a non-vertical fault are called the _____ and footwall. By definition, the _____ occurs above the fault and the footwall occurs below the fault.
a. 1700 Cascadia earthquake
c. 1703 Genroku earthquake
b. 1509 Istanbul earthquake
d. Hanging wall

17. A _____ is a large, slow-moving mass of ice, formed from compacted layers of snow, that slowly deforms and flows in response to gravity and high pressure.

_____ ice is the largest reservoir of fresh water on Earth, and second only to oceans as the largest reservoir of total water.

a. Glacier
c. Geologic temperature record
b. Keeling Curve
d. Little Ice Age

18. The _____ is a geologic fault structure of the Rocky Mountains within Glacier National Park in Montana, USA and Waterton Lakes National Park in Alberta, Canada, as well as into Lewis and Clark National Forest. It provides scientific insight into geologic processes happening in other parts of the world, like the Andes and the Himalaya Mountains. Scientific study of this region is practical because the original rock characteristics were well-preserved and recently sculptured by glaciers.
a. 1700 Cascadia earthquake
c. 1509 Istanbul earthquake
b. 1703 Genroku earthquake
d. Lewis Overthrust

19. _____ describes the large scale motions of Earth's lithosphere. The theory encompasses the older concepts of continental drift, developed during the first decades of the 20th century by Alfred Wegener, and seafloor spreading, understood during the 1960s.

The outermost part of the Earth's interior is made up of two layers: the lithosphere and the asthenosphere.

a. Plate tectonics
c. Subduction
b. Thrust fault
d. Copperbelt Province

Chapter 9. Folds, Faults, and Mountains

20. A _____ is the opposite of a normal fault -- the hanging wall moves up relative to the footwall. They are indicative of shortening of the crust. The dip of a _____ is relatively steep, greater than 45>°.
   a. 1700 Cascadia earthquake
   b. 1509 Istanbul earthquake
   c. 1703 Genroku earthquake
   d. Reverse fault

21. A _____ is a type of fault in which rocks of lower stratigraphic position are pushed up and over higher strata. They are often recognized because they place older rocks above younger. Thrust faults are the result of compressional forces.
   a. Copperbelt Province
   b. Thrust fault
   c. Juan de Fuca Ridge
   d. Gorda Ridge

22. The _____ a natural area in New York State northwest of New York City and southwest of Albany, are a mature dissected plateau, an uplifted region that was subsequently eroded into sharp relief. They are an eastward continuation, and the highest representation, of the Allegheny Plateau.

The history of the _____ is a geologic story come full circle, from erosion, deposition and uplift back to erosion. The _____ are more of a dissected plateau than a series of mountain ranges. The sediments that make up the rocks in the Catskills were deposited when the ancient Acadian Mountains in the east were rising and subsequently eroding. The sediments traveled westward and formed a great delta into the sea that was in the area at that time.

   a. 1509 Istanbul earthquake
   b. 1703 Genroku earthquake
   c. 1700 Cascadia earthquake
   d. Catskill Mountains

23. _____ is the largest volcano on earth in terms of area covered and one of five volcanoes that form the Island of Hawaii in the U.S. state of Hawai>Ê»i in the Pacific Ocean. It is an active shield volcano, with a volume estimated at approximately 18,000 cubic miles (75,000 kmÂ³), although its peak is about 120 feet (37 m) lower than that of its neighbor, Mauna Kea. The Hawaiian name '_____' means 'Long Mountain'.
   a. 1700 Cascadia earthquake
   b. 1509 Istanbul earthquake
   c. 1703 Genroku earthquake
   d. Mauna Loa

24. The physical manifestations of _____ are orogenic belts or orogens. An orogen is different from a mountain range in that an orogen may be almost completely eroded away, and only recognizable by studying (old) rocks that bear traces of _____. Orogens are usually long, thin, arcuate tracts of rock that have a pronounced linear structure resulting in terranes or blocks of deformed rocks, separated generally by dipping thrust faults.
   a. Orogeny
   b. Alpine orogeny
   c. Alleghenian orogeny
   d. Orogenesis

25. The _____ is the earliest of three geologic eras of the Phanerozoic eon. The _____ spanned from roughly 542 to 251 million years ago (ICS, 2004), and is subdivided into six geologic periods; from oldest to youngest they are: the Cambrian, Ordovician, Silurian, Devonian, Carboniferous, and Permian.

The _____ covers the time from the first appearance of abundant, soft-shelled fossils to the time when the continents were beginning to be dominated by large, relatively sophisticated reptiles and modern plants. The lower (oldest) boundary was classically set at the first appearance of creatures known as trilobites and archeocyathids.

Chapter 9. Folds, Faults, and Mountains

a. 1703 Genroku earthquake
c. 1509 Istanbul earthquake
b. 1700 Cascadia earthquake
d. Paleozoic

26. _____ is a geologic term for a type of topography characterized by a series of separate and parallel mountain ranges with broad valleys interposed, extending over a more or less wide area. It is typified by the topography found in the Great Basin in the western United States, which is part of a larger regional topography known as the _____ Province. _____ topography results from crustal extension.
a. Cap carbonates
c. Cross-cutting relationships
b. Basin and Range
d. Bediasite

27. The _____ is a large geologic province which includes parts of the southwestern United States and northwestern Mexico, typified by basin and range topography.

The topography of the _____ is a result of crustal extension within this part of the North American Plate. The cause of this extension is as yet not fully understood, although several hypotheses have been offered. The crust here has been stretched up to 100% of its original width. In fact, the crust underneath the _____, especially under the Great Basin, is some of the thinnest in the world.

a. Musgrave Block
c. Basin and Range province
b. Yilgarn Craton
d. Canadian Shield

28. A _____ is a series of mountainous foothills, adjacent to an orogenic belt, that form due to compression. They commonly form in the forelands adjacent to major orogens as deformation propagates outwards. They usually comprise both folds and thrust faults, commonly interrelated.
a. Nevadan orogeny
c. Pan-African orogeny
b. Trans-Hudson orogeny
d. Fold and thrust belt

29. The _____ is a tectonic plate covering most of North America, Greenland and part of Siberia. It extends eastward to the Mid-Atlantic Ridge and westward to the Chersky Range in eastern Siberia. The plate includes both continental and oceanic crust. The interior of the main continental landmass includes an extensive granitic core called a craton. Along most of the edges of this craton are fragments of crustal material called terranes, accreted to the craton by tectonic actions over the long span of geologic time. It is believed that much of North America west of the Rockies is composed of such terranes.
a. Gorda Plate
c. North American plate
b. North Bismarck Plate
d. Conway Reef Plate

30. A _____ is generally a large area of exposed Precambrian crystalline igneous and high-grade metamorphic rocks that form tectonically stable areas. In all cases, the age of these rocks is greater than 570 million years and sometimes dates back 2 to 3.5 billion years. They have been little affected by tectonic events following the end of the Precambrian Era, and are relatively flat regions where mountain building, faulting, and other tectonic processes are greatly diminished compared with the activity that occurs at the margins of the shields and the boundaries between tectonic plates.
a. 1703 Genroku earthquake
c. 1700 Cascadia earthquake
b. 1509 Istanbul earthquake
d. Shield

31. A _____ is a large volcano with shallow-sloping sides.

Chapter 9. Folds, Faults, and Mountains

They are formed by lava flows of low viscosity - lava that flows easily. Consequently, a volcanic mountain having a broad profile is built up over time by flow after flow of relatively fluid basaltic lava issuing from vents or fissures on the surface of the volcano

a. 1700 Cascadia earthquake
b. 1703 Genroku earthquake
c. 1509 Istanbul earthquake
d. Shield volcano

32. A _____ is an opening in a planet's surface or crust, which allows hot, molten rock, ash, and gases to escape from below the surface. Volcanic activity involving the extrusion of rock tends to form mountains or features like mountains over a period of time.
a. Volcano
b. 1700 Cascadia earthquake
c. 1703 Genroku earthquake
d. 1509 Istanbul earthquake

33. _____ is the removal of solids (sediment, soil, rock and other particles) in the natural environment. It usually occurs due to transport by wind, water, or ice; by down-slope creep of soil and other material under the force of gravity; or by living organisms, such as burrowing animals, in the case of bioerosion.

_____ is distinguished from weathering, which is the process of chemical or physical breakdown of the minerals in the rocks, although the two processes may occur concurrently.

a. Erosion
b. AASHTO Soil Classification System
c. AL 129-1
d. AL 333

34. The _____ is a a term for a geologic period 65 million to 1.8 million years ago. The _____ covered the time span between the superseded Secondary period and an out-of-date definition of the Quaternary period. The period began with the demise of the non-avian dinosaurs in the Cretaceous-_____ extinction event, at start of the Cenozoic era, spanning to beginning of the most recent Ice Age, at the end of the Pliocene epoch.
a. Historical geology
b. Tertiary
c. Suspended load
d. Rockall

35. The _____ is a middle Paleozoic mountain building event (orogeny), especially in the northern Appalachians, between New York and Newfoundland. The _____ most greatly affected the Northern Appalachian region (New England northeastward into the Gasp>é region of Canada.) The _____ should not be regarded as a single tectonic event, but rather as an orogenic era.
a. Alice Springs Orogeny
b. Alpine orogeny
c. Orogenesis
d. Acadian orogeny

36. _____ was the supercontinent that is theorized to have existed during the Paleozoic and Mesozoic eras about 250 million years ago, before the component continents were separated into their current configuration.

The name was first used by the German originator of the continental drift theory, Alfred Wegener, in the 1920 edition of his book The Origin of Continents and Oceans , in which a postulated supercontinent _____ played a key role.

The single enormous ocean which surrounded Pangaea is known as Panthalassa.

a. 1700 Cascadia earthquake b. 1703 Genroku earthquake
c. 1509 Istanbul earthquake d. Pangea

Chapter 10. Earthquakes and the Earth's Interior

1. The _____ or epicentre is the point on the Earth's surface that is directly above the hypocenter or focus, the point where an earthquake or underground explosion originates.

   The _____ is usually the location of greatest damage. However, in some cases the _____ is above the start of a much larger event.

   a. AL 333
   b. AASHTO Soil Classification System
   c. Epicenter
   d. AL 129-1

2. An _____ is the result of a sudden release of energy in the Earth's crust that creates seismic waves. They are recorded with a seismometer or the related and mostly obsolete Richter magnitude, with a magnitude 3 or lower _____ being mostly imperceptible and magnitude 7 causing serious damage over large areas.
   a. AASHTO Soil Classification System
   b. AL 333
   c. AL 129-1
   d. Earthquake

3. An _____ is an earthquake that occurs after a previous earthquake (the main shock.) An _____ is in the same region of the main shock but is always of smaller magnitude strength. If an _____ is larger than the main shock, the _____ is redesignated as the main shock and the original main shock is redesignated as a foreshock.
   a. Aftershock
   b. AL 129-1
   c. AL 333
   d. AASHTO Soil Classification System

4. _____ are type of elastic wave, also called seismic waves, that can travel through gases, elastic solids and liquids, including the Earth. _____ can be produced by earthquakes and recorded by seismometers.
   a. 1703 Genroku earthquake
   b. P-waves
   c. 1700 Cascadia earthquake
   d. 1509 Istanbul earthquake

5. A type of seismic wave, the _____, secondary wave or shear wave (sometimes called an elastic _____) is one of the two main types of elastic body waves, so named because they move through the body of an object, unlike surface waves.

   The _____ move as a shear or transverse wave, so motion is perpendicular to the direction of wave propagation: S-waves, like waves in a rope, as opposed to waves moving through a slinky, the P-wave. The wave moves through elastic media, and the main restoring force comes from shear effects.

   a. 1509 Istanbul earthquake
   b. 1700 Cascadia earthquake
   c. 1703 Genroku earthquake
   d. S-wave

6. _____ are waves that travel through the Earth or other elastic body, for example as the result of an earthquake, explosion, or some other process that imparts forces to the body. _____ are also continually excited on Earth by the incessant pounding of ocean waves (referred to as the microseism) and the wind. _____ are studied by seismologists, and measured by a seismograph, which records the output of a seismometer, or geophone.
   a. Hypocenter
   b. Seismic waves
   c. Strong ground motion
   d. Fault friction

Chapter 10. Earthquakes and the Earth's Interior

7. _____ is the scientific study of earthquakes and the propagation of elastic waves through the Earth. The field also includes studies of earthquake effects, such as tsunamis as well as diverse seismic sources such as volcanic, tectonic, oceanic, atmospheric, and artificial processes . A related field that uses geology to infer information regarding past earthquakes is paleoseismology.
   - a. 1700 Cascadia earthquake
   - b. 1509 Istanbul earthquake
   - c. 1703 Genroku earthquake
   - d. Seismology

8. In physics, a _____ is a mechanical wave that propagates along the interface between differing media, usually two fluids with different densities. A _____ can also be an electromagnetic wave guided by a refractive index gradient. In radio transmission, a ground wave is a _____ that propagates close to the surface of the Earth.
   - a. 1509 Istanbul earthquake
   - b. 1700 Cascadia earthquake
   - c. 1703 Genroku earthquake
   - d. Surface wave

9. The _____ is a scale used for measuring the intensity of an earthquake. The scale quantifies the effects of an earthquake on the Earth's surface, humans, objects of nature, and man-made structures on a scale of I through XII, with I denoting not felt, and XII one that causes almost complete destruction. The values will differ based on the distance to the earthquake, with the highest intensities being around the epicentral area.
   - a. Rossi-Forel scale
   - b. Richter magnitude scale
   - c. Mercalli intensity scale
   - d. Seismic scale

10. The _____ is used by seismologists to measure the size of earthquakes in terms of the energy released. The magnitude is based on the moment of the earthquake, which is equal to the rigidity of the Earth multiplied by the average amount of slip on the fault and the size of the area that slipped. The scale was developed in the 1970s to succeed the 1930s-era Richter magnitude scale, M_L.
    - a. Surface wave magnitude
    - b. Seismic scale
    - c. Moment magnitude scale
    - d. Mercalli intensity scale

11. The _____, also known as the local magnitude (M_L) scale, assigns a single number to quantify the amount of seismic energy released by an earthquake. It is a base-10 logarithmic scale obtained by calculating the logarithm of the combined horizontal amplitude of the largest displacement from zero on a Wood-Anderson torsion seismometer output. So, for example, an earthquake that measures 5.0 on the Richter scale has a shaking amplitude 10 times larger than one that measures 4.0.
    - a. Richter magnitude scale
    - b. China Seismic Intensity Scale
    - c. Medvedev-Sponheuer-Karnik scale
    - d. Moment magnitude scale

12. _____ is a quantity used by earthquake seismologists to measure the size of an earthquake. The scalar _____ M_0 is defined by the equation $M_0 = >\mu A u$, where

    - $>\mu$ is the shear modulus of the rocks involved in the earthquake, typically 30 gigapascals
    - A is the area of the rupture along the geologic fault where the earthquake occurred, and
    - u is the average displacement on A.

The _____ of an earthquake is typically estimated using whatever information is available to constrain its factors. For modern earthquakes, moment is usually estimated from ground motion recordings of earthquakes known as seismograms. For earthquakes that occurred in times before modern instruments were available, moment may be estimated from geologic estimates of the size of the fault rupture and the displacement.

Chapter 10. Earthquakes and the Earth's Interior

    a. Coulomb stress transfer
    b. Reflection seismology
    c. Gutenberg-Richter law
    d. Seismic moment

13. _____ are instruments that measure and record motions of the ground, including those of seismic waves generated by earthquakes, nuclear explosions, and other seismic sources. Records of seismic waves allow seismologists to map the interior of the Earth, and locate and measure the size of these different sources. Seismograph is another Greek term from seismós and γρÎ¬φω, gráphÄ, to draw.
    a. 1700 Cascadia earthquake
    b. 1509 Istanbul earthquake
    c. Seismometers
    d. 1703 Genroku earthquake

14. In geology, a _____ or _____ line is a planar fracture in rock in which the rock on one side of the fracture has moved with respect to the rock on the other side. Large faults within the Earth's crust are the result of differential or shear motion and active _____ zones are the causal locations of most earthquakes. Earthquakes are caused by energy release during rapid slippage along a _____.
    a. 1703 Genroku earthquake
    b. Fault
    c. 1509 Istanbul earthquake
    d. 1700 Cascadia earthquake

15. The _____ is a continental transform fault that runs a length of roughly 800 miles (1,300 km) through California in the United States. The fault's motion is right-lateral strike-slip (horizontal motion.) It forms the tectonic boundary between the Pacific Plate and the North American Plate.
    a. 1703 Genroku earthquake
    b. 1509 Istanbul earthquake
    c. 1700 Cascadia earthquake
    d. San Andreas fault

16. _____ is the naturally occurring, unconsolidated or loose covering on the Earth's surface. _____ is composed of particles of broken rock that have been altered by chemical, biological and environmental processes including weathering and erosion. _____ is different from its parent rock(s) source(s), altered by interactions between the lithosphere, hydrosphere, atmosphere, and the biosphere.
    a. 1509 Istanbul earthquake
    b. Soil
    c. Topsoil
    d. 1700 Cascadia earthquake

17. _____ describes the behavior of soils that, when loaded, suddenly go from a solid state to a liquefied state, or having the consistency of a heavy liquid. Liquefaction is more likely to occur in loose to moderate saturated granular soils with poor drainage, such as silty sands or sands and gravels capped or containing seams of impermeable sediments . During loading, usually cyclic undrained loading, e.g. earthquake loading, loose sands tend to decrease in volume, which produces an increase in their porewater pressures and consequently a decrease in shear strength, i.e. reduction in effective stress.
    a. 1703 Genroku earthquake
    b. 1700 Cascadia earthquake
    c. 1509 Istanbul earthquake
    d. Soil liquefaction

18. A _____ is a standing wave in an enclosed or partially enclosed body of water. Seiches and _____-related phenomena have been observed on lakes, reservoirs, swimming pools, bays and seas. The key requirement for formation of a _____ is that the body of water be at least partially bounded, allowing the formation of the standing wave.
    a. Seiche
    b. 1700 Cascadia earthquake
    c. 1509 Istanbul earthquake
    d. 1703 Genroku earthquake

Chapter 10. Earthquakes and the Earth's Interior

19. The _____ is the earliest of three geologic eras of the Phanerozoic eon. The _____ spanned from roughly 542 to 251 million years ago (ICS, 2004), and is subdivided into six geologic periods; from oldest to youngest they are: the Cambrian, Ordovician, Silurian, Devonian, Carboniferous, and Permian.

The _____ covers the time from the first appearance of abundant, soft-shelled fossils to the time when the continents were beginning to be dominated by large, relatively sophisticated reptiles and modern plants. The lower (oldest) boundary was classically set at the first appearance of creatures known as trilobites and archeocyathids.

   a. 1700 Cascadia earthquake
   c. 1703 Genroku earthquake
   b. 1509 Istanbul earthquake
   d. Paleozoic

20. A _____ is a deep active seismic area in a subduction zone. Differential motion along the zone produces deep-seated earthquakes, the foci of which may be as deep as about 700 kilometres (435 miles.) They develop beneath volcanic island arcs and continental margins above active subduction zones.
   a. 1703 Genroku earthquake
   c. 1509 Istanbul earthquake
   b. 1700 Cascadia earthquake
   d. Wadati-Benioff zone

21. In geology, _____ is the process that takes place at convergent boundaries by which one tectonic plate moves under another tectonic plate, sinking into the Earth's mantle, as the plates converge. A _____ zone is an area on Earth where two tectonic plates move towards one another and _____ occurs. Rates of _____ are typically measured in centimeters per year, with the average rate of convergence being approximately 2 to 8 centimeters per year (about the rate a fingernail grows.)
   a. Mirovia
   c. Plate tectonics
   b. Continental crust
   d. Subduction

22. The lithosphere is broken up into what are called _____. In the case of Earth, there are eight major and many minor plates The lithospheric plates ride on the asthenosphere. These plates move in relation to one another at one of three types of plate boundaries: convergent, or collisional boundaries; divergent boundaries, also called spreading centers; and transform boundaries.
   a. Juan de Fuca Ridge
   c. Lithosphere
   b. Thrust fault
   d. Tectonic plates

23. A _____ is a mountain rising from the ocean seafloor that does not reach to the water's surface (sea level), and thus is not an island. These are typically formed from extinct volcanoes, that rise abruptly and are usually found rising from a seafloor of 1,000-4,000 meters depth. They are defined by oceanographers as independent features that rise to at least 1,000 meters above the seafloor.
   a. 1700 Cascadia earthquake
   c. 1509 Istanbul earthquake
   b. 1703 Genroku earthquake
   d. Seamount

24. The _____ is a geologic fault zone capable of generating significantly destructive earthquakes. About 60 kilometers long, it lies mainly along the western base of the hills on the east side of San Francisco Bay. It runs through densely-populated areas, including the cities of Richmond, El Cerrito, Berkeley, Oakland, San Leandro, Hayward, Fremont, and San Jose.

The _____ is parallel to its more famous (and much longer) westerly neighbor, the San Andreas Fault, which lies offshore and through the San Francisco peninsula.

a. 1700 Cascadia earthquake
b. Hayward Fault Zone
c. 1509 Istanbul earthquake
d. 1703 Genroku earthquake

25. A _____ is a segment of an active fault that has not slipped in an unusually long time when compared with other segments along the same structure. _____ hypothesis/theory states that, over long periods of time, the displacement on any segment must be equal to that experienced by all the other parts of the fault. Any large and longstanding gap is therefore considered to be the fault segment most likely to suffer future earthquakes.
a. Receiver function
b. Teleseism
c. Seismic shadowing
d. Seismic gap

26. The _____, is a geologic eon before the Proterozoic and Paleoproterozoic, before 2.5 Ga (billion years ago, or 2,500 Ma.) Instead of being based on stratigraphy, this date is defined chronometrically. The lower boundary (starting point) has not been officially recognized by the International Commission on Stratigraphy, but it is usually set to 3.8 Ga, at the end of the Hadean eon.
a. AASHTO Soil Classification System
b. AL 333
c. AL 129-1
d. Archean

27. The _____ is a major branch of the San Andreas Fault located in northern California in the San Francisco Bay Area. It runs east of the San Andreas, diverging from it in the vicinity of Hollister, California, and is responsible for the formation of the Calaveras Valley there. Between the San Andreas Fault and the _____ lies the Hayward Fault, which diverges from the _____ east of San Jose, California.
a. 1703 Genroku earthquake
b. 1509 Istanbul earthquake
c. 1700 Cascadia earthquake
d. Calaveras fault

28. A _____ material is one in which viscosity increases with the rate of shear. Such a shear thickening fluid, also known by the acronym STF, is an example of a non-Newtonian fluid.

The _____ effect occurs when closely packed particles are combined with enough liquid to fill the gaps between them.

a. 1509 Istanbul earthquake
b. 1700 Cascadia earthquake
c. 1703 Genroku earthquake
d. Dilatant

29. The _____ Era is one of three geologic eras of the Phanerozoic eon. The division of time into eras dates back to Giovanni Arduino, in the 18th century, although his original name for the era now called the '_____' was 'Secondary' (making the modern era the 'Tertiary'.)

The _____ was a time of tectonic, climatic and evolutionary activity. The continents gradually shifted from a state of connectedness into their present configuration; the drifting provided for speciation and other important evolutionary developments.

Chapter 10. Earthquakes and the Earth's Interior

a. 1509 Istanbul earthquake
b. 1700 Cascadia earthquake
c. 1703 Genroku earthquake
d. Mesozoic

30. The _____ is the layer of igneous, sedimentary, and metamorphic rocks which form the continents and the areas of shallow seabed close to their shores, known as continental shelves. This layer is sometimes called sial due to more felsic, or granitic, bulk composition, which lies in contrast to the oceanic crust, called sima due to its mafic, or basaltic rock. (Based on the change in velocity of seismic waves, it is believed that at a certain depth sial becomes close in its physical properties to sima.

a. Tectonic plates
b. Mirovia
c. Thrust fault
d. Continental crust

31. The _____, usually referred to as the Moho, is the boundary between the Earth's crust and the mantle. The Moho serves to separate both oceanic crust and continental crust from underlying mantle. The Moho mostly lies entirely within the lithosphere; only beneath mid-ocean ridges does it define the lithosphere-asthenosphere boundary.

a. Copperbelt Province
b. Gorda Ridge
c. Panthalassa
d. Mohorovičić discontinuity

32. _____ is the part of Earth's lithosphere that surfaces in the ocean basins. _____ is primarily composed of mafic rocks, or sima. It is thinner than continental crust, or sial, generally less than 10 kilometers thick, however it is denser, having a mean density of about 3.3 grams per cubic centimeter.

a. AL 129-1
b. AASHTO Soil Classification System
c. AL 333
d. Oceanic crust

33. _____ is the decomposition of Earth rocks, soils and their minerals through direct contact with the planet's atmosphere. _____ occurs in situ, or 'with no movement', and thus should not be confused with erosion, which involves the movement of rocks and minerals by agents such as water, ice, wind and gravity.

Two important classifications of _____ processes exist -- physical and chemical _____.

a. 1703 Genroku earthquake
b. 1509 Istanbul earthquake
c. 1700 Cascadia earthquake
d. Weathering

34. The _____ lies between the Earth's silicate mantle and its liquid iron-nickel outer core. This boundary is located at approximately 2900 km of depth beneath the Earth's surface. The boundary is observed via the discontinuity in seismic wave velocities at that depth. This discontinuity is due to the differences between the acoustic impedances of the solid mantle and the molten outer core. P-wave velocities are much slower in the outer core than in the deep mantle while S-waves do not exist at all in the liquid portion of the core.

a. Seismogenic layer
b. Brittle-ductile transition zone
c. 1509 Istanbul earthquake
d. Core-mantle boundary

35. The _____ is the mechanically weak ductily-deforming region of the upper mantle of the Earth. It lies below the lithosphere, at depths between 100 and 200 km (~ 62 and 124 miles) below the surface, but perhaps extending as deep as 400 km (~ 249 miles.)

The _____ is a portion of the upper mantle just below the lithosphere that is involved in plate movements and isostatic adjustments. In spite of its heat, pressures keep it plastic, and it has a relatively low density. Seismic waves pass relatively slowly through the _____, compared to the overlying lithospheric mantle, thus it has been called the low-velocity zone. This was the observation that originally alerted seismologists to its presence and gave some information about its physical properties, as the speed of seismic waves decreases with decreasing rigidity.

a. AL 129-1
b. AASHTO Soil Classification System
c. AL 333
d. Asthenosphere

36. The mineral _____ is a magnesium iron silicate with the formula $(Mg,Fe)_2SiO_4$. It is one of the most common minerals on Earth, and has also been identified in meteorites and on the Moon, Mars, and comet Wild 2.

The ratio of magnesium and iron varies between the two endmembers of the solid solution series: forsterite (Mg-endmember) and fayalite (Fe-endmember.)

a. AL 333
b. AASHTO Soil Classification System
c. Olivine
d. AL 129-1

37. The _____ is part of the Earth's mantle, and is located between the lower mantle and the upper mantle, between a depth of 410 and 660 km. The Earth's mantle, including the _____, consists primarily of peridotite, a course grained, ultramafic, igneous rock.

The mantle was divided into the upper mantle, _____, and lower mantle as a result of sudden seismic-velocity discontinuities at depths of 410 and 660 km.

a. Dissolved load
b. Basin and Range
c. Primordial water
d. Transition zone

38. A _____ is an area in which an S-Wave (secondary seismic wave) is not detected due to it not being able to pass through the outer core of the earth due to it being liquid. When an earthquake occurs, seismographs near the epicenter, out to about 90° distance, are able to record both Primary and Secondary waves, but those at a greater distance no longer detect the S-wave. This is because shear waves cannot pass through liquids.

a. Rayleigh waves
b. Receiver function
c. Seismic shadowing
d. Shadow zone

Chapter 11. Plate Tectonics: Creating Oceans and Continents

1. _____ describes the large scale motions of Earth's lithosphere. The theory encompasses the older concepts of continental drift, developed during the first decades of the 20th century by Alfred Wegener, and seafloor spreading, understood during the 1960s.

The outermost part of the Earth's interior is made up of two layers: the lithosphere and the asthenosphere.

a. Thrust fault
b. Subduction
c. Copperbelt Province
d. Plate tectonics

2. _____ is the movement of the Earth's continents relative to each other. The hypothesis that continents 'drift' was first put forward by Abraham Ortelius in 1596 and was fully developed by Alfred Wegener in 1912. However, it was not until the development of the theory of plate tectonics in the 1960s, that a sufficient geological explanation of that movement was found.

a. Copperbelt Province
b. Continental drift
c. Tectonic plates
d. Panthalassa

3. The _____ Period is the last geological period of the Neoproterozoic Era and of the Proterozoic Eon, immediately preceding the Cambrian Period, the first period of the Paleozoic Era and of the Phanerozoic Eon. Its status as an official geological period was ratified in 2004 by the International Union of Geological Sciences (IUGS), making it the first new geological period declared in 120 years. The type section is in the Flinders Ranges in South Australia.

a. AASHTO Soil Classification System
b. AL 333
c. AL 129-1
d. Ediacaran

4. The _____ is the earliest of three geologic eras of the Phanerozoic eon. The _____ spanned from roughly 542 to 251 million years ago (ICS, 2004), and is subdivided into six geologic periods; from oldest to youngest they are: the Cambrian, Ordovician, Silurian, Devonian, Carboniferous, and Permian.

The _____ covers the time from the first appearance of abundant, soft-shelled fossils to the time when the continents were beginning to be dominated by large, relatively sophisticated reptiles and modern plants. The lower (oldest) boundary was classically set at the first appearance of creatures known as trilobites and archeocyathids.

a. 1703 Genroku earthquake
b. 1509 Istanbul earthquake
c. 1700 Cascadia earthquake
d. Paleozoic

5. _____ was the supercontinent that is theorized to have existed during the Paleozoic and Mesozoic eras about 250 million years ago, before the component continents were separated into their current configuration.

The name was first used by the German originator of the continental drift theory, Alfred Wegener, in the 1920 edition of his book The Origin of Continents and Oceans , in which a postulated supercontinent _____ played a key role.

The single enormous ocean which surrounded Pangaea is known as Panthalassa.

a. 1700 Cascadia earthquake
b. 1509 Istanbul earthquake
c. 1703 Genroku earthquake
d. Pangea

Chapter 11. Plate Tectonics: Creating Oceans and Continents

6. _____ was the vast global ocean that surrounded the supercontinent Pangaea, during the late Paleozoic and the early Mesozoic eras. It included the Pacific Ocean to the west and north and the Tethys Ocean to the southeast. It became the Pacific Ocean, following the closing of the Tethys basin and the breakup of Pangaea, which created the Atlantic, Arctic, and Indian Ocean basins.
   a. Juan de Fuca Ridge
   b. Mohorovičić discontinuity
   c. Tectonic plates
   d. Panthalassa

7. In geology, _____ is transported rock debris overlying the solid bedrock. The term is also sometimes refers to organic debris so-transported. In the largest sense, it refers to the material left behind by retreating continental glaciers.
   a. Drift
   b. Dispersion
   c. Georeactor
   d. Compression

8. The _____, is a geologic eon before the Proterozoic and Paleoproterozoic, before 2.5 Ga (billion years ago, or 2,500 Ma.) Instead of being based on stratigraphy, this date is defined chronometrically. The lower boundary (starting point) has not been officially recognized by the International Commission on Stratigraphy, but it is usually set to 3.8 Ga, at the end of the Hadean eon.
   a. AL 333
   b. Archean
   c. AASHTO Soil Classification System
   d. AL 129-1

9. _____ is one of the three main rock types (the others being igneous and metamorphic rock.) _____ is formed by deposition and consolidation of mineral and organic material and from precipitation of minerals from solution. The processes that form _____ occur at the surface of the Earth and within bodies of water.
   a. Felsic
   b. Rock cycle
   c. Serpentinite
   d. Sedimentary rock

10. The _____ is a a term for a geologic period 65 million to 1.8 million years ago. The _____ covered the time span between the superseded Secondary period and an out-of-date definition of the Quaternary period. The period began with the demise of the non-avian dinosaurs in the Cretaceous-_____ extinction event, at start of the Cenozoic era, spanning to beginning of the most recent Ice Age, at the end of the Pliocene epoch.
    a. Historical geology
    b. Tertiary
    c. Rockall
    d. Suspended load

11. The lithosphere is broken up into what are called _____. In the case of Earth, there are eight major and many minor plates The lithospheric plates ride on the asthenosphere. These plates move in relation to one another at one of three types of plate boundaries: convergent, or collisional boundaries; divergent boundaries, also called spreading centers; and transform boundaries.
    a. Juan de Fuca Ridge
    b. Lithosphere
    c. Thrust fault
    d. Tectonic plates

12. _____ is an active undersea volcano that lies approximately 48 km (30 mi) off the southeast coast of the island of Hawaiʻi. It is located on the flank of Mauna Loa, the largest shield volcano on Earth. _____ is the newest volcano in the Hawaiian-Emperor seamount chain, a string of volcanoes that stretches over 5,800 km (3,604 mi) northwest of Lōʻihi and the island of Hawaiʻi. In 1996, Loihi was the site of the first ever directly observed eruption of an active underwater volcano in Hawaiʻi.

Chapter 11. Plate Tectonics: Creating Oceans and Continents

a. Loihi Seamount
c. 1509 Istanbul earthquake
b. 1703 Genroku earthquake
d. 1700 Cascadia earthquake

13. A _____ is a mountain rising from the ocean seafloor that does not reach to the water's surface (sea level), and thus is not an island. These are typically formed from extinct volcanoes, that rise abruptly and are usually found rising from a seafloor of 1,000-4,000 meters depth. They are defined by oceanographers as independent features that rise to at least 1,000 meters above the seafloor.

a. Seamount
c. 1509 Istanbul earthquake
b. 1700 Cascadia earthquake
d. 1703 Genroku earthquake

14. In geology, a _____ is a location on the Earth's surface that has experienced active volcanism for a long period of time.

J. Tuzo Wilson came up with the idea in 1963 that volcanic chains like the Hawaiian Islands result from the slow movement of a tectonic plate across a 'fixed' _____ deep beneath the surface of the planet.

a. 1509 Istanbul earthquake
c. 1700 Cascadia earthquake
b. 1703 Genroku earthquake
d. Hotspot

15. The _____ Era is one of three geologic eras of the Phanerozoic eon. The division of time into eras dates back to Giovanni Arduino, in the 18th century, although his original name for the era now called the '_____' was 'Secondary' (making the modern era the 'Tertiary'.)

The _____ was a time of tectonic, climatic and evolutionary activity. The continents gradually shifted from a state of connectedness into their present configuration; the drifting provided for speciation and other important evolutionary developments.

a. 1703 Genroku earthquake
c. 1509 Istanbul earthquake
b. 1700 Cascadia earthquake
d. Mesozoic

16. In geology, a _____ is a place where the Earth's crust and lithosphere are being pulled apart and is an example of extensional tectonics.

Typical _____ features are a central linear downdropped fault segment, called a graben, with parallel normal faulting and _____-flank uplifts on either side forming a _____ valley, where the _____ remains above sea level. The axis of the _____ area commonly contains volcanic rocks and active volcanism is a part of many, but not all active _____ systems.

a. Rift
c. 1509 Istanbul earthquake
b. 1703 Genroku earthquake
d. 1700 Cascadia earthquake

17. In geology, an _____ is a failed arm of a triple junction of a plate tectonics rift system. A triple junction beneath a continental plate initiates a three way breakup of the continental plate. As the continental break-up develops one of the three spreading ridges typically fails or stops spreading. The resulting failed rift is called an _____ and becomes a filled graben within the continent. However, the crust in an _____ region remains weakened by previous rifting activity and thus seismic activity and, occasionally, volcanic activity may re-occur subsequently from time to time.

Chapter 11. Plate Tectonics: Creating Oceans and Continents

a. AL 129-1
c. AL 333

b. AASHTO Soil Classification System
d. Aulacogen

18. The _____ is the zone of the ocean floor that separates the thin oceanic crust from thick continental crust. Continental margins constitute about 28% of the oceanic area.

The transition from continental to oceanic crust commonly occurs within the outer part of the margin, called continental rise.

a. Longshore drift
c. Continental margin

b. Cuspate forelands
d. 1509 Istanbul earthquake

19. In plate tectonics, a _____ is a linear feature that exists between two tectonic plates that are moving away from each other. These areas can form in the middle of continents but eventually form ocean basins. Divergent boundaries within continents initially produce rifts which produce rift valleys. Therefore, most active divergent plate boundaries are between oceanic plates and are often called mid-oceanic ridges. Divergent boundaries also form Volcanic Islands which occur when the plates move apart to produce gaps which molten lava rises to fill. Thus creating a shield volcano which would eventually build up to become a volcanic island.

a. 1509 Istanbul earthquake
c. 1700 Cascadia earthquake

b. 1703 Genroku earthquake
d. Divergent boundary

20. The _____ is a name given in the late 19th century by British explorer John Walter Gregory to the continuous geographic trough, approximately 6,000 kilometres (3,700 mi) in length, that runs from northern Syria in Southwest Asia to central Mozambique in East Africa. The name continues in some usages, although it is today considered geologically imprecise as it includes what are today regarded as separate, since 1869 due to the Suez Canal Company project, although related rift and fault systems. Today, the term is most often used to refer to the valley of the East African Rift, the divergent plate boundary which extends from the Afar Triple Junction southward across eastern Africa, and is in the process of splitting the African Plate into two new separate plates.

a. 1509 Istanbul earthquake
c. 1703 Genroku earthquake

b. Great Rift Valley
d. 1700 Cascadia earthquake

21. A _____ is an underwater mountain range, typically having a valley known as a rift running along its spine, formed by plate tectonics. This type of oceanic ridge is characteristic of what is known as an oceanic spreading center, which is responsible for seafloor spreading. The uplifted sea floor results from convection currents which rise in the mantle as magma at a linear weakness in the oceanic crust, and emerge as lava, creating new crust upon cooling.

a. Wave pounding
c. Downcutting

b. Spheroidal weathering
d. Mid-ocean ridge

22. A _____ or sea vent, is a type of hydrothermal vent found on the ocean floor. They are formed in fields hundreds of meters wide when superheated water from below Earth's crust comes through the ocean floor. This water is rich in dissolved minerals from the crust, most notably sulfides.

a. 1700 Cascadia earthquake
c. 1509 Istanbul earthquake

b. Black smoker
d. 1703 Genroku earthquake

Chapter 11. Plate Tectonics: Creating Oceans and Continents 83

23. The _____ is a mid-oceanic ridge, a divergent tectonic plate boundary located along the floor of the Pacific Ocean. It separates the Pacific Plate to the west from (north to south) the North American Plate, the Rivera Plate, the Cocos Plate, the Nazca Plate, and the Antarctic Plate. It runs from an undefined point near Antarctica in the south northward to its termination at the northern end of the Gulf of California in the Salton Sea basin in southern California.
   a. Azores-Gibraltar Transform Fault
   b. Obduction
   c. Elastic rebound theory
   d. East Pacific rise

24. The _____ is a tectonic spreading center located off the coasts of the state of Washington in the United States and the province of British Columbia in Canada. It runs northward from a transform boundary, the Blanco Fracture Zone, to a triple junction with the Nootka Fault and the Sovanco Fracture Zone. To its east is the Juan de Fuca Plate, which together with the Gorda Plate to its south and the Explorer Plate to its north, is what remains of the once-vast Farallon Plate which has been largely subducted under the North American Plate.
   a. Copperbelt Province
   b. Juan de Fuca ridge
   c. Lithosphere
   d. Mohorovičić discontinuity

25. An _____ or accretionary prism is formed from sediments that are accreted onto the non-subducting tectonic plate at a convergent plate boundary. Most of the material in the _____ consists of marine sediments scraped off from the downgoing slab of oceanic crust but in some cases includes the erosional products of volcanic island arcs formed on the overriding plate.

The internal structure of an _____ is similar to that found in a thin-skinned foreland thrust belt.

   a. AL 129-1
   b. AL 333
   c. Accretionary wedge
   d. AASHTO Soil Classification System

26. _____ are geologic features, submarine basins associated with island arcs and subduction zones. They are found at some convergent plate boundaries, presently concentrated in the Western Pacific ocean. Most of them result from tensional forces caused by oceanic trench rollback and the collapse of the edge of the continent.
   a. 1703 Genroku earthquake
   b. 1509 Istanbul earthquake
   c. 1700 Cascadia earthquake
   d. Back-arc basins

27. _____ is a rock that forms by the metamorphism of basalt and rocks with similar composition at high pressures and low temperatures, approximately corresponding to a depth of 15 to 30 kilometers and 200 to ~500 degrees Celsius. The blue color of the rock comes from the presence of the mineral glaucophane.

They are typically found within orogenic belts as terranes of lithology in faulted contact with greenschist or rarely eclogite facies rocks.

   a. Granoblastic
   b. Jadeitite
   c. Prehnite-pumpellyite facies
   d. Blueschist

28. In plate tectonics, a _____ is an actively deforming region where two tectonic plates or fragments of lithosphere move toward one another and collide. As a result of pressure and friction and plate material melting in the mantle, earthquakes and volcanoes are common near convergent boundaries.

a. Thrust fault
b. Plate tectonics
c. Convergent boundary
d. Mirovia

29. A _____ is a depression in the sea floor located between a subduction zone and an associated volcanic arc. It is typically filled with sediments from the adjacent landmass and the island arc in addition to trapped oceanic crustal material. The oceanic crustal fragments may be obducted as ophiolites onto the continent during terrane accretion.
a. 1703 Genroku earthquake
b. 1700 Cascadia earthquake
c. 1509 Istanbul earthquake
d. Forearc

30. In geology, a _____ is a large scale breccia, a mappable body of rock characterized by a lack of continuous bedding and the inclusion of fragments of rock of all sizes, contained in a fine-grained deformed matrix. The _____ typically consists of a jumble of large blocks of varied lithologies of altered oceanic crustal material and blocks of continental slope sediments in a sheared mudstone matrix. Some larger blocks of rock may be as much as 1 km across.
a. 1700 Cascadia earthquake
b. 1703 Genroku earthquake
c. 1509 Istanbul earthquake
d. Melange

31. In geology, _____ is the process that takes place at convergent boundaries by which one tectonic plate moves under another tectonic plate, sinking into the Earth's mantle, as the plates converge. A _____ zone is an area on Earth where two tectonic plates move towards one another and _____ occurs. Rates of _____ are typically measured in centimeters per year, with the average rate of convergence being approximately 2 to 8 centimeters per year (about the rate a fingernail grows.)
a. Continental crust
b. Plate tectonics
c. Subduction
d. Mirovia

32. A _____ is a chain of volcanic islands or mountains formed by plate tectonics as an oceanic tectonic plate subducts under another tectonic plate and produces magma. There are two types of these: oceanic arcs (commonly called island arcs, a type of archipelago) and continental arcs. In the former, oceanic crust subducts beneath other oceanic crust on an adjacent plate, while in the latter case the oceanic crust subducts beneath continental crust. In some situations, a single subduction zone may show both aspects along its length, as part of a plate subducts beneath a continent and part beneath adjacent oceanic crust.
a. 1700 Cascadia earthquake
b. 1703 Genroku earthquake
c. Volcanic arc
d. 1509 Istanbul earthquake

33. _____ is the wearing away of land or the removal of beach or dune sediments by wave action, tidal currents, wave currents generated by storms, wind, or fast moving motor craft cause _____, which may take the form of long-term losses of sediment and rocks, or merely the temporary redistribution of coastal sediments; erosion in one location may result in accretion nearby. The study of erosion and sediment redistribution is called 'coastal morphodynamics'.
a. Coastal erosion
b. Bradyseism
c. Shutter ridge
d. Fault scarp

34. _____ is the removal of solids (sediment, soil, rock and other particles) in the natural environment. It usually occurs due to transport by wind, water, or ice; by down-slope creep of soil and other material under the force of gravity; or by living organisms, such as burrowing animals, in the case of bioerosion.

_____ is distinguished from weathering, which is the process of chemical or physical breakdown of the minerals in the rocks, although the two processes may occur concurrently.

a. AL 333
b. AL 129-1
c. AASHTO Soil Classification System
d. Erosion

35. _____ is a phenomenon of the plate tectonics of Earth that occurs at convergent boundaries. _____ is a variation on the fundamental process of subduction, whereby the subduction zone is destroyed, mountains produced, and two continents sutured together. _____ is known only from this planet and is an interesting example of how our different crusts, oceanic and continental, behave during subduction.
a. 1700 Cascadia earthquake
b. 1509 Istanbul earthquake
c. 1703 Genroku earthquake
d. Continental collision

36. _____ refers to natural mountain building, and may be studied as a tectonic structural event, (b) as a geographical event, and (c) a chronological event. Orogenic events (a) cause distinctive structural phenomena and related tectonic activity, (b) affect certain regions of rocks and crust, and (c) happen within a specific period of time.
a. Antler orogeny
b. Orogeny
c. Alice Springs Orogeny
d. Orogenesis

37. The _____ was an ocean that existed between the continents of Gondwana and Laurasia during the Mesozoic era before the opening of the Indian Ocean.

About 250 million years ago, during the Triassic, a new ocean began forming in the southern end of the Paleo-_____. A rift formed along the northern continental shelf of Southern Pangaea (Gondwana.) Over the next 60 million years, that piece of shelf, known as Cimmeria, traveled north, pushing the floor of the Paleo-_____ under the eastern end of Northern Pangaea (Laurasia). The _____ formed between Cimmeria and Gondwana, directly over where the Paleo-Tethys used to be.

a. 1700 Cascadia earthquake
b. 1509 Istanbul earthquake
c. 1703 Genroku earthquake
d. Tethys Ocean

38. The _____ -- also called the Laurentian Plateau, or Bouclier Canadien -- is a massive geological shield covered by a thin layer of soil that forms the nucleus of the North American or Laurentia craton. It has a deep, common, joined bedrock region in eastern and central Canada and stretches North from the Great Lakes to the Arctic Ocean, covering over half of Canada; it also extends south into the northern reaches of the United States. Population is scarce, and industrial development is minimal, although the region has a large hydroelectric power potential.
a. Canadian Shield
b. Quaternary
c. Sahara pump theory
d. Great Artesian Basin

39. In geology, a _____ is a continental area covered by relatively flat or gently tilted, mainly sedimentary strata, which overlie a basement of consolidated igneous or metamorphic rocks of an earlier deformation. They as well as, shields and the basement rocks together constitute cratons.

It is also common practice to use the term _____ as a very general term for a sequence of shallow water carbonate _____.

a. Geometallurgy
b. Paralithic
c. Platform
d. Schreyerite

40. A _____ is generally a large area of exposed Precambrian crystalline igneous and high-grade metamorphic rocks that form tectonically stable areas. In all cases, the age of these rocks is greater than 570 million years and sometimes dates back 2 to 3.5 billion years. They have been little affected by tectonic events following the end of the Precambrian Era, and are relatively flat regions where mountain building, faulting, and other tectonic processes are greatly diminished compared with the activity that occurs at the margins of the shields and the boundaries between tectonic plates.
  a. 1700 Cascadia earthquake
  b. 1509 Istanbul earthquake
  c. Shield
  d. 1703 Genroku earthquake

41. A _____ is an old and stable part of the continental crust that has survived the merging and splitting of continents and supercontinents for at least 500 million years. Some are over two billion years old. They are generally found in the interiors of continents and are characteristically composed of ancient crystalline basement crust of lightweight felsic igneous rock such as granite.
  a. Superior craton
  b. Kalahari craton
  c. Craton
  d. Wyoming craton

42. _____ , originally Gondwanaland is the name given to a southern precursor-supercontinent and then as a remnant separated from Laurasia 180->200 million years ago during the breakup of the Pangaea supercontinent that existed about 500 to 200 Ma ago into two large segments. While the corresponding northern hemisphere continent Laurasia moved further north, the nearly equal in area _____ included most of the landmasses in today's southern hemisphere, including Antarctica, South America, Africa, Madagascar, Australia-New Guinea, and New Zealand, as well as Arabia and the Indian subcontinent, which have now moved into the Northern Hemisphere.
  a. 1509 Istanbul earthquake
  b. 1703 Genroku earthquake
  c. 1700 Cascadia earthquake
  d. Gondwana

43. _____ was a supercontinent that most recently existed as a part of the split of the Pangaean supercontinent in the late Mesozoic era. It included most of the landmasses which make up today's continents of the northern hemisphere, chiefly Laurentia (the name given to the North American craton), Baltica, Siberia, Kazakhstania, and the North China and East China cratons.
  a. 1700 Cascadia earthquake
  b. 1509 Istanbul earthquake
  c. 1703 Genroku earthquake
  d. Laurasia

44. The _____ is the rigid outermost shell of a rocky planet.

In the Earth, the _____ includes the crust and the uppermost mantle, which constitute the hard and rigid outer layer of the planet. The _____ is underlain by the asthenosphere, the weaker, hotter, and deeper part of the upper mantle.

  a. Thrust fault
  b. Continental crust
  c. Lithosphere
  d. Continental drift

45. _____, is the process of coastal sediments returning to the visible portion of a beach or foreshore following a submersion event. A sustainable beach or foreshore often goes through a cycle of submersion during rough weather then _____ during calmer periods. If a coastline is not in a healthy sustainable condition, then erosion can be more serious and _____ does not fully restore the original volume of the visible beach or foreshore leading to permanent beach or foreshore loss.

Chapter 11. Plate Tectonics: Creating Oceans and Continents

a. AASHTO Soil Classification System
b. AL 333
c. AL 129-1
d. Accretion

46. _____, partially synonymous with microcontinents, are fragments of continents thought to have been broken off from the main continental mass forming distinct islands, possibly several hundred kilometers from their place of origin. All continents are fragments; the terms 'continental fragment' and 'microcontinent' are restricted to those smaller than Sahul (Australia-New Guinea.) Other than perhaps Zealandia, they are not known to contain a craton or fragment of a craton.
 a. Continental crustal fragments
 b. 1509 Istanbul earthquake
 c. 1703 Genroku earthquake
 d. 1700 Cascadia earthquake

47. A _____ is a phenomenon of fluid dynamics that occurs in situations where there are temperature differences within a body of liquid or gas.

Fluids are materials that exhibit the property of flow. Both gases and liquids have fluid properties, and in sufficient quantity, even particulate solids such as salt, grain, and gravel show some fluid properties. When a volume of fluid is heated, it expands and becomes less dense and thus more buoyant than the surrounding fluid. The colder, denser fluid settles underneath the warmer, less dense fluid and forces it to rise. Such movement is called convection, and the moving body of liquid is referred to as a _____.

 a. 1703 Genroku earthquake
 b. Convection cell
 c. 1700 Cascadia earthquake
 d. 1509 Istanbul earthquake

48. A _____ column (or _____) is a column of rising air in the lower altitudes of the Earth's atmosphere. They are created by the uneven heating of the Earth's surface from solar radiation, and an example of convection. The Sun warms the ground, which in turn warms the air directly above it.
 a. 1700 Cascadia earthquake
 b. 1703 Genroku earthquake
 c. 1509 Istanbul earthquake
 d. Thermal

49. A _____ is an upwelling of abnormally hot rock within the Earth's mantle. As the heads of mantle plumes can partly melt when they reach shallow depths, they are thought to be the cause of volcanic centers known as hotspots and probably also to have caused flood basalts. It is a secondary way that Earth loses heat, much less important in this regard than is heat loss at plate margins.
 a. 1509 Istanbul earthquake
 b. 1703 Genroku earthquake
 c. 1700 Cascadia earthquake
 d. Mantle plume

Chapter 12. Mass Movement

1. _____ is the geomorphic process by which soil, regolith, and rock move downslope under the force of gravity. Types of _____ include creep, slides, flows, topples, and falls, each with its own characteristic features, and taking place over timescales from seconds to years. _____ occurs on both terrestrial and submarine slopes, and has been observed on Earth, Mars, and Venus.
   a. 1703 Genroku earthquake
   b. 1509 Istanbul earthquake
   c. 1700 Cascadia earthquake
   d. Mass wasting

2. An _____ is the result of a sudden release of energy in the Earth's crust that creates seismic waves. They are recorded with a seismometer or the related and mostly obsolete Richter magnitude, with a magnitude 3 or lower _____ being mostly imperceptible and magnitude 7 causing serious damage over large areas.
   a. Earthquake
   b. AL 333
   c. AL 129-1
   d. AASHTO Soil Classification System

3. The _____ is an engineering property of granular materials. The _____ is the maximum angle of a stable slope determined by friction, cohesion and the shapes of the particles.

   When bulk granular materials are poured onto a horizontal surface, a conical pile will form. The internal angle between the surface of the pile and the horizontal surface is known as the _____ and is related to the density, surface area, and coefficient of friction of the material.

   a. AASHTO Soil Classification System
   b. AL 129-1
   c. AL 333
   d. Angle of repose

4. _____ is a term given to an accumulation of broken rock fragments at the base of crags, mountain cliffs, or valley shoulders. Landforms associated with these materials are sometimes called _____ slopes or talus piles. These deposits typically have a concave upwards form, while the maximum inclination of such deposits corresponds to the angle of repose of the mean debris size.
   a. Scree
   b. 1509 Istanbul earthquake
   c. 1700 Cascadia earthquake
   d. 1703 Genroku earthquake

5. Two important classifications of weathering processes exist -- physical and _____. Mechanical or physical weathering involves the breakdown of rocks and soils through direct contact with atmospheric conditions, such as heat, water, ice and pressure. The second classification, _____, involves the direct effect of atmospheric chemicals or biologically produced chemicals (also known as biological weathering) in the breakdown of rocks, soils and minerals.
   a. Chemical weathering
   b. 1703 Genroku earthquake
   c. 1509 Istanbul earthquake
   d. 1700 Cascadia earthquake

6. _____ or tree-ring dating is the method of scientific dating based on the analysis of tree-ring growth patterns. This technique was developed during the first half of the 20th century originally by the astronomer A. E. Douglass, the founder of the Laboratory of Tree-Ring Research at the University of Arizona. Douglass sought to better understand cycles of sunspot activity and reasoned that changes in solar activity would affect climate patterns on earth which would subsequently be recorded by tree-ring growth patterns (i.e., sunspots >→ climate >→ tree rings.)
   a. 1700 Cascadia earthquake
   b. Dendrochronology
   c. 1703 Genroku earthquake
   d. 1509 Istanbul earthquake

Chapter 12. Mass Movement

7. _____ is the decomposition of Earth rocks, soils and their minerals through direct contact with the planet's atmosphere. _____ occurs in situ, or 'with no movement', and thus should not be confused with erosion, which involves the movement of rocks and minerals by agents such as water, ice, wind and gravity.

Two important classifications of _____ processes exist -- physical and chemical _____.

   a. 1700 Cascadia earthquake   b. 1703 Genroku earthquake
   c. Weathering   d. 1509 Istanbul earthquake

8. _____ is water located beneath the ground surface in soil pore spaces and in the fractures of lithologic formations. A unit of rock or an unconsolidated deposit is called an aquifer when it can yield a usable quantity of water. The depth at which soil pore spaces or fractures and voids in rock become completely saturated with water is called the water table.

   a. 1700 Cascadia earthquake   b. 1509 Istanbul earthquake
   c. Depression focused recharge   d. Groundwater

9. The _____ Era is one of three geologic eras of the Phanerozoic eon. The division of time into eras dates back to Giovanni Arduino, in the 18th century, although his original name for the era now called the '_____' was 'Secondary' (making the modern era the 'Tertiary'.)

The _____ was a time of tectonic, climatic and evolutionary activity. The continents gradually shifted from a state of connectedness into their present configuration; the drifting provided for speciation and other important evolutionary developments.

   a. 1703 Genroku earthquake   b. 1509 Istanbul earthquake
   c. 1700 Cascadia earthquake   d. Mesozoic

10. In geology, _____ is a type of mass wasting where waterlogged sediment slowly moves downslope over impermeable material. It can occur in any climate where the ground is saturated by water, though it is most often found in periglacial environments where the ground is permanently frozen, under which conditions the process is often called gelifluction. During warm seasonal periods the surface layer melts and slides over the frozen underlayer, slowly moving downslope due to frost heave that occurs normal to the slope.

   a. Sturzstrom   b. Solifluction
   c. Geohazard   d. Debris flow

11. In geology, _____ or _____ soil is soil at or below the freezing point of water (0 >°C or 32 >°F) for two or more years. Ice is not always present, as may be in the case of nonporous bedrock, but it frequently occurs and it may be in amounts exceeding the potential hydraulic saturation of the ground material. Most _____ is located in high latitudes (i.e. land in close proximity to the North and South poles), but alpine _____ may exist at high altitudes in much lower latitudes.

   a. 1703 Genroku earthquake   b. 1509 Istanbul earthquake
   c. 1700 Cascadia earthquake   d. Permafrost

12. The field of _____ encompasses the analysis of static and dynamic stability of slopes of earth and rock-fill dams, slopes of other types of embankments, excavated slopes, and natural slopes in soil and soft rock.

Earthen slopes can develop a cut-spherical weakness zone. The probability of this happening can be calculated in advance using a simple 2-D circular analysis package. A primary difficulty with analysis is locating the most-probable slip plane for any given situation. Many landslides have only been analyzed after the fact.

a. Reynolds' dilatancy
b. Shear strength
c. Soil mechanics
d. Slope stability

13. _____ is a form of mass wasting event that occurs when loosely consolidated materials or rock layers move a short distance down a slope. The landmass and the surface it slumps upon is called a failure surface. When the movement occurs in soil, there is often a distinctive rotational movement to the mass, that cuts vertically through bedding planes (landslides take place along a bedding plane or fault). This rotational movement moves along a curved slip surface of regolith (the failure surface) which overlies bedrock. This results in internal deformation of the moving mass consisting chiefly of overturned folds called 'sheath folds.'

a. 1703 Genroku earthquake
b. 1700 Cascadia earthquake
c. 1509 Istanbul earthquake
d. Slump

14. An _____ is a downslope viscous flow of fine grained materials that have been saturated with water, and moves under the pull of gravity. They are an intermediate type of mass wasting that is between downhill creep and mudflow. The types of materials that are susceptible to earthflows are clay, fine sand and silt, and fine-grained pyroclastic material.

a. AL 129-1
b. Earthflow
c. AASHTO Soil Classification System
d. AL 333

15. A _____ or mudslide is the most rapid (up to 80 km/h, or 50 mph) and fluid type of downhill mass wasting. It is a rapid movement of a large mass of mud formed from loose earth and water. Similar terms are mudslide (not very liquid), mud stream, debris flow (e.g. in high mountains), j>ökulhlaup, and lahar

a. 1509 Istanbul earthquake
b. 1700 Cascadia earthquake
c. Mudflow
d. 1703 Genroku earthquake

16. _____ describes the large scale motions of Earth's lithosphere. The theory encompasses the older concepts of continental drift, developed during the first decades of the 20th century by Alfred Wegener, and seafloor spreading, understood during the 1960s.

The outermost part of the Earth's interior is made up of two layers: the lithosphere and the asthenosphere.

a. Plate tectonics
b. Copperbelt Province
c. Thrust fault
d. Subduction

17. A _____ is the topographic expression of faulting attributed to the displacement of the land surface by movement along the fault. It can be caused by differential erosion along an old inactive geologic fault (a sort of old rupture) with hard and weak rock, or by a movement on an active fault. In many cases, bluffs form from the upthrown block and can be very steep.

a. Bed load
b. Bradyseism
c. Coastal erosion
d. Fault scarp

Chapter 12. Mass Movement

18. The lithosphere is broken up into what are called _____. In the case of Earth, there are eight major and many minor plates The lithospheric plates ride on the asthenosphere. These plates move in relation to one another at one of three types of plate boundaries: convergent, or collisional boundaries; divergent boundaries, also called spreading centers; and transform boundaries.
    a. Lithosphere
    b. Juan de Fuca Ridge
    c. Thrust fault
    d. Tectonic plates

19. A _____ is a fast moving mass of unconsolidated, saturated debris that looks like flowing concrete. They differentiate from a mudflow by terms of the viscosity of the flow. Flows can carry clasts ranging in size from clay particles to boulders, and also often contains a large amount of woody debris.
    a. Rockfall
    b. Geohazard
    c. Predator trap
    d. Debris flow

20. A _____ is a type of mudflow or landslide composed of pyroclastic material and water that flows down from a volcano, typically along a river valley. The term '_____' originated in the Javanese language of Indonesia. They can be best described as volcanic mudflows. They may not necessarily be caused by volcanic activity, but at the very least do originate from some type of volcanism.
    a. Lahar
    b. 1703 Genroku earthquake
    c. 1700 Cascadia earthquake
    d. 1509 Istanbul earthquake

21. _____ is a unique form of highly sensitive marine clay, with the tendency to change from a relatively stiff condition to a liquid mass when it is disturbed.

    Undisturbed _____ resembles a water-saturated gel. When a mass of _____ undergoes sufficient stress, however, it instantly turns into a flowing ooze, a process known as liquefaction.

    a. Boulder clay
    b. Salt glacier
    c. Sediment
    d. Quick clay

22. An _____ is a rapid flow of snow down a slope, from either natural triggers or human activity. Typically occurring in mountainous terrain, an _____ can mix air and water with the descending snow. Powerful avalanches have the capability to entrain ice, rocks, trees, and other material on the slope; however avalanches are always initiated in snow, are primarily composed of flowing snow, and are distinct from mudslides, rock slides, rock avalanches, and serac collapses from an icefall.
    a. AASHTO Soil Classification System
    b. AL 333
    c. AL 129-1
    d. Avalanche

23. _____ is a naturally occurring material composed primarily of fine-grained minerals, which show plasticity through a variable range of water content, and which can be hardened when dried and/or fired. _____ deposits are mostly composed of _____ minerals (phyllosilicate minerals), minerals which impart plasticity and harden when fired and/or dried, and variable amounts of water trapped in the mineral structure by polar attraction. Organic materials which do not impart plasticity may also be a part of _____ deposits.
    a. 1700 Cascadia earthquake
    b. 1703 Genroku earthquake
    c. 1509 Istanbul earthquake
    d. Clay

24. The _____, is a geologic eon before the Proterozoic and Paleoproterozoic, before 2.5 Ga (billion years ago, or 2,500 Ma.) Instead of being based on stratigraphy, this date is defined chronometrically. The lower boundary (starting point) has not been officially recognized by the International Commission on Stratigraphy, but it is usually set to 3.8 Ga, at the end of the Hadean eon.

   a. AASHTO Soil Classification System   b. AL 333
   c. AL 129-1   d. Archean

Chapter 13. Streams and Floods

1. The _____ describes the continuous movement of water on, above, and below the surface of the Earth. Since the _____ is truly a 'cycle,' there is no beginning or end. Water can change states among liquid, vapor, and ice at various places in the _____.
   a. Hydraulic conductivity
   b. Water cycle
   c. Stemflow
   d. Specific storage

2. _____ is the natural or artificial removal of surface and sub-surface water from an area. Many agricultural soils need _____ to improve production or to manage water supplies.

   The earliest archaeological record of an advanced system of _____ comes from the Indus Valley Civilization from around 3100 BC in what is now Pakistan and North India.

   a. Drainage
   b. 1703 Genroku earthquake
   c. 1509 Istanbul earthquake
   d. 1700 Cascadia earthquake

3. A _____ is an extent of land where water from rain or snow melt drains downhill into a body of water, such as a river, lake, reservoir, estuary, wetland, sea or ocean. The _____ includes both the streams and rivers that convey the water as well as the land surfaces from which water drains into those channels, and is separated from adjacent basins by a drainage divide.

   The _____ acts like a funnel, collecting all the water within the area covered by the basin and channelling it into a waterway.

   a. 1509 Istanbul earthquake
   b. 1700 Cascadia earthquake
   c. Drainage basin
   d. 1703 Genroku earthquake

4. A _____, is the line separating neighbouring drainage basins (catchments.) In hilly country, the divide lies along topographical peaks and ridges, but in flat country (especially where the ground is marshy) the divide may be invisible - just a more or less notional line on the ground on either side of which falling raindrops will start a journey to different rivers, and even to different sides of a region or continent.
   a. 1703 Genroku earthquake
   b. 1700 Cascadia earthquake
   c. 1509 Istanbul earthquake
   d. Drainage divide

5. _____ occurs when the rate of rainfall on a surface exceeds the rate at which water can infiltrate the ground, and any depression storage has already been filled. This is called infiltration excess _____, Hortonian _____, or unsaturated _____. This more commonly occurs in arid and semi-arid regions, where rainfall intensities are high and the soil infiltration capacity is reduced because of surface sealing, or in paved areas.
   a. AASHTO Soil Classification System
   b. Overland flow
   c. Intertidal
   d. AL 129-1

6. A _____ is a stream that branches off and flows away from a main stream channel. They are a common feature of river deltas. The phenomenon is known as river bifurcation.
   a. 1700 Cascadia earthquake
   b. 1703 Genroku earthquake
   c. 1509 Istanbul earthquake
   d. Distributary

7. A _____ is a narrow and shallow incision into soil resulting from erosion by overland flow that has been focused into a thin thread by soil surface roughness. Rilling, the process of _____ formation, is common on agricultural land and unvegetated ground.

   a. 1509 Istanbul earthquake
   b. 1700 Cascadia earthquake
   c. 1703 Genroku earthquake
   d. Rill

8. _____ is the removal of solids (sediment, soil, rock and other particles) in the natural environment. It usually occurs due to transport by wind, water, or ice; by down-slope creep of soil and other material under the force of gravity; or by living organisms, such as burrowing animals, in the case of bioerosion.

_____ is distinguished from weathering, which is the process of chemical or physical breakdown of the minerals in the rocks, although the two processes may occur concurrently.

   a. AASHTO Soil Classification System
   b. Erosion
   c. AL 333
   d. AL 129-1

9. _____ is mechanical scraping of a rock surface by friction between rocks and moving particles during their transport in wind, glacier, waves, gravity or running water, after friction, the moving particles dislodge loose and weak debris from the side of the rock, these particles can be dissolved in the water source.

The intensity of _____ depends on the hardness, concentration, velocity and mass of moving particles.

A virtually smooth marine platform cut by the ocean waves at a coastline.

   a. AASHTO Soil Classification System
   b. Abrasion
   c. AL 333
   d. AL 129-1

10. In geomorphology, a _____ is the pattern formed by the streams, rivers, and lakes in a particular drainage basin. They are governed by the topography of the land, whether a particular region is dominated by hard or soft rocks, and the gradient of the land.

They can fall into one of several categories, depending on the topography and geology of the land:

Dendritic drainage systems are the most common form of _____.

   a. 1509 Istanbul earthquake
   b. 1703 Genroku earthquake
   c. Drainage system
   d. 1700 Cascadia earthquake

11. _____ is a term for a formation in rivers caused by a whirlpool eroding a hole into rock. The abrasion is mainly caused by the circular motion of small sediments such as small stones in the river. The interiors of potholes tend to be smooth and regular, unlike a plunge pool.

   a. 1509 Istanbul earthquake
   b. 1700 Cascadia earthquake
   c. Subsidence
   d. Pothole

Chapter 13. Streams and Floods

12. A _____ is flat or nearly flat land adjacent to a stream or river that experiences occasional or periodic flooding. It includes the floodway, which consists of the stream channel and adjacent areas that carry flood flows, and the flood fringe, which are areas covered by the flood, but which do not experience a strong current.

They generally contain unconsolidated sediments, often extending below the bed of the stream.

   a. 1703 Genroku earthquake
   b. 1509 Istanbul earthquake
   c. 1700 Cascadia earthquake
   d. Floodplain

13. In geology a _____ is the smallest division of a geologic formation or stratigraphic rock series marked by well-defined divisional planes (bedding planes) separating it from layers above and below. A _____ is the smallest lithostratigraphic unit, usually ranging in thickness from a centimeter to several meters and distinguishable from beds above and below it. Beds can be differentiated in various ways, including rock or mineral type and particle size.
   a. 1703 Genroku earthquake
   b. 1509 Istanbul earthquake
   c. 1700 Cascadia earthquake
   d. Bed

14. The term _____ describes particles in a flowing fluid (usually a river) that are transported along the bed. This is in opposition to suspended load and wash load which are carried entirely in suspension.

_____ moves by a variety of methods, including rolling, sliding, traction, and saltation.

   a. Coastal erosion
   b. Shutter ridge
   c. Rejuvenated
   d. Bed load

15. In geology, _____ is a specific type of particle transport by fluids such as wind, or the denser fluid water. It occurs when loose material is removed from a bed and carried by the fluid, before being transported back to the surface. Examples include pebble transport by rivers, sand drift over desert surfaces, soil blowing over fields, or even snow drift over smooth surfaces such as those in the Arctic or Canadian Prairies.
   a. Saltation
   b. Stoping
   c. Spheroidal weathering
   d. Seafloor spreading

16. _____ is the term for the fine particles that are light enough to be carried in a stream without touching the stream bed. These particles are generally of the fine sand, silt and clay size, although they can be larger, especially in cases of high discharge, such as during floods. This is in contrast to bed load which is carried along the bottom of the stream.
   a. Suspended load
   b. Tertiary
   c. Logarithmic Spiral Beach
   d. Historical geology

17. _____ is any particulate matter that can be transported by fluid flow, and which eventually is deposited.

They are most often transported by water (fluvial processes) transported by wind (aeolian processes) and glaciers. Beach sands and river channel deposits are examples of fluvial transport and deposition, though _____ also often settles out of slow-moving or standing water in lakes and oceans.

   a. Sediment
   b. Dry quicksand
   c. Brickearth
   d. Bovey Beds

Chapter 13. Streams and Floods

18. _____ is soil or sediments deposited by a river or other running water. _____ is typically made up of a variety of materials, including fine particles of silt and clay and larger particles of sand and gravel.

Flowing water associated with glaciers may also deposit _____, but deposits directly from ice are not _____ .

   a. Alluvium
   c. AL 129-1
   b. AASHTO Soil Classification System
   d. AL 333

19. _____ is the geological process by which material is added to a landform or land mass. Fluids such as wind and water, as well as sediment gravity flows, transport previously eroded sediment, which, at the loss of enough kinetic energy in the fluid, is deposited, building up layers of sediment.

_____ occurs when the forces responsible for sediment transportation are no longer sufficient to overcome the forces of particle weight and friction, which resist motion.

   a. Permineralization
   c. Seafloor spreading
   b. Headward erosion
   d. Deposition

20. _____ is the term for material, especially ions from chemical weathering, that are carried in solution by a stream.
   a. Teilzone
   c. Dissolved load
   b. Zechstein
   d. Salt tectonics

21. In geology _____ is the section of a floodplain where deposits of fine silts and clays settle after a flood. They usually lie behind a stream's natural levees.
   a. Morton Gneiss
   c. Transition zone
   b. Basin and Range
   d. Backswamp

22. _____ or tree-ring dating is the method of scientific dating based on the analysis of tree-ring growth patterns. This technique was developed during the first half of the 20th century originally by the astronomer A. E. Douglass, the founder of the Laboratory of Tree-Ring Research at the University of Arizona. Douglass sought to better understand cycles of sunspot activity and reasoned that changes in solar activity would affect climate patterns on earth which would subsequently be recorded by tree-ring growth patterns (i.e., sunspots >→ climate >→ tree rings.)
   a. Dendrochronology
   c. 1700 Cascadia earthquake
   b. 1509 Istanbul earthquake
   d. 1703 Genroku earthquake

23. An _____ is a fan-shaped deposit formed where a fast flowing stream flattens, slows, and spreads typically at the exit of a canyon onto a flatter plain. A convergence of neighboring fans into a single apron of deposits against a slope is called a bajada, or compound _____.
   a. AL 129-1
   c. AASHTO Soil Classification System
   b. AL 333
   d. Alluvial fan

24. The _____, is a geologic eon before the Proterozoic and Paleoproterozoic, before 2.5 Ga (billion years ago, or 2,500 Ma.) Instead of being based on stratigraphy, this date is defined chronometrically. The lower boundary (starting point) has not been officially recognized by the International Commission on Stratigraphy, but it is usually set to 3.8 Ga, at the end of the Hadean eon.

Chapter 13. Streams and Floods

a. AL 129-1
b. AL 333
c. AASHTO Soil Classification System
d. Archean

25. The _____ is the earliest of three geologic eras of the Phanerozoic eon. The _____ spanned from roughly 542 to 251 million years ago (ICS, 2004), and is subdivided into six geologic periods; from oldest to youngest they are: the Cambrian, Ordovician, Silurian, Devonian, Carboniferous, and Permian.

The _____ covers the time from the first appearance of abundant, soft-shelled fossils to the time when the continents were beginning to be dominated by large, relatively sophisticated reptiles and modern plants. The lower (oldest) boundary was classically set at the first appearance of creatures known as trilobites and archeocyathids.

a. 1700 Cascadia earthquake
b. 1509 Istanbul earthquake
c. 1703 Genroku earthquake
d. Paleozoic

26. _____ describes the large scale motions of Earth's lithosphere. The theory encompasses the older concepts of continental drift, developed during the first decades of the 20th century by Alfred Wegener, and seafloor spreading, understood during the 1960s.

The outermost part of the Earth's interior is made up of two layers: the lithosphere and the asthenosphere.

a. Copperbelt Province
b. Subduction
c. Thrust fault
d. Plate tectonics

27. _____ is water located beneath the ground surface in soil pore spaces and in the fractures of lithologic formations. A unit of rock or an unconsolidated deposit is called an aquifer when it can yield a usable quantity of water. The depth at which soil pore spaces or fractures and voids in rock become completely saturated with water is called the water table.

a. Groundwater
b. 1700 Cascadia earthquake
c. Depression focused recharge
d. 1509 Istanbul earthquake

Chapter 14. Groundwater, Caves, and Karst

1. _____ or deep drainage or deep percolation is a hydrologic process where water moves downward from surface water to groundwater. This process usually occurs in the vadose zone below plant roots and is often expressed as a flux to the water table surface. Recharge occurs both naturally (through the water cycle) and anthropologically (i.e., 'artificial _____'), where rainwater and or reclaimed water is routed to the subsurface.
    a. Permeability
    b. Saltwater intrusion
    c. 1509 Istanbul earthquake
    d. Groundwater recharge

2. _____ is water located beneath the ground surface in soil pore spaces and in the fractures of lithologic formations. A unit of rock or an unconsolidated deposit is called an aquifer when it can yield a usable quantity of water. The depth at which soil pore spaces or fractures and voids in rock become completely saturated with water is called the water table.
    a. Groundwater
    b. 1700 Cascadia earthquake
    c. Depression focused recharge
    d. 1509 Istanbul earthquake

3. The _____, is a geologic eon before the Proterozoic and Paleoproterozoic, before 2.5 Ga (billion years ago, or 2,500 Ma.) Instead of being based on stratigraphy, this date is defined chronometrically. The lower boundary (starting point) has not been officially recognized by the International Commission on Stratigraphy, but it is usually set to 3.8 Ga, at the end of the Hadean eon.
    a. AL 333
    b. Archean
    c. AASHTO Soil Classification System
    d. AL 129-1

4. The _____ is the subsurface layer in which groundwater seeps up from a water table by capillary action to fill pores. Pores at the base of the _____ are filled with water due to tension saturation. This saturated portion of the _____ is less than total capillary rise because of the presence of a mix in pore size.
    a. Suspended load
    b. Logarithmic Spiral Beach
    c. Historical geology
    d. Capillary fringe

5. _____ is a measure of the void spaces in a material, and is measured as a fraction, between 0-1, or as a percentage between 0-100%. The term is used in multiple fields including ceramics, metallurgy, materials, manufacturing, earth sciences and construction.

Used in geology, hydrogeology, soil science, and building science, the _____ of a porous medium (such as rock or sediment) describes the fraction of void space in the material, where the void may contain, for example, air or water.

    a. Saltwater intrusion
    b. Porosity
    c. 1509 Istanbul earthquake
    d. Permeability

6. The _____ is the area in an aquifer, below the water table, in which relatively all pores and fractures are saturated with water. The _____ may fluctuate with changes of season and during wet and dry periods.
    a. 1700 Cascadia earthquake
    b. 1703 Genroku earthquake
    c. 1509 Istanbul earthquake
    d. Phreatic zone

7. _____ is any particulate matter that can be transported by fluid flow, and which eventually is deposited.

They are most often transported by water (fluvial processes) transported by wind (aeolian processes) and glaciers. Beach sands and river channel deposits are examples of fluvial transport and deposition, though _____ also often settles out of slow-moving or standing water in lakes and oceans.

Chapter 14. Groundwater, Caves, and Karst

a. Sediment
b. Dry quicksand
c. Brickearth
d. Bovey Beds

8. _____ is the naturally occurring, unconsolidated or loose covering on the Earth's surface. _____ is composed of particles of broken rock that have been altered by chemical, biological and environmental processes including weathering and erosion. _____ is different from its parent rock(s) source(s), altered by interactions between the lithosphere, hydrosphere, atmosphere, and the biosphere.
   a. Topsoil
   b. 1700 Cascadia earthquake
   c. Soil
   d. 1509 Istanbul earthquake

9. The _____ is the level at which the ground water pressure is equal to atmospheric pressure. It may be conveniently visualized as the 'surface' of the ground water in a given vicinity. It usually coincides with the phreatic surface, but can be many feet above it. As water infiltrates through pore spaces in the soil, it first passes through the zone of aeration, where the soil is unsaturated. At increasing depths water fills in more spaces, until the zone of saturation is reached. The relatively horizontal plane atop this zone constitutes the _____.
   a. Crosshole sonic logging
   b. Rock bolt
   c. Water table
   d. Shaft construction

10. _____ in the earth sciences (commonly symbolized as κ a rock or k) is a measure of the ability of a material (typically unconsolidated material) to transmit fluids. It is of great importance in determining the flow characteristics of hydrocarbons in oil and gas reservoirs, and of groundwater in aquifers. It is typically measured in the lab by application of Darcy's law under steady state conditions or, more generally, by application of various solutions to the diffusion equation for unsteady flow conditions.
   a. 1509 Istanbul earthquake
   b. Saltwater intrusion
   c. Porosity
   d. Permeability

11. An _____ is an underground layer of water-bearing permeable rock or unconsolidated materials (gravel, sand, silt, or clay) from which groundwater can be usefully extracted using a water well. The study of water flow in aquifers and the characterization of aquifers is called hydrogeology. Related terms include: an aquitard, which is an impermeable layer along an _____, and an aquiclude (or aquifuge), which is a solid, impermeable area beneath an _____.
   a. AL 129-1
   b. AASHTO Soil Classification System
   c. AL 333
   d. Aquifer

12. The _____ is a vast yet shallow underground water table aquifer located beneath the Great Plains in the United States. One of the world's largest aquifers, it covers an area of approximately 174,000 mi^2 in portions of the eight states of South Dakota, Nebraska, Wyoming, Colorado, Kansas, Oklahoma, New Mexico, and Texas. It was named in 1898 by N.H. Darton from its type locality near the town of Ogallala, Nebraska.
   a. AL 333
   b. Ogallala Aquifer
   c. AASHTO Soil Classification System
   d. AL 129-1

13. A _____ column (or _____) is a column of rising air in the lower altitudes of the Earth's atmosphere. They are created by the uneven heating of the Earth's surface from solar radiation, and an example of convection. The Sun warms the ground, which in turn warms the air directly above it.
   a. 1700 Cascadia earthquake
   b. 1703 Genroku earthquake
   c. 1509 Istanbul earthquake
   d. Thermal

14. A _____ occurs in an aquifer when groundwater is pumped from a well. In an unconfined (water table) aquifer, this is an actual depression of the water levels. In confined (artesian) aquifers, the _____ is a reduction in the pressure head surrounding the pumped well.
   a. Specific storage
   b. Cone of depression
   c. Water cycle
   d. Flownet

15. _____ in geology is a landform sunken or depressed below the surrounding area. Depressions may be formed by various mechanisms, and may be referred to by a variety of technical terms.

   - A basin may be any large sediment filled _____. In tectonics, it may refer specifically to a circular, syncline-like _____: a geologic basin; while in sedimentology, it may refer to an area thickly filled with sediment: sedimentary basin.

   - A blowout is a _____ created by wind erosion typically in either a desert sand or dry soil (such as a post-glacial loess environment.)

   - A graben is a down dropped and typically linear _____ or basin created by rifting in a region under tensional tectonic forces.

   - An impact crater is a _____ created by an impact such as a meteorite crater.
   - A pit crater is a _____ formed by a sinking, or caving in, of the ground surface lying over a void.
   - A kettle is left behind when a piece of ice left behind in glacial deposits melts.

   - A _____ may be an area of subsidence caused by the collapse of an underlying structure. Examples include sinkholes above caves in karst topography, or calderas.

   a. 1703 Genroku earthquake
   b. 1509 Istanbul earthquake
   c. 1700 Cascadia earthquake
   d. Depression

16. An _____, is a type of best management practice that is used to manage stormwater runoff, prevent flooding and downstream erosion, and improve water quality in an adjacent river, stream, lake or bay. It is essentially a shallow artificial pond that is designed to infiltrate stormwater though permeable soils into the groundwater aquifer. Infiltration basins do not discharge to a surface water body under most storm conditions, but are designed with overflow structures
   a. AL 129-1
   b. AASHTO Soil Classification System
   c. AL 333
   d. Infiltration basin

17. _____ is the movement of saline water into freshwater aquifers. Most often, it is caused by ground-water pumping from coastal wells, or from construction of navigation channels or oil field canals. The channels and canals provide conduits for salt water to be brought into fresh water marshes.
   a. Permeability
   b. 1509 Istanbul earthquake
   c. Porosity
   d. Saltwater intrusion

18. In geology, engineering, and surveying, _____ is the motion of a surface (usually, the Earth's surface) as it shifts downward relative to a datum such as sea-level. The opposite of _____ is uplift, which results in an increase in elevation. There are several types of _____.

a. Pothole
b. 1700 Cascadia earthquake
c. 1509 Istanbul earthquake
d. Subsidence

19. In geology, an _____ is a body of igneous rock that has crystallized from molten magma below the surface of the Earth. Bodies of magma that solidify underground before they reach the surface of the earth are called plutons the Roman god of the underworld. Correspondingly, rocks of this kind are also referred to as igneous plutonic rocks or igneous intrusive rocks.
a. AL 333
b. AL 129-1
c. AASHTO Soil Classification System
d. Intrusion

20. _____ is a landscape shaped by the dissolution of a layer or layers of soluble bedrock, usually carbonate rock such as limestone or dolomite.

Due to subterranean drainage, there may be very limited surface water, even to the absence of all rivers and lakes. Many karst regions display distinctive surface features, with sinkholes or dolines being the most common.

a. Karst topography
b. Ambulocetus
c. Andrija Mohorović ić
d. Amblypoda

21. Two important classifications of weathering processes exist -- physical and _____. Mechanical or physical weathering involves the breakdown of rocks and soils through direct contact with atmospheric conditions, such as heat, water, ice and pressure. The second classification, _____, involves the direct effect of atmospheric chemicals or biologically produced chemicals (also known as biological weathering) in the breakdown of rocks, soils and minerals.
a. Chemical weathering
b. 1703 Genroku earthquake
c. 1700 Cascadia earthquake
d. 1509 Istanbul earthquake

22. _____ is the decomposition of Earth rocks, soils and their minerals through direct contact with the planet's atmosphere. _____ occurs in situ, or 'with no movement', and thus should not be confused with erosion, which involves the movement of rocks and minerals by agents such as water, ice, wind and gravity.

Two important classifications of _____ processes exist -- physical and chemical _____.

a. 1700 Cascadia earthquake
b. 1509 Istanbul earthquake
c. 1703 Genroku earthquake
d. Weathering

23. _____ is the chemical element with the symbol Ca and atomic number 20. It has an atomic mass of 40.078 amu. _____ is a soft grey alkaline earth metal, and is the fifth most abundant element by mass in the Earth's crust.
a. 1703 Genroku earthquake
b. 1700 Cascadia earthquake
c. 1509 Istanbul earthquake
d. Calcium

24. A _____ is a speleothem found in limestone caves that changes its axis from the vertical at one or more stages during its growth. They have a curving or angular form that looks as if they were grown in zero gravity. They are most likely the result of capillary forces acting on tiny water droplets, a force often strong enough at this scale to defy gravity.
a. 1703 Genroku earthquake
b. 1509 Istanbul earthquake
c. 1700 Cascadia earthquake
d. Helictite

Chapter 14. Groundwater, Caves, and Karst

25. A _____, commonly known as a cave formation, is a secondary mineral deposit formed in a cave. They are typically formed in limestone or dolostone solutional caves.

Water seeping through cracks in a cave's surrounding bedrock may dissolve certain compounds, usually calcite and aragonite , or gypsum (calcium sulfate.)

- a. 1700 Cascadia earthquake
- b. 1703 Genroku earthquake
- c. 1509 Istanbul earthquake
- d. Speleothem

26. A _____ is a type of speleothem (secondary mineral) that hangs from the ceiling or wall of limestone caves. It is sometimes referred to as dripstone.

They are formed by the deposition of calcium carbonate and other minerals, which is precipitated from mineralized water solutions.

- a. 1509 Istanbul earthquake
- b. Stalactite
- c. 1700 Cascadia earthquake
- d. 1703 Genroku earthquake

27. A _____ is a type of speleothem that rises from the floor of a limestone cave due to the dripping of mineralized solutions and the deposition of calcium carbonate.

The corresponding formation on the ceiling of a cave is known as a stalactite. If these formations grow together, the result is known as a column.

- a. 1703 Genroku earthquake
- b. 1509 Istanbul earthquake
- c. 1700 Cascadia earthquake
- d. Stalagmite

28. _____ is a sedimentary rock. It is a natural chemical precipitate of carbonate minerals; typically aragonite, but often recrystallized to, or primarily, calcite.

_____ forms as calcium carbonate is deposited from the water of mineral springs or rivulets that are saturated with dissolved calcium bicarbonate. The spring water from which the calcium carbonate precipitates can be hot, warm or cold. The rate of deposition increases with the temperature of the water, or alternatively, when biotic material accelerates the process of precipitation.

- a. 1509 Istanbul earthquake
- b. 1703 Genroku earthquake
- c. Travertine
- d. 1700 Cascadia earthquake

29. In chemistry, a _____ is a salt or ester of carbonic acid.

To test for the presence of the _____ anion in a salt, the addition of dilute mineral acid (e.g. hydrochloric acid) will yield carbon dioxide gas.

_____-containing salts are industrially and mineralogically ubiquitous.

a. 1700 Cascadia earthquake
c. 1703 Genroku earthquake
b. Carbonate
d. 1509 Istanbul earthquake

30. A _____ is a natural depression or hole in the surface topography caused by the removal of soil or bedrock, often both, by water. They may vary in size from less than a meter to several hundred meters both in diameter and depth, and vary in form from soil-lined bowls to bedrock-edged chasms. They may be formed gradually or suddenly, and are found worldwide.

a. 1700 Cascadia earthquake
c. 1509 Istanbul earthquake
b. 1703 Genroku earthquake
d. Sinkhole

Chapter 15. Glaciers and Ice Ages

1. A _____ is a large, slow-moving mass of ice, formed from compacted layers of snow, that slowly deforms and flows in response to gravity and high pressure.

_____ ice is the largest reservoir of fresh water on Earth, and second only to oceans as the largest reservoir of total water.

   a. Geologic temperature record
   b. Little Ice Age
   c. Keeling Curve
   d. Glacier

2. A _____ is an amphitheatre-like valley formed at the head of a glacier by erosion. A _____ is also known as a coombe or coomb in England, a combe or comb in America, a corrie in Scotland and Ireland, and a cwm in Wales, although these terms apply to a specific feature of which several may be found in a _____. The term 'comb' is often found at the end of placenames such as Newcomb and Maycomb, where it is pronounced /kÉ™m/.

   a. 1703 Genroku earthquake
   b. Cirque
   c. 1509 Istanbul earthquake
   d. 1700 Cascadia earthquake

3. A _____ is formed in a cirque, bowl-shaped depressions on the side of mountains. Snow and ice accumulation in corries often occurs as the result of avalanching from higher surrounding slopes.

In these depressions, snow persists through summer months, and becomes glacier ice.

   a. 1509 Istanbul earthquake
   b. 1700 Cascadia earthquake
   c. 1703 Genroku earthquake
   d. Cirque glacier

4. _____ is partially-compacted n>év>é, a type of snow that has been left over from past seasons and has been recrystallized into a substance denser than n>év>é. It is ice that is at an intermediate stage between snow and glacial ice. _____ has the appearance of wet sugar, but has a hardness that makes it extremely resistant to shovelling. It generally has a density greater than 550 kg/mÂ³ and is often found underneath the snow that accumulates at the head of a glacier.

   a. Firn
   b. Bramertonian Stage
   c. Bull Lake glaciation
   d. Glaciolacustrine deposits

5. The general term '_____' or, more precisely, 'glacial age' denotes a geological period of long-term reduction in the temperature of the Earth's surface and atmosphere, resulting in an expansion of continental ice sheets, polar ice sheets and alpine glaciers. Within a long-term _____, individual pulses of extra cold climate are termed 'glaciations'. Glaciologically, _____ implies the presence of extensive ice sheets in the northern and southern hemispheres; by this definition we are still in an _____.

   a. Ice Age
   b. AL 333
   c. AASHTO Soil Classification System
   d. AL 129-1

6. _____ are the largest glaciers, enormous masses of ice that are not visibly affected by the landscape and that cover the entire surface beneath them, except possibly on the margins where they are thinnest. Antarctica and Greenland are the only places where continental _____ currently exist. These regions contain vast quantities of fresh water.

   a. AL 333
   b. AL 129-1
   c. AASHTO Soil Classification System
   d. Ice sheets

7. An _____ is an ice mass that covers less than 50 000 km^2 of land area (usually covering a highland area.) Masses of ice covering more than 50 000 km^2 are termed an ice sheet.

Chapter 15. Glaciers and Ice Ages

They are not constrained by topographical features (i.e., they will lie over the top of mountains) but their dome is usually centred on the highest point of a massif.

a. AL 129-1
b. AL 333
c. AASHTO Soil Classification System
d. Ice cap

8. Alpine glaciers form high on the mountain slopes and are niche, slope or cirque glaciers. As a mountain glacier increases in size it can begin to flow down valley, and are referred to as _____.
a. Valley glaciers
b. 1700 Cascadia earthquake
c. 1703 Genroku earthquake
d. 1509 Istanbul earthquake

9. Geologically, a _____ is a long, narrow inlet with steep sides, created in a valley carved by glacial activity.

The seeds of a _____ are laid when a glacier cuts a U-shaped valley through abrasion of the surrounding bedrock by the sediment it carries. Many such valleys were formed during the recent ice age.

a. 1703 Genroku earthquake
b. 1509 Istanbul earthquake
c. Fjord
d. 1700 Cascadia earthquake

10. _____ is a tidewater glacier in the U.S. state of Alaska and the Yukon Territory of Canada. From its source in the Yukon, the glacier stretches 122 km (76 mi) to the sea at Yakutat Bay and Disenchantment Bay. It is the longest tidewater glacier in Alaska, with an open calving face over ten kilometers (6 mi) wide.
a. 1700 Cascadia earthquake
b. Hubbard glacier
c. 1703 Genroku earthquake
d. 1509 Istanbul earthquake

11. An _____ is a region of an ice sheet that moves significantly faster than the surrounding ice. They are significant features of the Antarctic where they account for 10% of the volume of the ice. They are up to 50 km wide, 2 km thick, can stretch for hundreds of kilometres, and account for most of the ice leaving the ice sheet.
a. AL 129-1
b. AASHTO Soil Classification System
c. AL 333
d. Ice stream

12. A _____ is the end of a glacier at any given point in time. Although glaciers seem motionless to the observer, in reality glaciers are in endless motion and the _____ is always either advancing or retreating. The location of the terminus is often directly related to glacier mass balance, which is based on the amount of snowfall which occurs in the accumulation zone of a glacier, as compared to the amount that is melted in the ablation zone.
a. 1703 Genroku earthquake
b. 1700 Cascadia earthquake
c. 1509 Istanbul earthquake
d. Glacier terminus

13. On a glacier, the _____, zone of ablation or zone of wastage is the area in which annual loss of snow through melting, evaporation, iceberg calving and sublimation exceeds annual gain of snow and ice on the surface. Of these, melting is most important in most glaciers, but the others, especially iceberg calving, can be significant. Spatially, the zone of ablation can be identified as the part of the glacier below the snowline.
a. AL 129-1
b. AASHTO Soil Classification System
c. AL 333
d. Ablation zone

Chapter 15. Glaciers and Ice Ages

14. _____ is mechanical scraping of a rock surface by friction between rocks and moving particles during their transport in wind, glacier, waves, gravity or running water, after friction, the moving particles dislodge loose and weak debris from the side of the rock, these particles can be dissolved in the water source.

The intensity of _____ depends on the hardness, concentration, velocity and mass of moving particles.

A virtually smooth marine platform cut by the ocean waves at a coastline.

   a. AASHTO Soil Classification System
   c. AL 129-1
   b. Abrasion
   d. AL 333

15. _____ is the act of a glacier sliding over the bed before it due to meltwater under the ice acting as a lubricant. This movement very much depends on the temperature of the area, the slope of the glacier, the bed's sediment size, the amount of meltwater from the glacier, and the glacier's size.

The movement that happens to these glaciers as they slide is that of a jerky motion where any seismic events, especially at the base of glacier, can cause movement.

   a. Firn
   c. Basal sliding
   b. Bramertonian Stage
   d. Bull Lake glaciation

16. _____ is the removal of solids (sediment, soil, rock and other particles) in the natural environment. It usually occurs due to transport by wind, water, or ice; by down-slope creep of soil and other material under the force of gravity; or by living organisms, such as burrowing animals, in the case of bioerosion.

_____ is distinguished from weathering, which is the process of chemical or physical breakdown of the minerals in the rocks, although the two processes may occur concurrently.

   a. Erosion
   c. AL 333
   b. AASHTO Soil Classification System
   d. AL 129-1

17. _____ is caused by movement of ice, typically as glaciers. Glaciers erode predominantly by three different processes: abrasion/scouring, plucking, and ice thrusting. In an abrasion process, debris in the basal ice scrapes along the bed, polishing and gouging the underlying rocks, similar to sandpaper on wood. Glaciers can also cause pieces of bedrock to crack off in the process of plucking. In ice thrusting, the glacier freezes to its bed, then as it surges forward, it moves large sheets of frozen sediment at the base along with the glacier. This method produced some of the many thousands of lake basins that dot the edge of the Canadian Shield. These processes, combined with erosion and transport by the water network beneath the glacier, leave moraines, drumlins, eskers, ground moraine (till), kames, kame deltas, moulins, and glacial erratics in their wake, typically at the terminus or during glacier retreat.

   a. AASHTO Soil Classification System
   c. AL 333
   b. Ice erosion
   d. AL 129-1

18. A _____ is a mountain rising from the ocean seafloor that does not reach to the water's surface (sea level), and thus is not an island. These are typically formed from extinct volcanoes, that rise abruptly and are usually found rising from a seafloor of 1,000-4,000 meters depth. They are defined by oceanographers as independent features that rise to at least 1,000 meters above the seafloor.

Chapter 15. Glaciers and Ice Ages

a. 1509 Istanbul earthquake
c. 1700 Cascadia earthquake
b. Seamount
d. 1703 Genroku earthquake

19. _____ is a fine-grained, foliated, homogeneous metamorphic rock derived from an original shale-type sedimentary rock composed of clay or volcanic ash through low grade regional metamorphism. The result is a foliated rock in which the foliation may not correspond to the original sedimentary layering. _____ is frequently grey in colour especially when seen en masse covering roofs.
   a. Facies
   c. Geothermobarometry
   b. Shock metamorphism
   d. Slate

20. A _____ is a mountain lake or pool, formed in a cirque excavated by a glacier. A moraine may form a natural dam below a _____. A corrie may be called a cirque.
   a. Tarn
   c. 1509 Istanbul earthquake
   b. 1703 Genroku earthquake
   d. 1700 Cascadia earthquake

21. _____ is the geological process by which material is added to a landform or land mass. Fluids such as wind and water, as well as sediment gravity flows, transport previously eroded sediment, which, at the loss of enough kinetic energy in the fluid, is deposited, building up layers of sediment.

_____ occurs when the forces responsible for sediment transportation are no longer sufficient to overcome the forces of particle weight and friction, which resist motion.

   a. Deposition
   c. Permineralization
   b. Seafloor spreading
   d. Headward erosion

22. A _____ is a tributary valley with the floor at a higher relief than the main channel into which it flows. They are most commonly associated with U-shaped valleys when a tributary glacier flows into a glacier of larger volume. The main glacier erodes a deep U-shaped valley with nearly vertical sides while the tributary glacier, with a smaller volume of ice, makes a shallower U-shaped valley.
   a. 1509 Istanbul earthquake
   c. Hanging valley
   b. 1700 Cascadia earthquake
   d. 1703 Genroku earthquake

23. In geology, _____ is transported rock debris overlying the solid bedrock. The term is also sometimes refers to organic debris so-transported. In the largest sense, it refers to the material left behind by retreating continental glaciers.
   a. Drift
   c. Georeactor
   b. Compression
   d. Dispersion

24. _____ is any particulate matter that can be transported by fluid flow, and which eventually is deposited.

They are most often transported by water (fluvial processes) transported by wind (aeolian processes) and glaciers. Beach sands and river channel deposits are examples of fluvial transport and deposition, though _____ also often settles out of slow-moving or standing water in lakes and oceans.

   a. Dry quicksand
   c. Bovey Beds
   b. Brickearth
   d. Sediment

Chapter 15. Glaciers and Ice Ages

25. The phrase _____ is used to describe the movement of solid particles (sediment) and the processes that govern their motion. _____ is typically due to a combination of the force of gravity acting on the sediment, and/or the movement of the fluid in which the sediment is entrained. This is typically studied in natural systems, where the particles are clastic rocks (sand, gravel, boulders, etc.), mud, or clay; the fluid is air, water, or ice; and the force of gravity is due to the sloping surface on which the particles are resting.
  a. 1703 Genroku earthquake
  b. 1509 Istanbul earthquake
  c. 1700 Cascadia earthquake
  d. Sediment transport

26. A _____ is a piece of rock that differs from the size and type of rock native to the area in which it rests. They are carried by glacial ice, often over distances of hundreds of kilometres and can range in size from pebbles to large boulders such as Big Rock (16,500 tons) in Alberta.
  a. Glacial erratic
  b. 1703 Genroku earthquake
  c. 1509 Istanbul earthquake
  d. 1700 Cascadia earthquake

27. _____ is unsorted glacial sediment. Glacial drift is a general term for the coarsely graded and extremely heterogeneous sediments of glacial origin. Glacial _____ is that part of glacial drift which was deposited directly by the glacier. In cases where _____ has been indurated or lithified by subsequent burial into solid rock, it is known as the sedimentary rock tillite.
  a. 1700 Cascadia earthquake
  b. 1509 Istanbul earthquake
  c. 1703 Genroku earthquake
  d. Till

28. A _____ is any glacially formed accumulation of unconsolidated glacial debris (soil and rock) which can occur in currently glaciated and formerly glaciated regions, such as those areas acted upon by a past ice age. This debris may have been plucked off the valley floor as a glacier advanced or it may have fallen off the valley walls as a result of frost wedging. Moraines may be composed of silt like glacial flour to large boulders.
  a. Moraine
  b. 1509 Istanbul earthquake
  c. 1703 Genroku earthquake
  d. 1700 Cascadia earthquake

29. A _____ is a moraine that forms at the end of the glacier called the snout.

They mark the maximum advance of the glacier. An end moraine is at the present boundary of the glacier. They are one of the most prominent types of moraines in the Arctic. One famous _____ is the Giant's Wall in Norway.

  a. 1703 Genroku earthquake
  b. Terminal moraine
  c. 1509 Istanbul earthquake
  d. 1700 Cascadia earthquake

30. A _____ is an elongated whale-shaped hill formed by glacial action. Its long axis is parallel with the movement of the ice, with the blunter end facing into the glacial movement. They may be more than 45 m (150 ft) high and more than 0.8 km (1/2 mile) long, and are often in _____ fields of similarly shaped, sized and oriented hills. They usually have layers indicating that the material was repeatedly added to a core, which may be of rock or glacial till.
  a. 1509 Istanbul earthquake
  b. 1700 Cascadia earthquake
  c. Rogen moraine
  d. Drumlin

Chapter 15. Glaciers and Ice Ages

31. An _____ is a long winding ridge of stratified sand and gravel, examples of which occur in glaciated and formerly glaciated regions of Europe and North America. They are frequently several miles long and, because of their peculiar uniform shape, are somewhat like railroad embankments.

Most are believed to form in ice-walled tunnels by streams which flowed within (englacial) and under (subglacial) glaciers.

   a. AASHTO Soil Classification System
   b. AL 333
   c. AL 129-1
   d. Esker

32. _____ is a homogeneous, typically nonstratified, porous, friable, slightly coherent, often calcareous, fine-grained, silty, pale yellow or buff, windblown (aeolian) sediment. It generally occurs as a widespread blanket deposit that covers areas of hundreds of square kilometers and tens of meters thick. _____ often stands in either steep or vertical faces.
   a. 1703 Genroku earthquake
   b. Loess
   c. 1509 Istanbul earthquake
   d. 1700 Cascadia earthquake

33. A _____ is a glacial outwash plain formed of sediments deposited by meltwater at the terminus of a glacier.

_____ are found in glaciated areas, such as Svalbard, Kerguelen Islands, and Iceland. Glaciers and icecaps contain large amounts of silt and sediment, picked up as they erode the underlying rocks when they move slowly downhill, and at the snout of the glacier, meltwater can carry this sediment away from the glacier and deposit it on a broad plain.

   a. 1509 Istanbul earthquake
   b. 1700 Cascadia earthquake
   c. Rogen moraine
   d. Sandur

34. _____ in geology is a landform sunken or depressed below the surrounding area. Depressions may be formed by various mechanisms, and may be referred to by a variety of technical terms.

- A basin may be any large sediment filled _____. In tectonics, it may refer specifically to a circular, syncline-like _____: a geologic basin; while in sedimentology, it may refer to an area thickly filled with sediment: sedimentary basin.

- A blowout is a _____ created by wind erosion typically in either a desert sand or dry soil (such as a post-glacial loess environment.)

- A graben is a down dropped and typically linear _____ or basin created by rifting in a region under tensional tectonic forces.

- An impact crater is a _____ created by an impact such as a meteorite crater.
- A pit crater is a _____ formed by a sinking, or caving in, of the ground surface lying over a void.
- A kettle is left behind when a piece of ice left behind in glacial deposits melts.

- A _____ may be an area of subsidence caused by the collapse of an underlying structure. Examples include sinkholes above caves in karst topography, or calderas.

Chapter 15. Glaciers and Ice Ages

a. 1700 Cascadia earthquake
c. 1509 Istanbul earthquake
b. Depression
d. 1703 Genroku earthquake

35. In geology and climatology, a _____ was an extended period of abundant rainfall lasting many thousands of years. The term is especially applied to such periods during the Pleistocene Epoch. A minor, short _____ may be termed a 'subpluvial'.
a. 1700 Cascadia earthquake
c. 1509 Istanbul earthquake
b. 1703 Genroku earthquake
d. Pluvial

36. A _____ is a lake that experiences significant increase in depth and extent as a result of increased precipitation and reduced evaporation. Such lakes are likely to be endorheic.

They represent changes in the hydrological cycle -- wet cycles generate large lakes, whereas dry cycles cause the lakes to dry up leaving large flat plains.

a. 1703 Genroku earthquake
c. Pluvial lake
b. 1509 Istanbul earthquake
d. 1700 Cascadia earthquake

37. A _____ is an interval of time within an ice age that is marked by colder temperatures and glacier advances. Interglacials, on the other hand, are periods of warmer climate within an ice age. The last _____ ended about 10,000 to 15,000 years ago; the current Holocene epoch is the interglacial we are presently in.
a. Snowball Earth
c. Pastonian Stage
b. Wolstonian Stage
d. Glacial period

38. The _____ is the geologic eon before the Archean. It started at Earth's formation about 4.6 billion years ago (4,600 Ma), and ended roughly 3.8 billion years ago, though the latter date varies according to different sources.
a. 1509 Istanbul earthquake
c. 1703 Genroku earthquake
b. 1700 Cascadia earthquake
d. Hadean

39. An _____ is a geological interval of warmer global average temperature that separates glacial periods within an ice age. The current Holocene _____ has persisted since the Pleistocene, about 11,400 years ago.

During the 2.5 million year span of the Pleistocene, numerous glacials, or significant advances of continental ice sheets in North America and Europe have occurred at intervals of approximately 40,000 to 100,000 years.

a. Interglacial
c. AL 129-1
b. AL 333
d. AASHTO Soil Classification System

40. _____ is the geomorphic process by which soil, regolith, and rock move downslope under the force of gravity. Types of _____ include creep, slides, flows, topples, and falls, each with its own characteristic features, and taking place over timescales from seconds to years. _____ occurs on both terrestrial and submarine slopes, and has been observed on Earth, Mars, and Venus.
a. 1700 Cascadia earthquake
c. 1509 Istanbul earthquake
b. 1703 Genroku earthquake
d. Mass wasting

Chapter 15. Glaciers and Ice Ages

41. _____ are the collective effect of changes in the Earth's movements upon its climate axial tilt, and precession of the Earth's orbit determined climatic patterns on Earth, resulting in 100,000-year ice age cycles of the Quaternary glaciation over the last few million years. The Earth's axis completes one full cycle of precession approximately every 26,000 years. At the same time, the elliptical orbit rotates, more slowly, leading to a 23,000-year cycle between the seasons and the orbit.
- a. 1509 Istanbul earthquake
- b. 1703 Genroku earthquake
- c. 1700 Cascadia earthquake
- d. Milankovitch Theory

42. The _____ is the earliest of three geologic eras of the Phanerozoic eon. The _____ spanned from roughly 542 to 251 million years ago (ICS, 2004), and is subdivided into six geologic periods; from oldest to youngest they are: the Cambrian, Ordovician, Silurian, Devonian, Carboniferous, and Permian.

The _____ covers the time from the first appearance of abundant, soft-shelled fossils to the time when the continents were beginning to be dominated by large, relatively sophisticated reptiles and modern plants. The lower (oldest) boundary was classically set at the first appearance of creatures known as trilobites and archeocyathids.

- a. 1703 Genroku earthquake
- b. 1509 Istanbul earthquake
- c. Paleozoic
- d. 1700 Cascadia earthquake

43. _____ describes the large scale motions of Earth's lithosphere. The theory encompasses the older concepts of continental drift, developed during the first decades of the 20th century by Alfred Wegener, and seafloor spreading, understood during the 1960s.

The outermost part of the Earth's interior is made up of two layers: the lithosphere and the asthenosphere.

- a. Plate tectonics
- b. Thrust fault
- c. Copperbelt Province
- d. Subduction

44. The _____ is the epoch from 1.8 million to 11550 years BP covering the world's recent period of repeated glaciations. The _____ epoch follows the Pliocene epoch and is followed by the Holocene epoch. The _____ is the third epoch of the Neogene period or 6th epoch of the Cenozoic Era. The end of the _____ corresponds with the retreat of the last continental glacier. It also corresponds with the end of the Paleolithic age used in archaeology.
- a. Late Pleistocene
- b. Tyrrhenian
- c. Pleistocene
- d. Sicilian Stage

45. The _____ Period is the geologic time period after the Neogene Period, spanning 1.805 +/- 0.005 million years ago to the present. The _____ includes two geologic epochs: the Pleistocene and the Holocene Epoch.

There is an ongoing debate of the status of _____ -- a recent proposal from International Commission on Stratigraphy (ICS) was to make _____ a subperiod under Neogene, but that was retracted after criticism from International Union for _____ Research (INQUA), so instead ICS and INQUA agreed to erect _____ as an Era, above Neogene, and to place the base for _____ at 2.588 >± 3.005, the base for Gelasian Stage.

Chapter 15. Glaciers and Ice Ages

a. Canadian Shield
c. Musgrave Block
b. Quaternary
d. Gawler craton

46. The terms _____ and icehouse Earth refer to the prevailing global climate on a timescale of millions of years.

During a _____ Earth period, the planet's atmosphere contains sufficient _____ gases such as carbon dioxide and methane for ice to be entirely absent from the planet's surface.

During icehouse periods, glaciers are present in fluctuating amounts; variations in the Earth's orbit may result in many ice ages, glacials, and interglacials.

a. Greenhouse
c. 1703 Genroku earthquake
b. 1509 Istanbul earthquake
d. 1700 Cascadia earthquake

47. The terms greenhouse earth and _____ refer to the prevailing global climate on a timescale of millions of years.

During a greenhouse Earth period, the planet's atmosphere contains sufficient greenhouse gases such as carbon dioxide and methane for ice to be entirely absent from the planet's surface.

During _____ periods, glaciers are present in fluctuating amounts; variations in the Earth's orbit may result in many ice ages, glacials, and interglacials.

a. Icehouse earth
c. AASHTO Soil Classification System
b. AL 333
d. AL 129-1

48. The _____ Era is one of three geologic eras of the Phanerozoic eon. The division of time into eras dates back to Giovanni Arduino, in the 18th century, although his original name for the era now called the '_____' was 'Secondary' (making the modern era the 'Tertiary'.)

The _____ was a time of tectonic, climatic and evolutionary activity. The continents gradually shifted from a state of connectedness into their present configuration; the drifting provided for speciation and other important evolutionary developments.

a. 1509 Istanbul earthquake
c. Mesozoic
b. 1703 Genroku earthquake
d. 1700 Cascadia earthquake

49. In geology, _____ is the name of a supercontinent, a continent which contained most or all of Earth's landmass. According to plate tectonic reconstructions, _____ existed between 1100 and 750 million years ago, in the Neoproterozoic era.

In contrast with Pangaea, the last supercontinent about 300 million years ago, little is known yet about the exact configuration and geodynamic history of _____.

Chapter 15. Glaciers and Ice Ages

a. 1700 Cascadia earthquake
c. Rodinia
b. 1703 Genroku earthquake
d. 1509 Istanbul earthquake

50. _____ refers to hypotheses regarding paleoclimatic global-scale glaciation, claiming that the Earth's surface was nearly or entirely frozen at some points in its past. The occurrence of _____ remains controversial. Proponents claim it best explains sedimentary deposits generally regarded as of glacial origin at tropical latitudes and other enigmatic features of the geological record.
a. Glacial period
c. Snowball Earth
b. Pre-Pastonian Stage
d. Cordilleran Ice Sheet

51. The _____ is a a term for a geologic period 65 million to 1.8 million years ago. The _____ covered the time span between the superseded Secondary period and an out-of-date definition of the Quaternary period. The period began with the demise of the non-avian dinosaurs in the Cretaceous-_____ extinction event, at start of the Cenozoic era, spanning to beginning of the most recent Ice Age, at the end of the Pliocene epoch.
a. Rockall
c. Suspended load
b. Tertiary
d. Historical geology

52. The _____ was a major ice sheet that covered, during glacial periods of the Quaternary, a large area of North America. This included the following areas:

- Western Montana
- The Idaho Panhandle
- Northern Washington state down to about Seattle and Spokane, Washington
- All of British Columbia
- The southwestern third or so of Yukon territory
- All of the Alaska Panhandle
- South Central Alaska
- The Alaska Peninsula
- Almost all of the continental shelf north of the Strait of Juan de Fuca

The ice sheet covered up to two and a half million square kilometres at the Last Glacial Maximum and probably more than that in some previous periods, when it may have extended into the northeast extremity of Oregon and the Salmon River Mountains in Idaho. It is probable, though, that its northern margin also migrated south due to the influence of starvation caused by very low levels of precipitation.

At its eastern end the _____ merged with the Laurentide ice sheet at the Continental Divide, forming an area of ice that contained one and a half times as much water as the Antarctic ice sheet does today.

a. Snowball Earth
c. Cordilleran ice sheet
b. Bergschrund
d. Wolstonian Stage

53. The _____ was a massive sheet of ice that covered hundreds of thousands of square miles, including most of Canada and a large portion of the northern United States, between c. 95,000 and c. 20,000 years before the present day.
a. 1700 Cascadia earthquake
c. 1509 Istanbul earthquake
b. Laurentide ice sheet
d. 1703 Genroku earthquake

Chapter 15. Glaciers and Ice Ages

54. The _____ is one of the six principal 'toes' of the Columbia Icefield, located in the Canadian Rockies. Due to global warming, the glacier has receded more than 1.5 km in the past 125 years and lost over half of its volume. It currently recedes at a rate of 2-3 metres per year.
   a. AASHTO Soil Classification System
   b. AL 333
   c. Athabasca Glacier
   d. AL 129-1

55. The _____ was a period of cooling occurring after a warmer North Atlantic era known as the Medieval Warm Period. While not a true ice age, the term was introduced into scientific literature by Fran>çois E. Matthes in 1939. Climatologists and historians working with local records no longer expect to agree on either the start or end dates of this period, which varied according to local conditions.
   a. Glacier
   b. Keeling Curve
   c. Geologic temperature record
   d. Little Ice Age

Chapter 16. Deserts and Wind Action

1. Two important classifications of weathering processes exist -- physical and _____. Mechanical or physical weathering involves the breakdown of rocks and soils through direct contact with atmospheric conditions, such as heat, water, ice and pressure. The second classification, _____, involves the direct effect of atmospheric chemicals or biologically produced chemicals (also known as biological weathering) in the breakdown of rocks, soils and minerals.
   - a. 1700 Cascadia earthquake
   - b. 1703 Genroku earthquake
   - c. 1509 Istanbul earthquake
   - d. Chemical weathering

2. _____ is the decomposition of Earth rocks, soils and their minerals through direct contact with the planet's atmosphere. _____ occurs in situ, or 'with no movement', and thus should not be confused with erosion, which involves the movement of rocks and minerals by agents such as water, ice, wind and gravity.

   Two important classifications of _____ processes exist -- physical and chemical _____.

   - a. 1703 Genroku earthquake
   - b. 1700 Cascadia earthquake
   - c. 1509 Istanbul earthquake
   - d. Weathering

3. An _____ is a numerical indicator of the degree of dryness of the climate at a given location. A number of aridity indices have been proposed ; these indicators serve to identify, locate or delimit regions that suffer from a deficit of available water, a condition that can severely affect the effective use of the land for such activities as agriculture or stock-farming.

   At the turn of the 20th century, Wladimir K>öppen and Rudolf Geiger developed the concept of a climate classification where arid regions were defined as those places where the annual rainfall accumulation (in centimetres) is less than R / 2, where:

   - ☒ > if rainfall occurs mainly in the cold season,
   - ☒ > if rainfall is evenly distributed throughout the year, and
   - ☒ > if rainfall occurs mainly in the hot season.

   where T is the mean annual temperature in Celsius.

   This was one of the first attempts at defining an _____, one that reflects the effects of the thermal regime and the amount and distribution of precipitation in determining the native vegetation possible in an area.

   - a. AL 333
   - b. AASHTO Soil Classification System
   - c. AL 129-1
   - d. Aridity index

4. A _____ is the shadow a rain drop has before it lands on the ground, with respect to prevailing wind direction. In a more geographical sense, a _____ is an area of land that has suffered desertification from proximity to mountain ranges. The mountains block the passage of rain-producing weather systems, casting a 'shadow' of dryness behind them.
   - a. Rain shadow
   - b. 1700 Cascadia earthquake
   - c. 1703 Genroku earthquake
   - d. 1509 Istanbul earthquake

5. The _____ is a geologic formation that is spread across the U.S. states of northern Arizona, Nevada, Utah, western New Mexico, and western Colorado. The _____ is controversially considered to be synonymous to Dockum Group in eastern Colorado, eastern New Mexico, southwestern Kansas, the Oklahoma panhandle, and western Texas. The _____ is sometimes colloquially used as a geologic formation within the Dockum in New Mexico and occasionally in Texas.

   a. Fault   b. Chinle
   c. Cohesion   d. Submersion

6. _____ is water located beneath the ground surface in soil pore spaces and in the fractures of lithologic formations. A unit of rock or an unconsolidated deposit is called an aquifer when it can yield a usable quantity of water. The depth at which soil pore spaces or fractures and voids in rock become completely saturated with water is called the water table.

   a. Depression focused recharge   b. 1509 Istanbul earthquake
   c. 1700 Cascadia earthquake   d. Groundwater

7. _____ is the geological process by which material is added to a landform or land mass. Fluids such as wind and water, as well as sediment gravity flows, transport previously eroded sediment, which, at the loss of enough kinetic energy in the fluid, is deposited, building up layers of sediment.

_____ occurs when the forces responsible for sediment transportation are no longer sufficient to overcome the forces of particle weight and friction, which resist motion.

   a. Headward erosion   b. Deposition
   c. Seafloor spreading   d. Permineralization

8. _____ is the removal of solids (sediment, soil, rock and other particles) in the natural environment. It usually occurs due to transport by wind, water, or ice; by down-slope creep of soil and other material under the force of gravity; or by living organisms, such as burrowing animals, in the case of bioerosion.

_____ is distinguished from weathering, which is the process of chemical or physical breakdown of the minerals in the rocks, although the two processes may occur concurrently.

   a. AL 333   b. AL 129-1
   c. AASHTO Soil Classification System   d. Erosion

9. A _____ or inselberg is an isolated rock hill, knob, ridge, or small mountain that rises abruptly from a gently sloping or virtually level surrounding plain. The term '_____' is usually used in the United States, whereas 'inselberg' is the more common international term. In southern and southern-central Africa, a similar formation of granite is known as a kopje (in fact a Dutch word) from the Afrikaans word: koppie.

_____ is an originally Native American term for an isolated hill or a lone mountain that has risen above the surrounding area, typically by surviving erosion.

   a. 1509 Istanbul earthquake   b. Monadnock
   c. 1703 Genroku earthquake   d. 1700 Cascadia earthquake

Chapter 16. Deserts and Wind Action

10. A _____ is a gently inclined erosional surface carved into bedrock. It is thinly covered with Fluvial gravel that has developed at the foot of mountains. It develops when running water erodes most of the mass of the mountain. It is typically a concave surface gently sloping away from mountainous desert areas.

   a. Pediment
   b. Corrasion
   c. Lisasion
   d. Patterned ground

11. _____ is any particulate matter that can be transported by fluid flow, and which eventually is deposited.

They are most often transported by water (fluvial processes) transported by wind (aeolian processes) and glaciers. Beach sands and river channel deposits are examples of fluvial transport and deposition, though _____ also often settles out of slow-moving or standing water in lakes and oceans.

   a. Bovey Beds
   b. Sediment
   c. Dry quicksand
   d. Brickearth

12. _____ pertain to the activity of the winds and more specifically, to the winds' ability to shape the surface of the Earth and other planets. Winds may erode, transport, and deposit materials, and are effective agents in regions with sparse vegetation and a large supply of unconsolidated sediments. Although water is much more powerful than wind, _____ are important in arid environments such as deserts.

   a. AASHTO Soil Classification System
   b. AL 333
   c. AL 129-1
   d. Aeolian processes

13. _____ is mechanical scraping of a rock surface by friction between rocks and moving particles during their transport in wind, glacier, waves, gravity or running water, after friction, the moving particles dislodge loose and weak debris from the side of the rock, these particles can be dissolved in the water source.

The intensity of _____ depends on the hardness, concentration, velocity and mass of moving particles.

A virtually smooth marine platform cut by the ocean waves at a coastline.

   a. AL 333
   b. AL 129-1
   c. AASHTO Soil Classification System
   d. Abrasion

14. _____ are sandy depressions in a sand dune ecosystem (psammosere) caused by the removal of sediments by wind.

_____ occur in partially vegetated dunefields or sandhills. _____ form when a patch of protective vegetation is lost, allowing strong winds to 'blow out' sand and form a depression.

   a. 1700 Cascadia earthquake
   b. 1509 Istanbul earthquake
   c. Pothole
   d. Blowouts

15. A _____ is a desert surface that is covered with closely packed, interlocking angular or rounded rock fragments of pebble and cobble size.

Chapter 16. Deserts and Wind Action

Several theories have been proposed for their formation. The more common theory is that they form by the gradual removal of the sand, dust and other fine grained material by the wind and intermittent rain leaving only the larger fragments behind.

a. 1509 Istanbul earthquake
c. 1700 Cascadia earthquake
b. 1703 Genroku earthquake
d. Desert pavement

16. In geology, _____ is a specific type of particle transport by fluids such as wind, or the denser fluid water. It occurs when loose material is removed from a bed and carried by the fluid, before being transported back to the surface. Examples include pebble transport by rivers, sand drift over desert surfaces, soil blowing over fields, or even snow drift over smooth surfaces such as those in the Arctic or Canadian Prairies.

a. Seafloor spreading
c. Stoping
b. Spheroidal weathering
d. Saltation

17. _____ is a naturally occurring granular material composed of finely divided rock and mineral particles.

As the term is used by geologists, _____ particles range in diameter from 0.0625 (or $>^1\!\!/_{16}$ mm, or 62.5 micrometers) to 2 millimeters. An individual particle in this range size is termed a _____ grain.

a. 1509 Istanbul earthquake
c. 1703 Genroku earthquake
b. 1700 Cascadia earthquake
d. Sand

18. _____ are rocks that have been abraded, pitted, etched, grooved, or polished by wind-driven sand or ice crystals. These geomorphic features are most typically found in arid environments where there is little vegetation to interfere with aeolian particle transport, where there are frequently strong winds, and where there is a steady but not overwhelming supply of sand.

_____ can be abraded to eye-catching natural sculptures.

a. 1509 Istanbul earthquake
c. Coprolite
b. Ventifacts
d. Fault breccia

19. A _____ is a wind-abraded ridge found in a desert environment. They are elongate features typically three or more times longer than they are wide, and when viewed from above, resemble the hull of a boat. Facing the wind is a steep, blunt face that gradually gets lower and narrower toward the lee end.

a. 1509 Istanbul earthquake
c. 1703 Genroku earthquake
b. 1700 Cascadia earthquake
d. Yardang

20. _____ describes the large scale motions of Earth's lithosphere. The theory encompasses the older concepts of continental drift, developed during the first decades of the 20th century by Alfred Wegener, and seafloor spreading, understood during the 1960s.

The outermost part of the Earth's interior is made up of two layers: the lithosphere and the asthenosphere.

Chapter 16. Deserts and Wind Action

a. Thrust fault
c. Subduction
b. Copperbelt Province
d. Plate tectonics

21. The phrase _____ is used to describe the movement of solid particles (sediment) and the processes that govern their motion. _____ is typically due to a combination of the force of gravity acting on the sediment, and/or the movement of the fluid in which the sediment is entrained. This is typically studied in natural systems, where the particles are clastic rocks (sand, gravel, boulders, etc.), mud, or clay; the fluid is air, water, or ice; and the force of gravity is due to the sloping surface on which the particles are resting.
   a. 1700 Cascadia earthquake
   c. 1703 Genroku earthquake
   b. 1509 Istanbul earthquake
   d. Sediment transport

22. A _____ dune is an arc-shaped sand ridge, comprising well-sorted sand. This type of dune possesses two 'horns' that face downwind, with the slip face (the downwind slope) at the angle of repose, or approximately 32 degrees. The upwind side is packed by the wind, and stands at about 15 degrees. Simple _____ dunes may stretch from meters to a hundred meters or so between the tips of the horns.
   a. 1700 Cascadia earthquake
   c. 1703 Genroku earthquake
   b. 1509 Istanbul earthquake
   d. Barchan

23. _____ is a homogeneous, typically nonstratified, porous, friable, slightly coherent, often calcareous, fine-grained, silty, pale yellow or buff, windblown (aeolian) sediment. It generally occurs as a widespread blanket deposit that covers areas of hundreds of square kilometers and tens of meters thick. _____ often stands in either steep or vertical faces.
   a. 1700 Cascadia earthquake
   c. 1703 Genroku earthquake
   b. 1509 Istanbul earthquake
   d. Loess

24. Radially symmetrical, _____ are pyramidal sand mounds with slipfaces on three or more arms that radiate from the high center of the mound. They tend to accumulate in areas with multidirectional wind regimes. _____ grow upward rather than laterally. They dominate the Grand Erg Oriental of the Sahara. In other deserts, they occur around the margins of the sand seas, particularly near topographic barriers. In the southeast Badain Jaran Desert of China, the _____ are up to 500 meters tall and may be the tallest dunes on Earth.
   a. 1509 Istanbul earthquake
   c. 1700 Cascadia earthquake
   b. 1703 Genroku earthquake
   d. Star dunes

Chapter 17. Shores and Coastal Processes

1. _____ is the wearing away of land or the removal of beach or dune sediments by wave action, tidal currents, wave currents generated by storms, wind, or fast moving motor craft cause _____, which may take the form of long-term losses of sediment and rocks, or merely the temporary redistribution of coastal sediments; erosion in one location may result in accretion nearby. The study of erosion and sediment redistribution is called 'coastal morphodynamics'.

   a. Bradyseism
   b. Shutter ridge
   c. Coastal Erosion
   d. Fault scarp

2. _____ is the removal of solids (sediment, soil, rock and other particles) in the natural environment. It usually occurs due to transport by wind, water, or ice; by down-slope creep of soil and other material under the force of gravity; or by living organisms, such as burrowing animals, in the case of bioerosion.

   _____ is distinguished from weathering, which is the process of chemical or physical breakdown of the minerals in the rocks, although the two processes may occur concurrently.

   a. Erosion
   b. AASHTO Soil Classification System
   c. AL 333
   d. AL 129-1

3. _____ is water located beneath the ground surface in soil pore spaces and in the fractures of lithologic formations. A unit of rock or an unconsolidated deposit is called an aquifer when it can yield a usable quantity of water. The depth at which soil pore spaces or fractures and voids in rock become completely saturated with water is called the water table.

   a. Groundwater
   b. 1700 Cascadia earthquake
   c. Depression focused recharge
   d. 1509 Istanbul earthquake

4. _____, is the water that washes up on shore after an incoming wave has broken. This action will cause sand and other light particles to be transported up the beach. The direction of the _____ varies with the prevailing wind, whereas the backwash is always perpendicular to the coastline.

   a. 1509 Istanbul earthquake
   b. Cuspate forelands
   c. Swash
   d. Longshore drift

5. The _____ is the maximum depth at which a water wave's passage causes significant water motion. For water depths larger than the _____, bottom sediments are no longer stirred by the wave motion above.

   In deep water, the water particles are moved in a circular orbital motion when a wave passes.

   a. 1700 Cascadia earthquake
   b. 1703 Genroku earthquake
   c. 1509 Istanbul earthquake
   d. Wave base

6. _____, sometimes known as shore drift, is a geological process by which sediments such as sand or other materials, move along a beach shore. It uses the process of swash to push the material up the beach and backwash down the beach; until it reaches a groyne or another obstacle.

   Where waves approach the coastline at an angle, when they break their swash pushes beach material up the beach at the same angle.

   a. Swash
   b. 1509 Istanbul earthquake
   c. Cuspate forelands
   d. Longshore drift

Chapter 17. Shores and Coastal Processes

7. The _____ is the earliest of three geologic eras of the Phanerozoic eon. The _____ spanned from roughly 542 to 251 million years ago (ICS, 2004), and is subdivided into six geologic periods; from oldest to youngest they are: the Cambrian, Ordovician, Silurian, Devonian, Carboniferous, and Permian.

The _____ covers the time from the first appearance of abundant, soft-shelled fossils to the time when the continents were beginning to be dominated by large, relatively sophisticated reptiles and modern plants. The lower (oldest) boundary was classically set at the first appearance of creatures known as trilobites and archeocyathids.

   a. 1700 Cascadia earthquake
   b. Paleozoic
   c. 1509 Istanbul earthquake
   d. 1703 Genroku earthquake

8. The _____ is the vertical difference between the highest high tide and the lowest low tide. In other words, it is the difference in height between high and low tides. The most extreme _____ will occur around the time of the full or new moons, when gravity of both the Sun and Moon are pulling the same way (new moon), or exact opposite way (full.)
   a. 1703 Genroku earthquake
   b. 1700 Cascadia earthquake
   c. 1509 Istanbul earthquake
   d. Tidal range

9. _____ is the process of determining a specific date for an archaeological or palaeontological site or artifact. Some archaeologists prefer the terms chronometric or calendar dating, as use of the word 'absolute' implies a certainty and precision that is rarely possible in archaeology. _____ is usually based on the physical or chemical properties of the materials of artifacts, buildings, or other items that have been modified by humans.
   a. AASHTO Soil Classification System
   b. Uranium-lead dating
   c. Absolute dating
   d. Erathem

10. _____ is the geological process by which material is added to a landform or land mass. Fluids such as wind and water, as well as sediment gravity flows, transport previously eroded sediment, which, at the loss of enough kinetic energy in the fluid, is deposited, building up layers of sediment.

_____ occurs when the forces responsible for sediment transportation are no longer sufficient to overcome the forces of particle weight and friction, which resist motion.

   a. Seafloor spreading
   b. Headward erosion
   c. Permineralization
   d. Deposition

11. A _____ is a mountain rising from the ocean seafloor that does not reach to the water's surface (sea level), and thus is not an island. These are typically formed from extinct volcanoes, that rise abruptly and are usually found rising from a seafloor of 1,000-4,000 meters depth. They are defined by oceanographers as independent features that rise to at least 1,000 meters above the seafloor.
   a. 1703 Genroku earthquake
   b. 1509 Istanbul earthquake
   c. 1700 Cascadia earthquake
   d. Seamount

Chapter 17. Shores and Coastal Processes

12. A _____ is a natural formation (or landform) where a rock arch forms, with a natural passageway through underneath. Most natural arches form as a narrow ridge, walled by cliffs, become narrower from erosion, with a softer rock stratum under the cliff-forming stratum gradually eroding out until the rock shelters thus formed meet underneath the ridge, thus forming the arch. They commonly form where cliffs are subject to erosion from the sea, rivers or weathering (sub-aerial processes); the processes 'find' weaknesses in rocks and work on them, making them bigger until they break through.
    a. 1703 Genroku earthquake
    b. 1509 Istanbul earthquake
    c. 1700 Cascadia earthquake
    d. Natural arch

13. A _____ is a type of cave formed primarily by the wave action of the sea. The primary process involved is erosion. Sea caves are found throughout the world, actively forming along present coastlines and as relict sea caves on former coastlines.
    a. 1700 Cascadia earthquake
    b. 1509 Istanbul earthquake
    c. 1703 Genroku earthquake
    d. Sea cave

14. A _____ is a geological landform consisting of a steep and often vertical column or columns of rock in the sea near a coast. They are formed when part of a headland is eroded by hydraulic action, which is the force of the sea or water crashing against the rock. The force of the water weakens cracks in the headland, causing them to later collapse, forming free-standing stacks and even a small island.
    a. 1509 Istanbul earthquake
    b. 1700 Cascadia earthquake
    c. 1703 Genroku earthquake
    d. Stack

15. _____ is any particulate matter that can be transported by fluid flow, and which eventually is deposited.

They are most often transported by water (fluvial processes) transported by wind (aeolian processes) and glaciers. Beach sands and river channel deposits are examples of fluvial transport and deposition, though _____ also often settles out of slow-moving or standing water in lakes and oceans.

    a. Brickearth
    b. Bovey Beds
    c. Dry quicksand
    d. Sediment

16. The phrase _____ is used to describe the movement of solid particles (sediment) and the processes that govern their motion. _____ is typically due to a combination of the force of gravity acting on the sediment, and/or the movement of the fluid in which the sediment is entrained. This is typically studied in natural systems, where the particles are clastic rocks (sand, gravel, boulders, etc.), mud, or clay; the fluid is air, water, or ice; and the force of gravity is due to the sloping surface on which the particles are resting.
    a. Sediment transport
    b. 1509 Istanbul earthquake
    c. 1700 Cascadia earthquake
    d. 1703 Genroku earthquake

17. The _____ zone is the area that is exposed to the air at low tide and submerged at high tide, for example, the area between tide marks. This area can include many different types of habitats, including steep rocky cliffs, sandy beaches, or wetlands The area can be a narrow strip, as in Pacific islands that have only a narrow tidal range, or can include many meters of shoreline where shallow beach slope interacts with high tidal excursion.
    a. Intertidal
    b. AL 129-1
    c. Overland flow
    d. AASHTO Soil Classification System

Chapter 17. Shores and Coastal Processes

18. _____ are structures constructed on coasts as part of coastal defence or to protect an anchorage from the effects of weather and longshore drift.

Offshore _____, also called bulkheads, reduce the intensity of wave action in inshore waters and thereby reduce coastal erosion. They are constructed some distance away from the coast or built with one end linked to the coast.

  a. 1703 Genroku earthquake
  b. 1700 Cascadia earthquake
  c. 1509 Istanbul earthquake
  d. Breakwaters

19. A _____ or sometimes ayre is a deposition landform in which an island is attached to the mainland by a narrow piece of land such as a spit or bar. They usually form because the island causes wave refraction, depositing sand and shingle moved by longshore drift in each direction around the island where the waves meet. Eustatic sea level rise may also contribute to accretion as material is pushed up with rising sea levels.
  a. 1509 Istanbul earthquake
  b. Tombolo
  c. 1703 Genroku earthquake
  d. 1700 Cascadia earthquake

20. In geology, _____ is transported rock debris overlying the solid bedrock. The term is also sometimes refers to organic debris so-transported. In the largest sense, it refers to the material left behind by retreating continental glaciers.
  a. Dispersion
  b. Compression
  c. Georeactor
  d. Drift

21. A _____ or sandbar is a somewhat linear landform within or extending into a body of water, typically composed of sand, silt or small pebbles. A bar is characteristically long and narrow and develops where a stream or ocean current promotes deposition of granular material, resulting in localized shallowing of the water. Bars can appear in the sea, in a lake, or in a river.

The term _____ can be applied to larger geological units that form off a coastline as part of the process of coastal erosion. These include spits and baymouth bars that form across the front of embayments and rias. A tombolo is a bar that forms an isthmus between an island or offshore rock and a mainland shore.

  a. 1700 Cascadia earthquake
  b. 1509 Istanbul earthquake
  c. 1703 Genroku earthquake
  d. Shoal

22. Geologically, a _____ is a long, narrow inlet with steep sides, created in a valley carved by glacial activity.

The seeds of a _____ are laid when a glacier cuts a U-shaped valley through abrasion of the surrounding bedrock by the sediment it carries. Many such valleys were formed during the recent ice age.

  a. 1703 Genroku earthquake
  b. Fjord
  c. 1700 Cascadia earthquake
  d. 1509 Istanbul earthquake

23. _____ are coastal wetlands that form when mud is deposited by tides or rivers. They are found in sheltered areas such as bays, bayous, lagoons, and estuaries. _____ may be viewed geologically as exposed layers of bay mud, resulting from deposition of estuarine silts, clays and marine animal detritus.

a. 1703 Genroku earthquake
b. Mudflats
c. 1509 Istanbul earthquake
d. 1700 Cascadia earthquake

24. _____ describes the large scale motions of Earth's lithosphere. The theory encompasses the older concepts of continental drift, developed during the first decades of the 20th century by Alfred Wegener, and seafloor spreading, understood during the 1960s.

The outermost part of the Earth's interior is made up of two layers: the lithosphere and the asthenosphere.

a. Thrust fault
b. Subduction
c. Copperbelt Province
d. Plate tectonics

25. _____ -- also known as rip rap, rubble, shot rock or rock armour -- is rock or other material used to armor shorelines, streambeds, bridge abutments, pilings and other shoreline structures against scour, water or ice erosion.

It is made from a variety of rock types, commonly granite, limestone or occasionally concrete rubble from building and paving demolition. It is used to protect coastlines and structures from erosion by the sea, rivers, or streams.

a. Geologic preliminary investigation
b. Riprap
c. Mitigation of seismic motion
d. Sediment control

Chapter 18. Human Use of the Earth's Resources

1. _____ are the preserved remains or traces of animals, plants, and other organisms from the remote past. The totality of _____, both discovered and undiscovered, and their placement in fossiliferous rock formations and sedimentary layers (strata) is known as the fossil record. The study of _____ across geological time, how they were formed, and the evolutionary relationships between taxa (phylogeny) are some of the most important functions of the science of paleontology.
   - a. 1700 Cascadia earthquake
   - b. 1703 Genroku earthquake
   - c. Fossils
   - d. 1509 Istanbul earthquake

2. The _____, is a geologic eon before the Proterozoic and Paleoproterozoic, before 2.5 Ga (billion years ago, or 2,500 Ma.) Instead of being based on stratigraphy, this date is defined chronometrically. The lower boundary (starting point) has not been officially recognized by the International Commission on Stratigraphy, but it is usually set to 3.8 Ga, at the end of the Hadean eon.
   - a. AL 129-1
   - b. AL 333
   - c. AASHTO Soil Classification System
   - d. Archean

3. _____ or extra heavy oil, is a type of bitumen deposit. The sands are naturally occurring mixtures of sand or clay, water and an extremely dense and viscous form of petroleum called bitumen. They are found in large amounts in many countries throughout the world, but are found in extremely large quantities in Canada and Venezuela.
   - a. AL 129-1
   - b. AASHTO Soil Classification System
   - c. AL 333
   - d. Oil sands

4. _____ is an organic-rich fine-grained sedimentary rock. It contains significant amounts of kerogen, a solid mixture of organic chemical compounds from which liquid hydrocarbons can be extracted. Deposits of _____ occur around the world, including major deposits in the United States of America. Estimates of global deposits range from 2.8 trillion to 3.3 trillion barrels >(450 >× 10^9 to 520 >× 10^9 m^3) of recoverable oil.
   - a. AL 333
   - b. Oil shale
   - c. AASHTO Soil Classification System
   - d. AL 129-1

5. _____ is a naturally occurring granular material composed of finely divided rock and mineral particles.

   As the term is used by geologists, _____ particles range in diameter from 0.0625 (or >^{1}⁄$_{16}$ mm, or 62.5 micrometers) to 2 millimeters. An individual particle in this range size is termed a _____ grain.
   - a. 1703 Genroku earthquake
   - b. 1700 Cascadia earthquake
   - c. Sand
   - d. 1509 Istanbul earthquake

6. _____ is a fine-grained sedimentary rock whose original constituents were clay minerals or muds. It is characterized by thin laminae breaking with an irregular curving fracture, often splintery and usually parallel to the often-indistinguishable bedding plane. This property is called fissility.
   - a. Sandstone
   - b. Dolomite
   - c. Dolostone
   - d. Shale

7. _____ or kerogen oil is a non-conventional oil produced by the destructive distillation of oil shale. This process, a controlled form of pyrolysis, converts the organic matter within the rock (kerogen) into synthetic oil and gas. The resulting oil can be used immediately as a fuel or upgraded to meet refinery feedstock specifications by adding hydrogen and removing impurities such as sulfur and nitrogen.

Chapter 18. Human Use of the Earth's Resources

a. 1509 Istanbul earthquake
c. Shale oil
b. 1700 Cascadia earthquake
d. 1703 Genroku earthquake

8. _____ is a hard, compact variety of mineral coal that has a high lustre. It has the highest carbon count and contains the fewest impurities of all coals, despite its lower calorific content.

_____ is the highest of the metamorphic rank, in which the carbon content is between 92% and 98%.

a. AL 333
c. AASHTO Soil Classification System
b. AL 129-1
d. Anthracite

9. _____ is a relatively soft coal containing a tarlike substance called bitumen. It is of higher quality than lignite coal but of poorer quality than anthracite coal.

_____ is a sedimorphic rock formed by diagenetic and submetamorphic compression of peat bog material.

a. 1700 Cascadia earthquake
c. 1509 Istanbul earthquake
b. 1703 Genroku earthquake
d. Bituminous coal

10. _____ is an accumulation of partially decayed vegetation matter. _____ forms in wetlands or peatlands, variously called bogs, moors, muskegs, pocosins, mires, and _____ swamp forests. By volume there are about 4 trillion mÂÂ³ of _____ in the world covering a total of around 2% of global land mass (about 3 million km^2), containing about 8 billion terajoules of energy.

a. 1509 Istanbul earthquake
c. 1700 Cascadia earthquake
b. 1703 Genroku earthquake
d. Peat

11. The _____ is a region in southeast Montana and northeast Wyoming about 120 miles (190 km) east to west and 200 miles (320 km) north to south known for its coal deposits. It is both a topographic drainage and geologic structural basin. The basin is so named because it is drained by the Powder River, although it is also drained in part by the Cheyenne River, Tongue River, Bighorn River, Little Missouri River, Platte River, and their tributaries.

a. 1700 Cascadia earthquake
c. 1509 Istanbul earthquake
b. Raton Basin
d. Powder River basin

12. A _____ is an extent of land where water from rain or snow melt drains downhill into a body of water, such as a river, lake, reservoir, estuary, wetland, sea or ocean. The _____ includes both the streams and rivers that convey the water as well as the land surfaces from which water drains into those channels, and is separated from adjacent basins by a drainage divide.

The _____ acts like a funnel, collecting all the water within the area covered by the basin and channelling it into a waterway.

a. 1509 Istanbul earthquake
c. 1703 Genroku earthquake
b. 1700 Cascadia earthquake
d. Drainage basin

13. The terms _____ and icehouse Earth refer to the prevailing global climate on a timescale of millions of years.

Chapter 18. Human Use of the Earth's Resources

During a _____ Earth period, the planet's atmosphere contains sufficient _____ gases such as carbon dioxide and methane for ice to be entirely absent from the planet's surface.

During icehouse periods, glaciers are present in fluctuating amounts; variations in the Earth's orbit may result in many ice ages, glacials, and interglacials.

- a. Greenhouse
- c. 1703 Genroku earthquake
- b. 1509 Istanbul earthquake
- d. 1700 Cascadia earthquake

14. _____ is the largest volcano on earth in terms of area covered and one of five volcanoes that form the Island of Hawaii in the U.S. state of Hawai>Ê»i in the Pacific Ocean. It is an active shield volcano, with a volume estimated at approximately 18,000 cubic miles (75,000 km³), although its peak is about 120 feet (37 m) lower than that of its neighbor, Mauna Kea. The Hawaiian name '_____' means 'Long Mountain'.

- a. 1703 Genroku earthquake
- c. Mauna Loa
- b. 1509 Istanbul earthquake
- d. 1700 Cascadia earthquake

15. The _____ Era is one of three geologic eras of the Phanerozoic eon. The division of time into eras dates back to Giovanni Arduino, in the 18th century, although his original name for the era now called the '_____' was 'Secondary' (making the modern era the 'Tertiary'.)

The _____ was a time of tectonic, climatic and evolutionary activity. The continents gradually shifted from a state of connectedness into their present configuration; the drifting provided for speciation and other important evolutionary developments.

- a. 1703 Genroku earthquake
- c. 1509 Istanbul earthquake
- b. Mesozoic
- d. 1700 Cascadia earthquake

16. The _____ is a a term for a geologic period 65 million to 1.8 million years ago. The _____ covered the time span between the superseded Secondary period and an out-of-date definition of the Quaternary period. The period began with the demise of the non-avian dinosaurs in the Cretaceous-_____ extinction event, at start of the Cenozoic era, spanning to beginning of the most recent Ice Age, at the end of the Pliocene epoch.

- a. Rockall
- c. Historical geology
- b. Suspended load
- d. Tertiary

17. In geology, _____ refers to heat sources within the planet. _____ is technically an adjective (e.g., _____ energy) but in U.S. English the word has attained frequent use as a noun.

The planet's internal heat was originally generated during its accretion, due to gravitational binding energy, and since then additional heat has continued to be generated by decay heat from the radioactive decay of elements.

- a. Diamond Head
- c. Combe
- b. Geothermal
- d. Compaction

Chapter 18. Human Use of the Earth's Resources

18. _____ is power extracted from heat stored in the earth. This geothermal energy originates from the original formation of the planet, from radioactive decay of minerals, and from solar energy absorbed at the surface. It has been used for space heating and bathing since ancient roman times, but is now better known for generating electricity.

   a. Geothermal gradient   b. Geothermal desalination
   c. Geothermal power   d. Geothermal heat pump

19. _____ is water located beneath the ground surface in soil pore spaces and in the fractures of lithologic formations. A unit of rock or an unconsolidated deposit is called an aquifer when it can yield a usable quantity of water. The depth at which soil pore spaces or fractures and voids in rock become completely saturated with water is called the water table.

   a. Groundwater   b. 1700 Cascadia earthquake
   c. Depression focused recharge   d. 1509 Istanbul earthquake

20. The _____ is the earliest of three geologic eras of the Phanerozoic eon. The _____ spanned from roughly 542 to 251 million years ago (ICS, 2004), and is subdivided into six geologic periods; from oldest to youngest they are: the Cambrian, Ordovician, Silurian, Devonian, Carboniferous, and Permian.

The _____ covers the time from the first appearance of abundant, soft-shelled fossils to the time when the continents were beginning to be dominated by large, relatively sophisticated reptiles and modern plants. The lower (oldest) boundary was classically set at the first appearance of creatures known as trilobites and archeocyathids.

   a. 1700 Cascadia earthquake   b. 1509 Istanbul earthquake
   c. 1703 Genroku earthquake   d. Paleozoic

21. In archaeology, the _____ was the stage in the development of any people in which tools and weapons whose main ingredient was iron were prominent. The adoption of this material often coincided with other changes in society, including differing agricultural practices, religious beliefs and artistic styles.

In history, the _____ is the last principal period in the three-age system for classifying prehistoric societies, preceded by the Bronze Age.

   a. AL 129-1   b. AL 333
   c. AASHTO Soil Classification System   d. Iron Age

22. A _____ is any metal that is found in its metallic form, either pure or as an alloy, in nature. Metals that can be found as native deposits include bismuth, cadmium, chromium, indium, iron, nickel, tellurium, tin, titanium, and zinc, as well as two groups of metals: the gold group, and the platinum group. The gold group consists of gold, copper, lead, mercury, and silver.

   a. 1509 Istanbul earthquake   b. Native metal
   c. 1703 Genroku earthquake   d. 1700 Cascadia earthquake

23. In geology, a _____ deposit or _____ is an accumulation of valuable minerals formed by deposition of dense mineral phases in a trap site. Types of _____ deposits include alluvium, eluvium, beach placers, and paleoplacers.

Chapter 18. Human Use of the Earth's Resources

Typical locations for alluvial _____ deposits are on the inside bends of rivers and creeks, in natural hollows, at the break of slope on a stream, the base of an escarpment, waterfall or other barrier, within sand dunes, beach profiles or in gravel beds.

a. 1703 Genroku earthquake
c. 1509 Istanbul earthquake
b. Placer
d. 1700 Cascadia earthquake

24. _____ are the materials left over after the process of separating the valuable fraction from the worthless fraction of an ore.

_____ represent external costs of mining. As mining techniques and the price of minerals improve, it is not unusual for _____ to be reprocessed using new methods, or more thoroughly with old methods, to recover additional minerals.

a. 1703 Genroku earthquake
c. 1509 Istanbul earthquake
b. 1700 Cascadia earthquake
d. Tailings

25. _____ is the most important aluminium ore. It consists largely of the minerals gibbsite Al(OH)$_3$, boehmite >γ-AlO(OH), and diaspore >α-AlO(OH), together with the iron oxides goethite and hematite, the clay mineral kaolinite and small amounts of anatase TiO$_2$. It was named after the village Les Baux in southern France, where it was first discovered in 1821 by the geologist Pierre Berthier.

a. Bauxite
c. 1703 Genroku earthquake
b. 1509 Istanbul earthquake
d. 1700 Cascadia earthquake

26. _____ is a naturally occurring material composed primarily of fine-grained minerals, which show plasticity through a variable range of water content, and which can be hardened when dried and/or fired. _____ deposits are mostly composed of _____ minerals (phyllosilicate minerals), minerals which impart plasticity and harden when fired and/or dried, and variable amounts of water trapped in the mineral structure by polar attraction. Organic materials which do not impart plasticity may also be a part of _____ deposits.

a. 1703 Genroku earthquake
c. 1509 Istanbul earthquake
b. 1700 Cascadia earthquake
d. Clay

27. _____ are hydrous aluminium phyllosilicates, sometimes with variable amounts of iron, magnesium, alkali metals, alkaline earths and other cations. Clays have structures similar to the micas and therefore form flat hexagonal sheets.
_____ are common weathering products (including weathering of feldspar) and low temperature hydrothermal alteration products.

a. 1700 Cascadia earthquake
c. 1509 Istanbul earthquake
b. Clay minerals
d. 1703 Genroku earthquake

28. _____ forms a group of medium-grade metamorphic rocks, chiefly notable for the preponderance of lamellar minerals such as micas, chlorite, talc, hornblende, graphite, and others. Quartz often occurs in drawn-out grains to such an extent that a particular form called quartz _____ is produced. By definition, _____ contains more than 50% platy and elongated minerals, often finely interleaved with quartz and feldspar.

Chapter 18. Human Use of the Earth's Resources

a. Mylonite
b. Jadeitite
c. Porphyroclast
d. Schist

29. _____ is a fine-grained, foliated, homogeneous metamorphic rock derived from an original shale-type sedimentary rock composed of clay or volcanic ash through low grade regional metamorphism. The result is a foliated rock in which the foliation may not correspond to the original sedimentary layering. _____ is frequently grey in colour especially when seen en masse covering roofs.
   a. Geothermobarometry
   b. Shock metamorphism
   c. Facies
   d. Slate

30. _____ or white asbestos is the most commonly encountered form of asbestos, accounting for approximately 95% of the asbestos in place in the United States and a similar proportion in other countries. It is a soft, fibrous silicate mineral in the serpentine group of phyllosilicates: as such, it is distinct from other asbestiform minerals in the amphibole group. Its idealized chemical formula is $Mg_3(Si_2O_5)(OH)_4$, in which some of the magnesium ions may be substituted by iron or other cations.
   a. 1509 Istanbul earthquake
   b. 1700 Cascadia earthquake
   c. 1703 Genroku earthquake
   d. Chrysotile

31. A _____ in petrology or mineralogy is a secondary structure, generally spherical or irregularly rounded in shape. They are typically solid replacement bodies of chert or iron oxides formed during diagenesis of a sedimentary rock. They may be hollow as geodes or vugs or filled with crystals and intricate geometric shrinkage patterns as in septarian nodules.
   a. 1703 Genroku earthquake
   b. 1700 Cascadia earthquake
   c. 1509 Istanbul earthquake
   d. Nodule

32. _____ is a silvery white and ductile member of the boron group of chemical elements. It has the symbol Al; its atomic number is 13. It is not soluble in water under normal circumstances. _____ is the most abundant metal in the Earth's crust, and the third most abundant element therein, after oxygen and silicon. It makes up about 8% by weight of the Earth'e;s solid surface.
   a. AL 333
   b. Aluminum
   c. AASHTO Soil Classification System
   d. AL 129-1

Chapter 19. A Brief History of Earth and Its Life Forms

1. The _____ is a chronologic schema (or idealized model) relating stratigraphy to time that is used by geologists, paleontologists and other earth scientists to describe the timing and relationships between events that have occurred during the history of the Earth. The table of geologic time spans presented here agrees with the dates and nomenclature proposed by the International Commission on Stratigraphy, and uses the standard color codes of the United States Geological Survey.

Evidence from radiometric dating indicates that the Earth is about 4.570 billion years old.

   a. Geologic time scale
   b. 1700 Cascadia earthquake
   c. 1509 Istanbul earthquake
   d. 1703 Genroku earthquake

2. The _____ is a rock outcrop of Archaean tonalite gneiss in the Slave craton in Northwest Territories, Canada. The rock exposed in the outcrop formed just over four billion (4×10^9) years ago; an age based on radiometric dating of zircon crystals at 4.03 Ga, which were the oldest rocks in the world at that time. It was the oldest known rock outcrop in the world until a McGill University team reported a 4.28 billion year old outcrop on the eastern shores of Hudson Bay, 40 kilometres south of Inukjuak, Quebec, Canada.

   a. AL 129-1
   b. AASHTO Soil Classification System
   c. AL 333
   d. Acasta Gneiss

3. The _____, is a geologic eon before the Proterozoic and Paleoproterozoic, before 2.5 Ga (billion years ago, or 2,500 Ma.) Instead of being based on stratigraphy, this date is defined chronometrically. The lower boundary (starting point) has not been officially recognized by the International Commission on Stratigraphy, but it is usually set to 3.8 Ga, at the end of the Hadean eon.

   a. AASHTO Soil Classification System
   b. AL 333
   c. Archean
   d. AL 129-1

4. _____, is a phylum of bacteria that obtain their energy through photosynthesis. The name '_____' comes from the color of the bacteria. They are a significant component of the marine nitrogen cycle and an important primary producer in many areas of the ocean, but are also found in habitats other than the marine environment; in particular _____ are known to occur in both freshwater, hypersaline inland lakes and in arid areas where they are a major component of biological soil crusts.

Stromatolites of fossilized oxygen-producing _____ have been found from 2.8 billion years ago. The ability of _____ to perform oxygenic photosynthesis is thought to have converted the early reducing atmosphere into an oxidizing one, which dramatically changed the composition of life forms on Earth by provoking an explosion of biodiversity and leading to the near-extinction of oxygen-intolerant organisms.

   a. 1700 Cascadia earthquake
   b. 1509 Istanbul earthquake
   c. 1703 Genroku earthquake
   d. Cyanobacteria

5. _____ are the preserved remains or traces of animals, plants, and other organisms from the remote past. The totality of _____, both discovered and undiscovered, and their placement in fossiliferous rock formations and sedimentary layers (strata) is known as the fossil record. The study of _____ across geological time, how they were formed, and the evolutionary relationships between taxa (phylogeny) are some of the most important functions of the science of paleontology.

   a. Fossils
   b. 1509 Istanbul earthquake
   c. 1700 Cascadia earthquake
   d. 1703 Genroku earthquake

Chapter 19. A Brief History of Earth and Its Life Forms

6. _____ is a common and widely distributed type of rock formed by high-grade regional metamorphic processes from pre-existing formations that were originally either igneous or sedimentary rocks. Gneissic rocks are usually medium to coarse foliated and largely recrystallized but do not carry large quantities of micas, chlorite or other platy minerals. Gneisses that are metamorphosed igneous rocks or their equivalent are termed granite gneisses, diorite gneisses, etc.
   - a. 1509 Istanbul earthquake
   - b. Gneiss
   - c. 1703 Genroku earthquake
   - d. 1700 Cascadia earthquake

7. The _____ is the geologic eon before the Archean. It started at Earth's formation about 4.6 billion years ago (4,600 Ma), and ended roughly 3.8 billion years ago, though the latter date varies according to different sources.
   - a. 1509 Istanbul earthquake
   - b. Hadean
   - c. 1703 Genroku earthquake
   - d. 1700 Cascadia earthquake

8. The _____ Eon is the current eon in the geologic timescale, and the one during which abundant animal life has existed. It covers roughly 545 million years and goes back to the time when diverse hard-shelled animals first appeared.
   - a. 1703 Genroku earthquake
   - b. Phanerozoic
   - c. 1509 Istanbul earthquake
   - d. 1700 Cascadia earthquake

9. The _____ is an informal name for the supereon comprising the eons of the geologic timescale that came before the current Phanerozoic eon. It spans from the formation of Earth around 4500 Mya (million years ago) to the evolution of abundant macroscopic hard-shelled animals, which marked the beginning of the Cambrian, the first period of the first era of the Phanerozoic eon, some 542 Mya. It is named after the Roman name for Wales - Cambria - where rocks from this age were first studied.
   - a. 1509 Istanbul earthquake
   - b. 1700 Cascadia earthquake
   - c. 1703 Genroku earthquake
   - d. Precambrian

10. The _____ is a geological eon representing a period before the first abundant complex life on Earth. The _____ extended from 2500 Ma to 542.0 >± 1.0 Ma (million years ago), and is the most recent part of the old, informally named 'e;Precambrian'e; time.

The Proterozoic consists of 3 geologic eras, from oldest to youngest:

- Paleoproterozoic
- Mesoproterozoic
- Neoproterozoic

The well-identified events were:

- The transition to an oxygenated atmosphere during the Mesoproterozoic.
- Several glaciations, including the hypothesized Snowball Earth during the Cryogenian period in the late Neoproterozoic.
- The Ediacaran Period (635 to 542 Ma) which is characterized by the evolution of abundant soft-bodied multicellular organisms.

Chapter 19. A Brief History of Earth and Its Life Forms 133

The geoloic record of the Proterozoic is much better than that for the preceding Archean. In contrast to the deep-water deposits of the Archean, the Proterozoic features many strata that were laid down in extensive shallow epicontinental seas; furthermore, many of these rocks are less metamorphosed than Archean-age ones, and plenty are unaltered.

- a. 1703 Genroku earthquake
- b. 1700 Cascadia earthquake
- c. 1509 Istanbul earthquake
- d. Proterozoic Eon

11. _____ are layered accretionary structures formed in shallow water by the trapping, binding and cementation of sedimentary grains by biofilms of microorganisms, especially cyanobacteria (commonly known as blue-green algae.)

A variety of stromatolite morphologies exist including conical, stratiform, branching, domal, and columnar types. _____ occur widely in the fossil record of the Precambrian, but are rare today.

- a. 1700 Cascadia earthquake
- b. 1703 Genroku earthquake
- c. 1509 Istanbul earthquake
- d. Stromatolites

12. Two important classifications of weathering processes exist -- physical and _____. Mechanical or physical weathering involves the breakdown of rocks and soils through direct contact with atmospheric conditions, such as heat, water, ice and pressure. The second classification, _____, involves the direct effect of atmospheric chemicals or biologically produced chemicals (also known as biological weathering) in the breakdown of rocks, soils and minerals.
- a. 1700 Cascadia earthquake
- b. 1703 Genroku earthquake
- c. 1509 Istanbul earthquake
- d. Chemical weathering

13. _____ is the decomposition of Earth rocks, soils and their minerals through direct contact with the planet's atmosphere. _____ occurs in situ, or 'with no movement', and thus should not be confused with erosion, which involves the movement of rocks and minerals by agents such as water, ice, wind and gravity.

Two important classifications of _____ processes exist -- physical and chemical _____.

- a. 1509 Istanbul earthquake
- b. 1700 Cascadia earthquake
- c. 1703 Genroku earthquake
- d. Weathering

14. _____ - also known as greenstone - is a general field petrologic term applied to metamorphic and/or altered mafic volcanic rock. The green is due to abundant green chlorite, actinolite and epidote minerals that dominate the rock. However, basalts may remain quite black if primary pyroxene does not revert to chlorite or actinolite.
- a. Greenschist
- b. Quartzite
- c. Cataclasite
- d. Granulites

15. The _____ -- also called the Laurentian Plateau, or Bouclier Canadien -- is a massive geological shield covered by a thin layer of soil that forms the nucleus of the North American or Laurentia craton. It has a deep, common, joined bedrock region in eastern and central Canada and stretches North from the Great Lakes to the Arctic Ocean, covering over half of Canada; it also extends south into the northern reaches of the United States. Population is scarce, and industrial development is minimal, although the region has a large hydroelectric power potential.

a. Canadian Shield
c. Great Artesian Basin
b. Quaternary
d. Sahara pump theory

16. A _____ is generally a large area of exposed Precambrian crystalline igneous and high-grade metamorphic rocks that form tectonically stable areas. In all cases, the age of these rocks is greater than 570 million years and sometimes dates back 2 to 3.5 billion years. They have been little affected by tectonic events following the end of the Precambrian Era, and are relatively flat regions where mountain building, faulting, and other tectonic processes are greatly diminished compared with the activity that occurs at the margins of the shields and the boundaries between tectonic plates.
   a. 1703 Genroku earthquake
   b. 1700 Cascadia earthquake
   c. 1509 Istanbul earthquake
   d. Shield

17. The _____ is a geologic period and system of the Paleozoic era spanning from >416 to 359.2 million years ago (ICS, 2004.).

During the _____ Period, which occurred in the Paleozoic era, the first fish evolved legsand started to walk on land as tetrapods around 365 Ma.

   a. Gogo Formation
   b. 1509 Istanbul earthquake
   c. Xitun Formation
   d. Devonian

18. _____ are a range of low hills in the northern part of the Flinders Ranges of South Australia, around 650 km north of Adelaide. The area has many old copper and silver mines from mining activity in the late 19th century. The hills also contain fossils of early life forms, the Ediacaran biota (lagerst>ätte), and have given their name to the Ediacaran geological period.
   a. AL 129-1
   b. AL 333
   c. AASHTO Soil Classification System
   d. Ediacara Hills

19. The _____ Period is the last geological period of the Neoproterozoic Era and of the Proterozoic Eon, immediately preceding the Cambrian Period, the first period of the Paleozoic Era and of the Phanerozoic Eon. Its status as an official geological period was ratified in 2004 by the International Union of Geological Sciences (IUGS), making it the first new geological period declared in 120 years. The type section is in the Flinders Ranges in South Australia.
   a. AL 333
   b. Ediacaran
   c. AASHTO Soil Classification System
   d. AL 129-1

20. The _____ is the first geological period of the Phanerozoic eon, lasting from 542 ± 0.3 million years ago to 488.3 ± 1.7 million years ago (ICS, 2004); it is succeeded by the Ordovician. Its subdivisions, and indeed its base, are somewhat in flux. The period was established by Adam Sedgwick, who named it after Cambria, the classical name for Wales, where Britain's _____ rocks are best exposed.
   a. 1509 Istanbul earthquake
   b. 1703 Genroku earthquake
   c. 1700 Cascadia earthquake
   d. Cambrian

21. The _____ is a geologic period and system, the second of six of the Paleozoic era, and covers the time between 488.3>±1.7 to 443.7>±1.5 million years ago (ICS, 2004.) It follows the Cambrian period and is followed by the Silurian period. The _____ was defined by Charles Lapworth in 1879, to resolve a dispute between followers of Adam Sedgwick and Roderick Murchison, who were placing the same rock beds in northern Wales into the Cambrian and Silurian periods respectively.

Chapter 19. A Brief History of Earth and Its Life Forms

a. AL 129-1
b. AL 333
c. AASHTO Soil Classification System
d. Ordovician

22. The _____ is the earliest of three geologic eras of the Phanerozoic eon. The _____ spanned from roughly 542 to 251 million years ago (ICS, 2004), and is subdivided into six geologic periods; from oldest to youngest they are: the Cambrian, Ordovician, Silurian, Devonian, Carboniferous, and Permian.

The _____ covers the time from the first appearance of abundant, soft-shelled fossils to the time when the continents were beginning to be dominated by large, relatively sophisticated reptiles and modern plants. The lower (oldest) boundary was classically set at the first appearance of creatures known as trilobites and archeocyathids.

a. Paleozoic
b. 1703 Genroku earthquake
c. 1509 Istanbul earthquake
d. 1700 Cascadia earthquake

23. _____ was the supercontinent that is theorized to have existed during the Paleozoic and Mesozoic eras about 250 million years ago, before the component continents were separated into their current configuration.

The name was first used by the German originator of the continental drift theory, Alfred Wegener, in the 1920 edition of his book The Origin of Continents and Oceans , in which a postulated supercontinent _____ played a key role.

The single enormous ocean which surrounded Pangaea is known as Panthalassa.

a. 1700 Cascadia earthquake
b. 1703 Genroku earthquake
c. Pangea
d. 1509 Istanbul earthquake

24. _____ is the naturally occurring, unconsolidated or loose covering on the Earth's surface. _____ is composed of particles of broken rock that have been altered by chemical, biological and environmental processes including weathering and erosion. _____ is different from its parent rock(s) source(s), altered by interactions between the lithosphere, hydrosphere, atmosphere, and the biosphere.

a. 1700 Cascadia earthquake
b. Soil
c. Topsoil
d. 1509 Istanbul earthquake

25. A marine _____ is a geologic event during which sea level rises relative to the land and the shoreline moves toward higher ground, resulting in flooding. They can be caused either by the land sinking or the ocean basins filling with water (or decreasing in capacity.) Transgresssions and regressions may be caused by tectonic events such as orogenies, severe climate change such as ice ages or isostatic adjustments following removal of ice or sediment load.

a. Deposition
b. Downcutting
c. Diagenesis
d. Transgression

26. _____ was a supercontinent that most recently existed as a part of the split of the Pangaean supercontinent in the late Mesozoic era. It included most of the landmasses which make up today's continents of the northern hemisphere, chiefly Laurentia (the name given to the North American craton), Baltica, Siberia, Kazakhstania, and the North China and East China cratons.

a. 1509 Istanbul earthquake
b. 1700 Cascadia earthquake
c. 1703 Genroku earthquake
d. Laurasia

27. The _____ was an ocean that existed in the Neoproterozoic and Paleozoic eras of the geologic timescale (between 600 and 400 million years ago.) The _____ was situated in the southern hemisphere, between the paleocontinents of Laurentia, Baltica and Avalonia. The ocean disappeared with the Caledonian, Taconic and Acadian orogenies, when these three continents joined to form one big landmass called Laurussia.
   a. AASHTO Soil Classification System
   b. AL 129-1
   c. AL 333
   d. Iapetus Ocean

28. The _____ is a geologic subperiod and stratigraphic subsystem of the Carboniferous Period. It is the later subperiod of the Carboniferous, lasting from roughly 318.1>± 1.3 to 299>± 0.8 Ma (million years ago.) As with most other geochronologic units, the rock beds that define the _____ are well identified, but the exact date of the start and end are uncertain by a few million years.
   a. Dinantian
   b. Mississippian
   c. Calciferous sandstone
   d. Pennsylvanian

29. The _____ is a mountain-building episode that extensively deformed Paleozoic rocks of the Great Basin in Nevada and western Utah during Late Devonian and Early Mississippian time. In the late Devonian, the Antler volcanic island arc terrane collided with was then the west coast of North America in the vicinity of today's border between Utah and Nevada.
   a. Alleghenian orogeny
   b. Antler orogeny
   c. Orogeny
   d. Orogenesis

30. _____ , originally Gondwanaland is the name given to a southern precursor-supercontinent and then as a remnant separated from Laurasia 180->200 million years ago during the breakup of the Pangaea supercontinent that existed about 500 to 200 Ma ago into two large segments. While the corresponding northern hemisphere continent Laurasia moved further north, the nearly equal in area _____ included most of the landmasses in today's southern hemisphere, including Antarctica, South America, Africa, Madagascar, Australia-New Guinea, and New Zealand, as well as Arabia and the Indian subcontinent, which have now moved into the Northern Hemisphere.
   a. 1700 Cascadia earthquake
   b. 1509 Istanbul earthquake
   c. 1703 Genroku earthquake
   d. Gondwana

31. The _____ was a period of mountain building in western North America, which started in the Late Cretaceous, 70 to 80 million years ago, and ended 35 to 55 million years ago. The exact duration and ages of beginning and end of the orogeny are in dispute, as is the cause. The _____ occurred in a series of pulses, with quiescent phases intervening. The major feature that was created by this orogeny was the Rocky Mountains, but evidence of this orogeny can be found from Alaska to northern Mexico, with the easternmost extent of the mountain-building represented by the Black Hills of South Dakota.
   a. Nevadan orogeny
   b. Kaikoura Orogeny
   c. Laramide orogeny
   d. Sevier orogeny

Chapter 19. A Brief History of Earth and Its Life Forms

32. The _____ was a major mountain building event that took place along the western edge of ancient North America between the Mid to Late Jurassic (between about 180 and 140 million years ago.) The _____ was the first of three major mountain building episodes to transform Western North America between the Late Mesozoic and Early Cenozoic Eras, the latter two being the Sevier and Laramide orogeny, chronologically. Much like the two orogenies that followed, the Nevadan was caused by the subduction of oceanic lithosphere at a subduction zone running along the edge of the North American continent.
    a. Sevier orogeny
    b. Kaikoura Orogeny
    c. Nevadan orogeny
    d. Pan-African orogeny

33. The _____ was a mountain-building event that affected western North America from Canada to the north to Mexico to the south. This orogeny was the result of convergent boundary tectonism between approximately 140 million years (Ma) ago, and 50 Ma. This orogeny was produced by the collision of the oceanic Farallon Plate and Kula Plate, predecessors of the Pacific Plate, and their subduction underneath the continental North American Plate. The _____ was preceded by several other mountain-building events including the Nevadan orogeny, the Sonoman orogeny, and the Antler orogeny, and partially overlapped in time and space with the Laramide orogeny.
    a. Trans-Hudson orogeny
    b. Kaikoura Orogeny
    c. Sevier orogeny
    d. Pan-African orogeny

34. The _____ has been defined as a Late Permian to Early Triassic tectonic event that deformed Upper Paleozoic oceanic facies rocks and emplaced them over the Upper Paleozoic margin of northern Nevada.
    a. Sonoma orogeny
    b. Rivera Plate
    c. Farallon Plate
    d. Fault trace

35. _____ refers to natural mountain building, and may be studied as a tectonic structural event, (b) as a geographical event, and (c) a chronological event. Orogenic events (a) cause distinctive structural phenomena and related tectonic activity, (b) affect certain regions of rocks and crust, and (c) happen within a specific period of time.
    a. Orogeny
    b. Antler orogeny
    c. Alice Springs Orogeny
    d. Orogenesis

36. The _____ Era is one of three geologic eras of the Phanerozoic eon. The division of time into eras dates back to Giovanni Arduino, in the 18th century, although his original name for the era now called the '_____' was 'Secondary' (making the modern era the 'Tertiary'.)

The _____ was a time of tectonic, climatic and evolutionary activity. The continents gradually shifted from a state of connectedness into their present configuration; the drifting provided for speciation and other important evolutionary developments.

    a. 1509 Istanbul earthquake
    b. 1700 Cascadia earthquake
    c. Mesozoic
    d. 1703 Genroku earthquake

37. _____ is one of the two orders, or basic divisions of dinosaurs. In 1888, Harry Seeley classified dinosaurs into two orders, based on their hip structure. Saurischians ('lizard-hipped') are distinguished from the ornithischians ('bird-hipped') by retaining the ancestral configuration of bones in the hip.
    a. 1509 Istanbul earthquake
    b. 1700 Cascadia earthquake
    c. 1703 Genroku earthquake
    d. Saurischia

Chapter 19. A Brief History of Earth and Its Life Forms

38. _____ describes the large scale motions of Earth's lithosphere. The theory encompasses the older concepts of continental drift, developed during the first decades of the 20th century by Alfred Wegener, and seafloor spreading, understood during the 1960s.

The outermost part of the Earth's interior is made up of two layers: the lithosphere and the asthenosphere.

- a. Thrust fault
- b. Plate tectonics
- c. Copperbelt Province
- d. Subduction

39. A _____ is an opening in a planet's surface or crust, which allows hot, molten rock, ash, and gases to escape from below the surface. Volcanic activity involving the extrusion of rock tends to form mountains or features like mountains over a period of time.
- a. 1703 Genroku earthquake
- b. Volcano
- c. 1509 Istanbul earthquake
- d. 1700 Cascadia earthquake

40. _____ is a geologic term for a type of topography characterized by a series of separate and parallel mountain ranges with broad valleys interposed, extending over a more or less wide area. It is typified by the topography found in the Great Basin in the western United States, which is part of a larger regional topography known as the _____ Province. _____ topography results from crustal extension.
- a. Bediasite
- b. Cap carbonates
- c. Cross-cutting relationships
- d. Basin and Range

41. The _____ is a large geologic province which includes parts of the southwestern United States and northwestern Mexico, typified by basin and range topography.

The topography of the _____ is a result of crustal extension within this part of the North American Plate. The cause of this extension is as yet not fully understood, although several hypotheses have been offered. The crust here has been stretched up to 100% of its original width. In fact, the crust underneath the _____, especially under the Great Basin, is some of the thinnest in the world.

- a. Canadian Shield
- b. Yilgarn Craton
- c. Basin and Range province
- d. Musgrave Block

42. The _____ Era, is the most recent of the three classic geological eras and covers the period from 65.5 million years ago to the present. It is marked by the Cretaceous-Tertiary extinction event at the end of the Cretaceous that saw the demise of the last non-avian dinosaurs and the end of the Mesozoic Era. The _____ era is ongoing.
- a. 1700 Cascadia earthquake
- b. 1509 Istanbul earthquake
- c. Cenozoic
- d. 1703 Genroku earthquake

43. The _____ is a physiographic region of the Intermontane Plateaus, roughly centered on the Four Corners region of the southwestern United States. The province covers an area of 337,000 km^2 within western Colorado, northwestern New Mexico, southern and eastern Utah, and northern Arizona. About 90% of the area is drained by the Colorado River and its main tributaries; the Green, San Juan and Little Colorado.

Chapter 19. A Brief History of Earth and Its Life Forms

Development of the province has in large part been influenced by structural features in its oldest rocks. Part of the Wasatch Line and its various faults form the western edge of the province. Faults that run parallel to the Wasatch Fault that lies along the Wasatch Range form the boundaries between the plateaus in the High Plateaus Section. The Uinta Basin, Uncompahgre Uplift, and the Paradox Basin were also created by movement along structural weaknesses in the region's oldest rock.

a. Colorado Plateau
b. 1509 Istanbul earthquake
c. 1703 Genroku earthquake
d. 1700 Cascadia earthquake

44. The _____ epoch (55.8 >± 0.2 - 33.9 >± 0.1 Ma) is a major division of the geologic timescale and the second epoch of the Palaeogene period in the Cenozoic era. The _____ spans the time from the end of the Paleocene epoch to the beginning of the Oligocene epoch. The start of the _____ is marked by the emergence of the first modern mammals.

a. AL 333
b. Eocene
c. AASHTO Soil Classification System
d. AL 129-1

45. The _____ was an ancient oceanic plate, which began subducting under the west coast of the North American Plate-- then located in modern Utah-- as Pangaea broke apart during the Jurassic period. It is named for the Farallon Islands which are located just west of San Francisco, California.

Over time the central part of the _____ was completely subducted under the southwestern part of the North American Plate. The remains of the _____ are the Juan de Fuca, Explorer and Gorda Plates, subducting under the northern part of the North American Plate, the Cocos Plate subducting under Central America and the Nazca Plate subducting under the South American Plate.

a. Cocos Plate
b. Rivera Plate
c. Fault trace
d. Farallon plate

46. The _____ is an oceanic tectonic plate beneath the Pacific Ocean.

To the north the easterly side is a divergent boundary with the Explorer Plate, the Juan de Fuca Plate and the Gorda Plate forming respectively the Explorer Ridge, the Juan de Fuca Ridge and the Gorda Ridge. In the middle the easterly side is a transform boundary with the North American Plate along the San Andreas Fault and a boundary with the Cocos Plate.

a. New Hebrides Plate
b. Bird's Head Plate
c. Niuafo'ou Plate
d. Pacific plate

47. The _____ is a a term for a geologic period 65 million to 1.8 million years ago. The _____ covered the time span between the superseded Secondary period and an out-of-date definition of the Quaternary period. The period began with the demise of the non-avian dinosaurs in the Cretaceous-_____ extinction event, at start of the Cenozoic era, spanning to beginning of the most recent Ice Age, at the end of the Pliocene epoch.

Chapter 19. A Brief History of Earth and Its Life Forms

a. Historical geology
b. Suspended load
c. Rockall
d. Tertiary

48. The _____ was an ocean that existed between the continents of Gondwana and Laurasia during the Mesozoic era before the opening of the Indian Ocean.

About 250 million years ago, during the Triassic, a new ocean began forming in the southern end of the Paleo-_____. A rift formed along the northern continental shelf of Southern Pangaea (Gondwana.) Over the next 60 million years, that piece of shelf, known as Cimmeria, traveled north, pushing the floor of the Paleo-_____ under the eastern end of Northern Pangaea (Laurasia). The _____ formed between Cimmeria and Gondwana, directly over where the Paleo-Tethys used to be.

a. 1703 Genroku earthquake
b. 1509 Istanbul earthquake
c. Tethys Ocean
d. 1700 Cascadia earthquake

49. The _____ is a geologic period and system that extends from about 251 to 199 Mya (million years ago.) As the first period of the Mesozoic Era, the _____ follows the Permian and is followed by the Jurassic. Both the start and end of the _____ are marked by major extinction events.

a. Triassic
b. Rhaetian
c. 1509 Istanbul earthquake
d. 1700 Cascadia earthquake

50. The _____ is an oceanic tectonic plate beneath the Pacific Ocean off the west coast of Central America which rides upon it.

The _____ is created by sea floor spreading along the East Pacific Rise and the Cocos Ridge, specifically in a complicated area geologists call the Cocos-Nazca spreading system. From the rise the plate is pushed eastward and pushed or dragged (perhaps both) under the less dense overriding Caribbean Plate, in the process called subduction.

a. Fault trace
b. Cocos plate
c. Rivera Plate
d. Sonoma orogeny

51. An _____ is the result of a sudden release of energy in the Earth's crust that creates seismic waves. They are recorded with a seismometer or the related and mostly obsolete Richter magnitude, with a magnitude 3 or lower _____ being mostly imperceptible and magnitude 7 causing serious damage over large areas.

a. AL 333
b. Earthquake
c. AASHTO Soil Classification System
d. AL 129-1

52. The _____ is a continental transform fault that runs a length of roughly 800 miles (1,300 km) through California in the United States. The fault's motion is right-lateral strike-slip (horizontal motion.) It forms the tectonic boundary between the Pacific Plate and the North American Plate.

a. 1509 Istanbul earthquake
b. 1703 Genroku earthquake
c. 1700 Cascadia earthquake
d. San Andreas fault

Chapter 19. A Brief History of Earth and Its Life Forms

53. In geology, a _____ or _____ line is a planar fracture in rock in which the rock on one side of the fracture has moved with respect to the rock on the other side. Large faults within the Earth's crust are the result of differential or shear motion and active _____ zones are the causal locations of most earthquakes. Earthquakes are caused by energy release during rapid slippage along a _____.
   - a. 1700 Cascadia earthquake
   - b. Fault
   - c. 1509 Istanbul earthquake
   - d. 1703 Genroku earthquake

54. The _____ is a name given in the late 19th century by British explorer John Walter Gregory to the continuous geographic trough, approximately 6,000 kilometres (3,700 mi) in length, that runs from northern Syria in Southwest Asia to central Mozambique in East Africa. The name continues in some usages, although it is today considered geologically imprecise as it includes what are today regarded as separate, since 1869 due to the Suez Canal Company project, although related rift and fault systems. Today, the term is most often used to refer to the valley of the East African Rift, the divergent plate boundary which extends from the Afar Triple Junction southward across eastern Africa, and is in the process of splitting the African Plate into two new separate plates.
   - a. 1703 Genroku earthquake
   - b. Great Rift Valley
   - c. 1509 Istanbul earthquake
   - d. 1700 Cascadia earthquake

55. The _____ is a geological epoch which began approximately 11‰700 years ago (10‰000 ^{14}C years ago). According to traditional geological thinking, the _____ continues to the present. The _____ is part of the Neogene and Quaternary periods.
   - a. 1700 Cascadia earthquake
   - b. Holocene
   - c. Neoglaciation
   - d. 1509 Istanbul earthquake

56. _____ is an extinct species of the genus Homo, believed to have been the first hominin to leave Africa.

   _____ originally migrated from Africa during the Early Pleistocene, possibly as a result of the operation of the Saharan pump, around 2.0 million years ago, and dispersed throughout most of the Old World.

   - a. 1700 Cascadia earthquake
   - b. 1509 Istanbul earthquake
   - c. 1703 Genroku earthquake
   - d. Homo erectus

57. The general term '_____' or, more precisely, 'glacial age' denotes a geological period of long-term reduction in the temperature of the Earth's surface and atmosphere, resulting in an expansion of continental ice sheets, polar ice sheets and alpine glaciers. Within a long-term _____, individual pulses of extra cold climate are termed 'glaciations'. Glaciologically, _____ implies the presence of extensive ice sheets in the northern and southern hemispheres; by this definition we are still in an _____.
   - a. Ice Age
   - b. AASHTO Soil Classification System
   - c. AL 333
   - d. AL 129-1

58. The _____ is an extinct member of the Homo genus that is known from Pleistocene specimens found in Europe and parts of western and central Asia. Neanderthals are either classified as a subspecies of humans (Homo sapiens neanderthalensis) or as a separate species (Homo neanderthalensis.) The first proto-_____ traits appeared in Europe as early as 600,000-350,000 years ago.
   - a. 1700 Cascadia earthquake
   - b. 1509 Istanbul earthquake
   - c. Neanderthal
   - d. 1703 Genroku earthquake

Chapter 19. A Brief History of Earth and Its Life Forms

59. The _____ is the epoch from 1.8 million to 11550 years BP covering the world's recent period of repeated glaciations. The _____ epoch follows the Pliocene epoch and is followed by the Holocene epoch. The _____ is the third epoch of the Neogene period or 6th epoch of the Cenozoic Era. The end of the _____ corresponds with the retreat of the last continental glacier. It also corresponds with the end of the Paleolithic age used in archaeology.

   a. Pleistocene
   b. Sicilian Stage
   c. Tyrrhenian
   d. Late Pleistocene

60. The _____ Period is the geologic time period after the Neogene Period, spanning 1.805 +/- 0.005 million years ago to the present. The _____ includes two geologic epochs: the Pleistocene and the Holocene Epoch.

There is an ongoing debate of the status of _____ -- a recent proposal from International Commission on Stratigraphy (ICS) was to make _____ a subperiod under Neogene, but that was retracted after criticism from International Union for _____ Research (INQUA), so instead ICS and INQUA agreed to erect _____ as an Era, above Neogene, and to place the base for _____ at 2.588 >± 3.005, the base for Gelasian Stage.

   a. Canadian Shield
   b. Musgrave Block
   c. Gawler craton
   d. Quaternary

61. In geology, a _____ is a place where the Earth's crust and lithosphere are being pulled apart and is an example of extensional tectonics.

Typical _____ features are a central linear downdropped fault segment, called a graben, with parallel normal faulting and _____-flank uplifts on either side forming a _____ valley, where the _____ remains above sea level. The axis of the _____ area commonly contains volcanic rocks and active volcanism is a part of many, but not all active _____ systems.

   a. Rift
   b. 1509 Istanbul earthquake
   c. 1700 Cascadia earthquake
   d. 1703 Genroku earthquake

62. _____ is the geological process by which material is added to a landform or land mass. Fluids such as wind and water, as well as sediment gravity flows, transport previously eroded sediment, which, at the loss of enough kinetic energy in the fluid, is deposited, building up layers of sediment.

_____ occurs when the forces responsible for sediment transportation are no longer sufficient to overcome the forces of particle weight and friction, which resist motion.

   a. Deposition
   b. Seafloor spreading
   c. Permineralization
   d. Headward erosion

ANSWER KEY

Chapter 1
1. c 2. d 3. d 4. a 5. d 6. c 7. d 8. d 9. b 10. b
11. d 12. c 13. d 14. d 15. b 16. d 17. d 18. a 19. d 20. b
21. a 22. d 23. c 24. d 25. c 26. b 27. c 28. b 29. c 30. d
31. c 32. c 33. a 34. d 35. d 36. d 37. d 38. d 39. d 40. b
41. a 42. a 43. d 44. d 45. b 46. c 47. b

Chapter 2
1. d 2. b 3. a 4. d 5. b 6. d 7. d 8. d 9. b 10. c
11. d 12. d 13. b 14. d 15. b 16. b 17. d 18. a 19. a 20. c
21. d 22. a 23. b 24. d 25. d 26. a 27. d 28. b 29. d 30. b
31. d 32. c 33. c 34. c

Chapter 3
1. c 2. d 3. c 4. a 5. c 6. d 7. b 8. d 9. a 10. d
11. d 12. c 13. d 14. c 15. a 16. d 17. d 18. d 19. d 20. a
21. d 22. b 23. d 24. a 25. d 26. b 27. d 28. b 29. c 30. b
31. c 32. a 33. c 34. d 35. b 36. c 37. d 38. a 39. d 40. d
41. a 42. b 43. c 44. a 45. b 46. d 47. b

Chapter 4
1. b 2. d 3. d 4. b 5. d 6. d 7. d 8. d 9. d 10. d
11. d 12. b 13. b 14. b 15. c 16. d 17. d 18. d 19. a 20. d
21. d 22. d 23. d 24. c 25. a 26. c 27. a 28. d 29. d 30. a
31. a 32. d 33. a 34. b 35. c 36. d 37. d 38. b 39. d 40. a
41. a 42. c 43. c 44. d 45. d 46. d 47. d 48. b 49. b 50. d
51. a 52. b

Chapter 5
1. d 2. b 3. d 4. d 5. c 6. d 7. c 8. d 9. d 10. b
11. d 12. d 13. d 14. c 15. a 16. d 17. d 18. c 19. c 20. d
21. d 22. d 23. d 24. d 25. d 26. c 27. d 28. d 29. c 30. b
31. a 32. d 33. a 34. d 35. d 36. d 37. a 38. a 39. d 40. d
41. d 42. d 43. b

Chapter 6
1. d 2. b 3. c 4. d 5. d 6. b 7. c 8. b 9. c 10. b
11. d 12. c 13. d 14. a 15. d 16. b 17. d 18. d 19. d 20. a
21. c 22. d 23. c 24. b 25. b 26. d 27. c 28. c 29. b 30. b
31. d 32. d 33. d 34. c 35. d 36. d 37. b 38. b 39. b 40. c
41. d 42. b 43. d 44. d 45. a 46. c 47. d

Chapter 7

1. d	2. b	3. d	4. d	5. d	6. d	7. d	8. b	9. d	10. d
11. c	12. d	13. a	14. d	15. d	16. c	17. d	18. d	19. d	20. c
21. d	22. b	23. d	24. b	25. b	26. d	27. c	28. d	29. d	30. b
31. a	32. d	33. d	34. c						

Chapter 8

1. d	2. c	3. d	4. d	5. a	6. d	7. a	8. d	9. d	10. d
11. d	12. d	13. b	14. d	15. d	16. d	17. c	18. c	19. b	20. d
21. d	22. d	23. d	24. b	25. d	26. b	27. b	28. d	29. c	30. d
31. c	32. b	33. d	34. d	35. a	36. d	37. d	38. a	39. b	40. a

Chapter 9

1. d	2. b	3. d	4. c	5. a	6. d	7. c	8. d	9. d	10. d
11. c	12. d	13. d	14. c	15. d	16. d	17. a	18. d	19. a	20. d
21. b	22. d	23. d	24. d	25. d	26. b	27. c	28. d	29. c	30. d
31. d	32. a	33. a	34. b	35. d	36. d				

Chapter 10

1. c	2. d	3. a	4. b	5. d	6. b	7. d	8. d	9. c	10. c
11. a	12. d	13. c	14. b	15. d	16. b	17. d	18. a	19. d	20. d
21. d	22. d	23. d	24. b	25. d	26. d	27. d	28. d	29. d	30. d
31. d	32. d	33. d	34. d	35. d	36. c	37. d	38. d		

Chapter 11

1. d	2. b	3. d	4. d	5. d	6. d	7. a	8. b	9. d	10. b
11. d	12. a	13. a	14. d	15. d	16. a	17. d	18. c	19. d	20. b
21. d	22. b	23. d	24. b	25. c	26. d	27. d	28. c	29. d	30. d
31. c	32. c	33. a	34. d	35. d	36. b	37. d	38. a	39. c	40. c
41. c	42. d	43. d	44. c	45. d	46. a	47. b	48. d	49. d	

Chapter 12

1. d	2. a	3. d	4. a	5. a	6. b	7. c	8. d	9. d	10. b
11. d	12. d	13. d	14. b	15. c	16. a	17. d	18. d	19. d	20. a
21. d	22. d	23. d	24. d						

Chapter 13

1. b	2. a	3. c	4. d	5. b	6. d	7. d	8. b	9. b	10. c
11. d	12. d	13. d	14. d	15. a	16. a	17. a	18. a	19. d	20. c
21. d	22. a	23. d	24. d	25. d	26. d	27. a			

ANSWER KEY

Chapter 14
1. d   2. a   3. b   4. d   5. b   6. d   7. a   8. c   9. c   10. d
11. d   12. b   13. d   14. b   15. d   16. d   17. d   18. d   19. d   20. a
21. a   22. d   23. d   24. d   25. d   26. b   27. d   28. c   29. b   30. d

Chapter 15
1. d   2. b   3. d   4. a   5. a   6. d   7. d   8. a   9. c   10. b
11. d   12. d   13. d   14. b   15. c   16. a   17. b   18. b   19. d   20. a
21. a   22. c   23. a   24. d   25. d   26. a   27. d   28. a   29. b   30. d
31. d   32. b   33. d   34. b   35. d   36. c   37. d   38. d   39. a   40. d
41. d   42. c   43. a   44. c   45. b   46. a   47. a   48. c   49. c   50. c
51. b   52. c   53. b   54. c   55. d

Chapter 16
1. d   2. d   3. d   4. a   5. b   6. d   7. b   8. d   9. b   10. a
11. b   12. d   13. d   14. d   15. d   16. d   17. d   18. b   19. d   20. d
21. d   22. d   23. d   24. d

Chapter 17
1. c   2. a   3. a   4. c   5. d   6. d   7. b   8. d   9. c   10. d
11. d   12. d   13. d   14. d   15. d   16. a   17. a   18. d   19. b   20. d
21. d   22. b   23. b   24. d   25. b

Chapter 18
1. c   2. d   3. d   4. b   5. c   6. d   7. c   8. d   9. d   10. d
11. d   12. d   13. a   14. c   15. b   16. d   17. b   18. c   19. a   20. d
21. d   22. b   23. b   24. d   25. a   26. d   27. b   28. d   29. d   30. d
31. d   32. b

Chapter 19
1. a   2. d   3. c   4. d   5. a   6. b   7. b   8. b   9. d   10. d
11. d   12. d   13. d   14. a   15. a   16. d   17. d   18. d   19. b   20. d
21. d   22. a   23. c   24. b   25. d   26. d   27. d   28. d   29. b   30. d
31. c   32. c   33. c   34. a   35. a   36. c   37. d   38. b   39. b   40. d
41. c   42. c   43. a   44. b   45. d   46. d   47. d   48. c   49. a   50. b
51. b   52. d   53. b   54. b   55. b   56. d   57. a   58. c   59. a   60. d
61. a   62. a

www.ingramcontent.com/pod-product-compliance
Lightning Source LLC
Chambersburg PA
CBHW082041230426
43670CB00016B/2736